A Straightforward Approach to CJ Research Methods

A Straightforward Approach to CJ Research Methods

Practices, Policies, and Procedures

Vanessa W. Griffin
University of West Georgia

Kyle A. Burgason
Iowa State University

Carolina Academic Press
Durham, North Carolina

Library of Congress Cataloging-in-Publication Data

Names: Griffin, Vanessa Woodward, author. | Burgason, Kyle A., author.
Title: A straightforward approach to CJ research methods : practices,
  policies, and procedures / by Vanessa Woodward Griffin, Kyle A. Burgason.
Description: Durham, North Carolina : Carolina Academic Press, 2019. |
  Includes bibliographical references and index.
Identifiers: LCCN 2019008903 | ISBN 9781611638622 (alk. paper)
Subjects: LCSH: Criminal justice, Administration of--Research--Methodology. |
  Criminology--Methodology.
Classification: LCC HV7419.5 .G75 2019 | DDC 364.072/1--dc23
LC record available at https://lccn.loc.gov/2019008903

 e-ISBN 978-1-5310-0736-2

Carolina Academic Press
700 Kent Street
Durham, North Carolina 27701
Telephone (919) 489-7486
Fax (919) 493-5668
www.cap-press.com

Contents

Section II · Designing Research in Criminology and Criminal Justice (Chapters 5–7)

Section III · Doing Research: Types, Applications, and Methods (Chapters 8–11)

A Guide to Using This Book

We do not want to lie: Research Methods is a tough course. I (Vanessa Griffin) have been fortunate (or unfortunate) enough to teach it several times over the past eight or so years. In fact, this past spring was my first semester *not* teaching Research Methods in over five years. In this time, I have come to realize that when first learning methodologies, it is important to keep the information simple and casual. It is hard enough to understand without a bunch of additional information added.

Over time, I have used different types of textbooks in Research Methods and have found that students seem to respond most to those that provide some explanations and examples, but not *too* many—otherwise, the original message might get lost in translation. In teaching the course, I have often found it is best to give the explanation and example before even introducing the terminology. I have observed that students grasp information more if the examples used are more "real life" type examples rather than "real research" examples. Lastly, I have discovered that sometimes professors (including myself) have assumed that the information you consume in Research Methods is easy to apply to your own research project, when, in fact, it is a lot more helpful to provide additional lessons on *how* to apply the information in developing your own research project.

Taking all this into account, Kyle Burgason and I have attempted to create a straight-forward text that is a comprehensive introduction to research methodology in the social sciences. We have attempted to write the chapters on a more personal level, and we use a lot of casual language. Our hope is that it reads as though we are having a conversation with you. Research Methods is formal and complex enough—we do not think that additional formal and complex language helps anyone!

Since we are both criminologists, we tend to use criminology-based research for some examples (where appropriate); however, we are often using more real-life and/or pop culture examples. You will see a lot of references to friends, pets, television shows, and movies. We realized that we cannot assume how far advanced you are in your education. Your university might require that you are a senior to take this course, or you may be a freshman in your first semester. We cannot assume you have taken a bunch of criminology courses, so it would be hard to apply research methodologies to a bunch of courses that you have not yet taken. Therefore, we focused more on real-life examples: most everyone, regardless of where they are in their college career, can relate to friends, pets, television, and movies.

Lastly, the last four chapters of your book (Chapters 12–15) are, in a lot of ways, a separate book—they are to serve as a "how to" guide for research proposals. These chapters are not there for material to cover in class, but as a reference guide for you if you need to (in this class, or in another class) write your own research proposal.

How to Read This Book

Authors

We often will write our own personal stories and accounts in the chapters—so it is probably important that you know whether the stories are about Kyle or me (Vanessa). Each chapter has a bit of both of our writing, but here is an overview of the primary author for each chapter.

Chapter Number	Primary Author
1	Vanessa
2	Vanessa
3	Vanessa
4	Vanessa
5	Vanessa
6	Vanessa
7	Vanessa
8	Vanessa
9	Kyle
10	Vanessa
11	Vanessa
12	Kyle
13	Kyle
14	Kyle
15	Kyle

Terms

Research Methods is not a course for the lazy student or the lazy teacher! You know how in some courses if you just make definition flashcards, you might be okay? Research Methods requires more than just naming and defining the term—you must understand it and apply it in examples. While important terms are marked in the textbook, you should read a few paragraphs before and a few paragraphs after the term to make sure you can define, explain, and apply the term. I know, I know—how annoying. One of the reasons to read a few paragraphs before is that we often will give you the example before we give you the term. Understanding something before having to be introduced to it can be helpful—you do not get wrapped up in fancy language and forget to understand its meaning.

Bob and Jane: Examples and Scenarios

One way that we have tried to simplify things is by using consistent names for examples/scenarios in the main textbook chapters (Chapters 1–11): Bob and Jane. So, we are putting a BOLO (be on the lookout) for Bob and Jane—they are hints that we are providing you with a scenario/explanation of the material we have presented. Bob and Jane are bolded and in a different style from the rest of the material, so that it is easy to spot them. They take on different roles (Offender Bob, Professor Jane, Shady Jane, Student Bob, etc.); however, you should know that when you see their names, we have provided you with further explanation.

Our Hope Is That You Do Not End Up Hating Us

We hope that you find this book useful in your Research Methods class (and other classes)—even if its utility is just as a doorstop. Thanks for reading this far—and we hope you find this book more helpful than harmful throughout your college career!

Section I

The Role of Research in Criminology and Criminal Justice (Chapters 1–4)

As an undergraduate, I remember not really realizing how much research mattered in criminal justice. I always associated criminal justice with the three C's—courts, cops, and corrections—and the *practice* of those people involved in the criminal justice system. What I never thought of was why they do the things they do. Police may try to get to know people on their beat because of research on community policing. Prison wardens may allow for certain privileges in prisons because of research on violence in prisons. Courts may sentence someone to prison for life because of research on career criminals. This is not to say that all practices in the criminal justice system are evidence-based (seriously—many are not). However, it is to say that research does play a role in all the cool, scary, action-packed, and tedious practices of those in the criminal justice system. Criminal justice research *matters*. Hey, even Buzzfeed has published articles on criminal justice research (Vergano, 2018)!

These first four chapters are intended to help introduce you to research and its role in criminology and criminal justice. To understand research, it's important to go back to middle school science lab reports (I know, I know); think hypotheses, procedures, etc. This book is focused on how you start research, by forming hypotheses and research questions and then the steps you need (procedure) to conduct that research. In Chapter 2, you will learn about how theory plays a role in criminological and criminal justice research: to see if an idea makes sense, it has to be tested! Research is how we test ideas to see whether they show any promise. In addition to making sure research makes sense and is designed well, we also want to make sure we are doing ethical research—you cannot hurt people just because you have an interesting idea! Research has to benefit people more than it puts people at risk. Chapter 4 is sort of a combination of a bunch of things that you need to know about research. It is a bit of a long, tedious chapter, but you'll (hopefully) be grateful that we introduced you to some of this stuff earlier on, so that certain terminology is familiar.

Try to remember that even though some of this stuff is boring (it is), we really tried to keep things that were important for you to know. So, think of your own research and keep that in mind as you begin to read. Start with an idea—either criminal-justice related or silly—and think about how you would test it as you learn about research. Just *please* make sure that idea is not something like "how to pass Research Methods without ever opening that textbook."

Trying It Out

Your professor may ask you to complete the following companion assignment available from the publisher. Using the supplied worksheet form, you are going to identify research questions and concepts in the examples provided.

Chapter 1

Why Do I Care about Research? A Guide to This Book

Learning Objectives

- Explain the role of research in everyday life
- Explain the importance of research in the social sciences
- Define epistemology
- Compare and contrast agreement and experiential realities
- Define empiricism
- Explain the process of making erroneous conclusions
- Name and define the five approaches to research
- Compare and contrast inductive and deductive reasoning
- Compare and contrast qualitative and quantitative research

Getting Started

In all likelihood, you have heard the saying, "Don't judge a book by its cover." Regardless, we (the authors) are going to guess that is exactly what you did. We are also going to guess that, most often, you do not like the textbooks you read. While we hope this book is an exception, we can guess that you have already decided. In fact, research has demonstrated we only had eight seconds to capture your attention (Statistic Brain Research Institute, 2017). Further, if you have already been to your first Research Methods class, you have likely decided whether you like the professor. In the *New York Times* best-seller, *Blink!*, Malcolm Gladwell described how Nalini Ambody determined that students still make conclusions about how effective a teacher is within two seconds of beginning a *silent videotape* (Gladwell, 2007).

So why are we telling you all this? Believe it or not, it has nothing to do with your impression of our book. What you are doing—making judgments and conclusions—is research. Perhaps not the soundest research, but research that is important to you. You questioned whether you would like this book, you then hypothesized whether you would or would not, and you have probably already tested that hypothesis (by reading these two paragraphs), and drawn a conclusion. Remember the scientific method from middle school and high school science? We are bringing it back. It is the foundation of *all* research, and is particularly important to remember throughout reading this book.

Do not get freaked out or begin hating us already. This is not a science course. We are social scientists (or we claim to be), and you are becoming a social scientist. We do things somewhat differently. First, we do not typically use labs or test tubes—the world is our laboratory. We are much more interested in examining people and their interactions, whether that be in context of criminal activity or Yik Yak usage (even if this is not a thing anymore). You also should not freak out because you already conduct research every day. Ever been at a bar or a restaurant and seen someone attractive? You question whether if you approach them they will be interested, you hypothesize that they either will or will not be, and then (if you have some guts), you test that hypothesis. They throw a drink in your face? You conclude that they are not interested. They give you their phone number? You conclude that they are interested. Moreover, you determine whether your hypothesis was "right" or "wrong." That is all we are going to do here—just with a few more people and a bit more complexity of situation.

It is important to remember that few things in research are simple—including explaining how to do research. There is a lot of terminology and a whole lot to remember. Further, a lot of the terminology is connected and requires real understanding—you cannot just memorize each term and "get" research. The real quandary is that it is quite challenging to understand research until you do research—but you cannot understand it until you do it. So, this book tries to do both at once, by allowing you to write your own research proposal as you learn about each section. It is also important to realize that conducting research is an ongoing research process. None of us (the authors) are perfect researchers—we tend to live by the motto that hindsight is 20/20. There is always an "I wish I had…," an "I really could have…," or a "Wow, I screwed up there …"

Learning Research Methods provides you with a guide to the research process—a set of tools to which you can refer when conducting your own research.

Knowing What We Know

There is always an exception to the rule—so much so that there is probably an exception to this exception. When we conduct research, we are trying to determine what is true for *most*—whether that be people, animals, or something else. Since most social science research deals with people, it is important to remember that people are complicated. For instance, you cannot perfectly predict or explain the behaviors of your best friend or significant other—so why could researchers, who are strangers to your best friend and significant other, be able to predict or explain these behaviors? To a certain extent, researchers can identify patterns and be able to see what works for most people. However, researchers are people, too! Meaning, they are complicated and have their own biases and own understanding of the world. This not only affects perceptions and observations in research (we will get back to this soon), but also affects our overall knowledge—how do we know what we know? *Epistemology* is the science of knowing, which really is just a fancy way to classify the process of questioning why we perceive certain information to be fact. Moreover, it is questioning if we really have any clue about who we are, where we are, or if this is even reality. Are we all just butterflies living a dream? Epistemology may sound boring, but the science of knowing is something that fascinates many people; in fact, there is a whole subgenre of science fiction movies devoted to it—think *Inception* or *The Matrix*—those kinds of mind-blown-type movies. So, what do people know and how do they know it? Generally, people either trust others and accept that something is true or they must experience it for themselves. These are referred to as ***agreement and experiential realities*** (Babbie, 2015).

I (Vanessa Griffin—one of the authors of your book) have a cat named Trouble (we will move past the fact that he completely lives up to his name). Trouble was the epitome of a curious kitten—he wanted to explore everything. It did not help that his best pal, a Jack Russell named Jinx, was just as curious, making them partners in crime. Most of our house was destroyed as they explored and experienced everything together. I could not tell them that eating an entire cake together would make them sick; they did not accept that as fact. Eating the vanilla cake—icing and all—and then getting sick was really what sealed the "fact" deal. For them to accept something as true, they had to *experience* it; meaning, they had to see it for themselves. To some extent, people are like that, too. Most kids have—at one point or another—screamed to their parents "I have to make my own mistakes!" This is a need to experience something to "make sure" it is true. Smoking a cigarette will, indeed, make your throat hurt. Excessive drinking (most often) will give you a horrible hangover the next day. In all likelihood, however, you needed to learn these things for yourself—the hard way.

On the other hand, people can be pretty accepting, and sometimes, too accepting. Throughout time, there have been certain items of information that we believed to be true and later discovered were pure and utter nonsense. One such example is that a woman cannot get pregnant when standing up. Even though there has been plenty to bust this myth wide open, one poll showed that in the UK, one in 10 still believe it to be true (*The Daily Telegraph*, 2009). Or perhaps you have heard that if you swallow gum, it stays in your system for seven years—not so (Matson, 2007)! However, there are plenty of things we believe to be true *because* experts believe it to be true. You know the earth is round, there are seven continents, and the Declaration of Independence was adopted by the Continental Congress in 1776. But wait—how do you actually *know* these things? Have you seen the Earth from space? Have you traveled back in time and witnessed Thomas Jefferson writing the Declaration of Independence? Have you seen all seven continents—have you traveled around the globe to ensure that there are seven continents? We are going to guess that you have not done these things (if you have, we really want to know about it), and that is all right. We accept certain things to be true, because *everybody* does. We *agree* on knowledge and make it a part of our reality. Who we are and what we know are comprised of both relying on faith and having to see to believe. So, what knowledge falls into an agreement reality?

Perhaps everyone already agreed about it before you were born—so you just followed along with what was already in place. Or, perhaps it matters from whom you learned of this information: we tend to agree with those close to us but also tend to agree or go along with those who seem like they know what they are talking about. For instance, you have probably accepted what we are saying in this book thus far as fact because you think (accurately, we hope) that two criminology and criminal justice researchers have some experience on how to conduct research. On the other hand, if we start dropping knowledge on how to design a bridge, you should probably laugh, write a horrible Amazon review about this book, and use this book as an excellent doorstop. This is because neither of your authors knows a *thing* about architecture or engineering.

Errors We Make: What You See Is Not Always What You Get, and What You Get Is Not Always What You See

If you remember in the last section, we said that researchers are people too, and we would get back to that soon—we were not lying. Researchers tend to be more like annoying, rebellious teenagers—they must go and learn something for themselves and do not just accept that something is true. And that is good, because there remains a lot of uncertainty about the world, and the only way to assuage that uncertainty is through experiences. Within research, we refer to this as *empiricism.* This means experiencing, or at the least, directly observing the phenomenon (thing) that we are researching. In the social sciences, this helps to create better, deeper, broader understandings of people and groups of people. However, there is a lot of error that can occur, and different types of error must be considered when conducting and/or interpreting social science research. Specifically, researchers cannot completely control their biases, nor can they control everything that happens within a study or everything that happens outside of it. Within the social sciences, we cannot lock people in a lab and observe their social interactions (besides being super unethical, it is also contradictory—how can you be isolated but socializing)?

Do not worry—we have got chapters of fun-filled material focusing on error. For now, however, we will just focus on error within observations. It is particularly important to remember that when observing any interaction, it can become pretty easy to make an erroneous conclusion if you do not **watch for context**, are **resistant to change**, use **illogical reasoning**, or **overgeneralize** (Bachman & Schutt, 2013).

Let's first think of these errors in an everyday type situation. Sometimes, we can make an inaccurate observation, because we are unaware of the context. For instance, say you tell your friends a joke about a dog—and it is *hilarious*—yet, none of your friends laugh. Your next thoughts will likely lead you down one of two paths. Within path one, first, you feel awkward. Then, you conclude that the joke is not funny. Then, you start worrying that maybe you are not funny at all (you have always fancied yourself quite the comedian). Within the second path, you may first still feel awkward. Second, you may conclude that—no matter what—that joke is so funny; you just cannot see it any other way. Thus, you decide that your friends all have horrible senses of humor and are idiots.

Either way, you have made a huge error. The reason being that one of your friends, Bob, just found out his dog died. Moments before you approached, Bob told all your other friends. If you had told the joke yesterday, your friends would have found it funny, and at least one of them would have commented that you should do standup. However, this is today, and you were unaware of the *context*, and did not consider that you could be missing a key component. Further, in the first path, you concluded that because your friends did not find that joke funny, perhaps they found none of your jokes funny, and in reality, you are not the comedian you thought you were. These are examples of generalization. (Typically, we think of generalization as generalizing to a group of people; however, if you are generalizing one interaction to all interactions it still fits the mold of generalizing!) In the second path, you still made an error, because of not considering the context—you used illogical reasoning and jumped to a conclusion that your friends do not find you funny and are therefore stupid. This is also an example of being resistant to change—believing that what you know to be fact (your amazing wit) is not subject to change (Babbie, 2015; Bachman & Schutt, 2013).

Within criminology and criminal justice, there are many examples of how researchers or any person could make errors within their observations. In his book, *Code of the Street*, Elijah Anderson (2000) argued that there are two types of families: street and decent. Decent families were those trying to live life on the "straight and narrow." However, in the streets of Chicago, being a decent family could open one up to victimization and make him or her look weak. So, decent families often disguise themselves as street families to receive respect and avoid harassment from street families. If one were to go observe juveniles in Chicago (or other cities), s/he may classify someone as street who is actually from a decent family, because the researcher does not have context and jumps to conclusions without all the facts.

Errors in research and observations are hard to grasp abstractly, but we hope this at least gives you an impression of how what you see is not always what you get. One of the biggest takeaways from this section is to realize that social science research is about observing events and interactions that do not occur within a vacuum. Thus, we generally avoid saying something "causes" something else (we will get into that more later), and we also avoid the word "proves." We discuss social science research within the ideas of relationships: one thing is related to another, but one thing does not *cause* another. Avoid using the words prove and cause, and your professor *may* be happier with you.

Get it? There is a relationship between not saying prove and cause and your professor's opinion of you—but not using prove and cause does not *cause* your professor to like you. On the other end of that—if your professor likes you, that does not *prove* that you did not use the words prove and cause!

Social Science Research: Purposes and Approaches

Research Methods is confusing all by itself. What we want to try to avoid in this book is confusing you even more by being ambiguous. For instance, social sciences can generally be divided into *types* of research. However, it is common for people to discuss "types of research" when they mean different things, including *the purpose of research*, the method(s) used to collect data, the research design, as well as the analytic approach. Within this chapter, we will just touch on the very basics of each these, but will get more detailed in later chapters.

Purpose of Research

As social science researchers, we want to make sure that what we are doing matters. Research takes a lot of time, energy, and money—we want to make sure there is a purpose to it. Generally, we develop a research question and plan, plan, plan. Sports teams practice repeatedly before the game—because there are no do-overs—and everyone is watching. For instance, let's say an NFL team did not practice once in the off season, and then had their first game. The team would likely lose (depending on how good they were and against whom they were playing). Also, it is probable that the members of the team would be disorganized and lack effective communication. Now, losing a game is bad enough—but if everyone were to find out that they had not been practicing, fans would be angry and the team's owner would probably be a bit ticked (that is an understatement!). So, as researchers, before we go and waste time and money—our own and others'—we should practice and plan!

A research question is usually part of the first step in planning a research project (to see all the steps in a research project, see the later section, "The Research Process"). Yet, within that research question should also be an understanding of the purpose of the research. It cannot just be "because it sounds interesting." Research is trying to do something to a phenomenon (or thing, if that is simpler): explore, describe, explain, evaluate, and/or apply.

These may sound complicated, but in fact, they are things we do in everyday life—and you started it as a toddler. Think of a toddler's (we will name her Suzie) first day of preschool. Suzie goes to preschool to *explore* things: she explores what preschool is all about, she explores toys, friends, the recess yard, the classroom, the teachers. Suzie learns how to *explain* how one thing leads and relates to another (after lunch is recess—but if I am not good, I will get a timeout and not get to play at recess). Suzie can *describe* her first day of preschool to her parents when they pick her up by telling them what they did (first we had playtime, then nap time), and by also describing the other people involved: her new classmates and her teacher. She can *evaluate* what she likes and does not like about preschool (playtime was great! I do not know about learning to read, and nap time is boring); and lastly, she can take what she learned in preschool and *apply* it to other parts of her life (today I learned how to color in the lines).

Keeping these simple ideas of each goal in mind, we can examine how these fit into research and our everyday lives.

Who, What, Where, and When: Explore and Describe

Research typically has more than one goal: we need to explore before we can describe, and we need to explore and describe before we can explain. At times, previous researchers may have done the exploring and describing for us—meaning, what we are looking at is not the "unknown." At other times, we may need to start at the very beginning and take the first step to discovering something that most people do not understand or have not experienced.

There are certain subjects in the social sciences with which we are pretty familiar—for instance, I imagine you could describe a college classroom without having to be in one—and that is because you are familiar with what a classroom looks like and what types of interactions take place in a classroom. Similarly, if I asked you to describe typical environments and interactions at a bar or restaurant, you would likely have no problem doing that. Thus, these things seem like common knowledge because the experiences (going to restaurants, bars, or classrooms on a college campus) appear normal and frequent. Now imagine being asked to describe the interactions that take place within an Army unit during an attack or how a community in a developing country organizes events and communicates with one another. Perhaps you have the experiences to answer these questions—perhaps you do not. In research, sometimes the question that the researcher seeks to answer is simply "what is going on here?" We simply want to *describe* an environment, its members, and their interactions. Within criminal justice, one may want to describe a prison cafeteria. There are two paths to take to achieve this goal: the researcher can write a long, detailed description of the place or event (like how an author would set up a scene), or the researcher could use *descriptive statistics* to present a description in numbers by using counts or averages to set up a scene. To describe a college class, a professor could provide a rich description of students' body language and interactions within a semester's class periods, or the professor could provide the students' average grade on the midterm. While the former provides more information, it also requires a lot more time; conversely, the latter is an efficient way of describing the classroom, but a lot of information is lost.

As criminological researchers, imagine that we wanted to describe how police interact with homicide suspects during interrogation. Before deciding how to describe these events and interactions, it is important to know what your research goals are and who your audience is. You could describe in detail 500 interrogations, but that would result in an overwhelming amount of information. Instead, during each interrogation, you could also count the number of times a detective raises their voice, curses, or leaves the room. You could also count the number of times the suspect raises their voice, curses, or avoids eye contact. Focusing on voice raising only, you might find that on average, a detective raised their voice three times, while suspects raised their voice four times. This is still informative, but brief. It all depends on the goals of your research and your audience.

Like description, *exploration* is important for phenomenon with which we are unfamiliar, either collectively or individually. Exploratory research provides a method to learn about something novel or unknown. If you became a college football coach, you would probably want to know what tactics the best college football coaches use. Perhaps you would want to explore what coaching looks like during games and practices with some of the best college football coaches (even though such judgements may be subjective). You may want to—assuming you can gain access—watch practices and interview coaches to explore what the best college football coaches are doing. In criminal justice and criminology research, you may want to explore how drug dealers create their networks of buyers when first beginning to deal.

How, Why, and What If: Explain, Evaluate, and Apply

One of the most common types of research is research that is used to explain something. Most often, explanatory research is examining relationships or differences. In the previous example on football coaches, one might want to know what Alabama's football coach, Nick Saban, has done differently. Nick Saban has won six national titles, the most of any coach currently working. One might observe Nick Saban's tactics and then compare them to the practices of other, not as successful, football coaches. Explanatory research seeks to answer *why*. In this example, why is Nick Saban so successful? What makes him different from the rest?

Putting this goal in the context of criminological research, we might want to examine crime rates in cities and see which ones have the highest and lowest crime rates. If we identified the ten most "dangerous" cities and the ten "safest" cities, we could then see what they all have in common and what characteristics are distinct about the dangerous cities and what characteristics are distinct about the safest cities. Within this example, the research would aim to *explain* the differences in safe and unsafe cities.

One of the most important aspects of research is how it can be applied. Research should not be conducted simply because it is interesting. It must *mean* something. At the end of a research project a researcher must be able to answer the "so what?" question—meaning, the results of the research need to have utility, which occurs when they are *applied*.

Going back to the football coaching example, say you (as a college football coach) observe that the best college football coaches take the time to have one-on-one weekly meetings with each player (we are not arguing, this is true!). After observing this, you describe it to your coaching staff and your athletic director, and you all decide to have weekly meetings with each player. This is an example of *application*: you took what you observed through your explorations, described it, and then applied it. Research is typically applied through programs or policies, either by implementing new ones or modifying those already in place.

We apply research quite often in criminal justice—otherwise, what good would it be? And that is why you are having to take this god-awful class—because research matters within criminal justice and criminology. Things like hotspot policing, juvenile interventions, and community policing were all implemented because *research was applied to policies and programs*. So yes—it matters!

Ideally, existing policies and programs were research driven; meaning, research demonstrated that the implementation of a policy or program would be effective at whatever it aimed to be effective at (e.g., decreasing crime, preventing abuse, and/ or treating substance use). However, policies and programs are not always implemented for rational, planned reasons! Regardless of why it was implemented, it is important to make sure said policy or program is accomplishing what it set out to accomplish. This is where the last goal of research is used: *evaluation*. In a general sense, evaluation is used to determine whether goals of the program or policy are being met, and if so, whether they are being effectively met.

So, as the football coach, you and your staff implement this new program. You find that you need to pay your coaching staff overtime for the extra hours, and you also should hire an additional administrative assistant to manage the weekly schedule of meetings. After a year, you sit down with the athletic director and find that the program is costing an extra million dollars a year—however, the team had an undefeated season, which generated about ten times the normal revenue. While the program required some money on the front end, it certainly showed its worth by the end of the year!

Most often, the benefit and utility of a program or policy is not so clear. One example of this is drug courts. Generally, evaluations of drug court programs have shown that they make a difference: those who participate in drug courts are less likely to reoffend. However, there is some question of whether those who were selected to participate in drug courts were really similar to those who were not selected. Additionally, drug courts that were evaluated based on how many offenders completed the program could have been motivated to make sure that their participants were completing the program—even when they clearly showed failure in the program (Wilson, Mitchell, & MacKenzie, 2006). Overall, while there appear to be positive effects, the degree of these effects is still unknown. That is why it is also important to *evaluate* cost and time in context of benefit and utility. For instance, if a program requires an extra $100 a year, requires 10 hours of extra work annually, and appears to reduce crime within a city by 1%, it is likely worth it—at worst, it has no real effect, but little is being wasted. However, a reduction in a city's crime by 15% that costs 10 billion dollars may be too expensive—even though its benefit (15% reduction in crime) is much greater than the other program (1% reduction in crime).

The goals of research show that research in the social sciences is a never-ending process. Once we begin to understand a phenomenon, we then need to describe it, explain why it is occurring in the way it is occurring, apply what we have learned to policy and/or programs, and then evaluated whether it is meeting its intended goals effectively. And just when we think we have a handle on things, something new comes around, and the whole thing changes. It is kind of like keeping up with fashion (especially as you get older). Just when you think you have a grip on what is in and out of style, something like UGGs are cool again, and you might just have to start all over.

Approaches to Research:
Inductive and Deductive Reasoning

As we discussed in the last section, the goal of research is often dependent on what we already know—meaning, what type of research is already out there? Say you wanted to know more about academic test performance. Is this an area that has been researched? If you go on Google Scholar (see our "how to" guide on writing a literature review), you can search "test performance." There are over one million published books, articles, and/or chapters that have the term "test performance" in them. Additionally, the first available publication is an article by Steele and Aronson (1995) about the test performance of African Americans (Steele & Aronson, 1995). It has been cited over 6,000 times. That means that there are over 6,000 other authors and researchers that decided, within their own publication, that what Steele and Aronson said was so important, they had to discuss it. While this quick search does not definitively tell you that test performance is a well-researched area, we promise that it is. However, there are some things that remain less researched within the social sciences. For instance, while there is certainly research on gang hierarchy and politics, this is not necessarily a fully understood phenomenon.

Generally, if we have a good idea why something is occurring (such as how studying is related to test performance), it is because there is already research out there. And when there is research, there is theory. We can guess that studying is going to increase test scores because studying allows test takers to retain knowledge, while failing to study typically results in a test taker retaining fewer facts than their studious counterpart. When starting with a base of knowledge, researchers typically use *deductive reasoning*—theory and past research already exist and that helps to guide the research. Deductive reasoning starts with what is already known (past research and theoretical developments), then uses that to make predictions, which, in turn, guides their actual research. After completing their research, they can then conclude whether what they found is what they expected and why. For instance, if a researcher (Tanya) examined how studying is related to test scores using deductive reasoning, she may observe how many hours students study and then record their test score. Tanya observes that most of her participants had a higher grade when they studied more. However, those students who studied the most (20+ hours) did *the worst* on the test. After reviewing

Imagine that you reside in a high-crime neighborhood (Seashore), and your neighbors have just appointed you to the head of the neighborhood watch. You really want to make a difference and lower crime, but are not sure how. You find out that three neighborhoods over (Lakeshore) the crime rate is less than half of what it was a year prior to that. You would likely want to go and **explore** what that neighborhood is doing about crime. Perhaps you will talk with the head of their neighborhood watch—if they have one. You'll ask what efforts they took. You may even observe how they conduct nightly walks or go door-to-door and interview residents. You may then do the same in your own neighborhood. In this example, you are exploring the similarities and differences between your neighborhood and another. Those distinctions may be the "answer" to lowering crime.

After exploring the other neighborhood, you would likely need to *describe what you observed* and provide this information to your audience: the residents of your neighborhood. You might use both descriptive statistics and written descriptions to describe what you observed and report on your interactions with residents of Lakeshore. Part of it might look like this.

Lakeshore has used several tactics to decrease crime in their neighborhood. First, after many meetings, the neighborhood residents decided their biggest problem was a lack of visibility: the neighborhood was poorly lit and there were many good hiding spots (behind large bushes and trees). The residents first volunteered to help one another trim bushes and trees and replace outdoor lightbulbs where needed. The head of Lakeshore's neighborhood watch told me this was certainly a great first step; however, they decided that more lighting was needed, and thought it would be best to have motion lights in yards. While this was too costly for each household to afford, the neighborhood members held multiple fundraisers (including a car wash and a bake sale) to raise the funds. Currently, each house has at least one motion detection light. Additionally, all households agreed to keep their porch lights on from 7pm to 7am. Within their neighborhood watch, all residents participate in shifts twice per month. There are, on average, two neighborhood residents patrolling the streets for two hours. However, on weekend nights, there are three to four residents patrolling in two-hour shifts. I observed active patrol with four teams over the course of one week. One thing I noticed was that each patrol team knew and greeted each resident by name, and the residents greeted them back by name.

In the report, you also include your observations about your neighborhood, Seashore.

In Seashore, our neighborhood watch has focused only on patrol during the weekend nights, with two people for a five-hour shift. After discussing it with you all, it appears that many residents were reluctant or unable to volunteer for these shifts because of time constraints.

Additionally, we have not made any efforts to change lighting or increase visibility.

From here, you may try to *explain* the differences you see: what is different about Lakeshore as compared to Seashore?

Lakeshore is doing a lot more to prevent crime than Seashore. It appears these prevention techniques may have helped in lowering their crime rate.

The next step would be to *apply* what you have learned to your own neighborhood. You suggest this to your neighbors and they agree. You all fundraise, fix lighting fixtures, replace lightbulbs, and install motion detectors. All residents volunteer for two-hour shifts that occur all day, every day. Within a year, you all **evaluate** your progress and find that cost (time and money) is minimal compared to the security each resident feels. Further, after consulting with the police department, you determine that Seashore has decreased crime by 25%. Keeping in mind that evaluation will need to continue, your neighborhood finds that—for the moment—the new program is effective at meeting its goal to decrease crime.

past theory and research, Tanya can theorize that this could be because of test anxiety. Tanya is suggesting what could be a focus of research in the future: how test anxiety affects test scores.

While there is an abundance of research on test performance, there are several topics within the social sciences that are less understood, often because they are hard to access (such as the inner workings of gangs) or because they are new (like the legalization of marijuana). If conducting exploratory research and just trying to observe and describe what is occurring, it is most likely that the researcher would use an inductive approach.

Generally speaking, an inductive approach starts with data collection—meaning, there is no theory, no hypotheses, no preconceived notion(s). Inductive reasoning is appropriate when a researcher is developing theory, not testing it. With deductive reasoning, the research is answering the question "is this [theory/fact/thing] true?" Within inductive reasoning, the research is asking "What is the fact/thing?" An inductive approach ends with theory, while a deductive approach starts with it. While this might sound complicated, think about being a homicide detective. In the first case, you are asked to find the murderer. In the second case, you are asked to reassess a case in which the offender has already been convicted. In the first case, you are not starting with a suspect; while in the second, you are. Imagine that you have a hunch and just lead with your gut. You may miss important evidence because you have "tunnel vision." If evidence reveals that it may not be the suspect you have in mind, you may dismiss it, because it does not support what you already believe. This is obviously problematic—which is why when you do not have a solid base of information (past research and theory), you should likely start as a blank slate and be open to all possibilities. Only when there appears to be a strong foundation (someone has already been found guilty of the homicide) should deductive reasoning be used to answer: is this [the person's guilt] true?

Methods of Data Collection and the Analytic Approach

Generally, there are two "types" of research: qualitative and quantitative—the same root words as quality and quantity. Typically, qualitative research deals with words and quantitative research deals with numbers. However, that is a simple breakdown of the two types of research, and both deserve a lot more attention. We want to touch on these types of research and explain the overall differences. Examples of qualitative data include interviews using open-ended questions, observations of a culture or subculture, or even rap lyrics. Quantitative research and quantitative data are those things that are numeric or easily assigned a number, such as interviews with closed-ended questions (how many times have you stolen from your parents), or an online survey instrument that asks multiple choice questions. When you take a multiple-choice exam, this is an example of quantitative data, while an essay test would be qualitative. However, there is a distinction between data and analysis—and this is important, because it is often confused or thought to be the same thing. Qualitative data can then be analyzed using qualitative methods *or* quantitative methods; however, quantitative data can typically only be analyzed using quantitative methods. You do not need to necessarily understand this right now—but keep it in mind for later chapters.

Qualitative data collection is important when researchers need to grasp a better understanding of something. Thus, it is particularly important within exploratory research, and is often used within research that aims to describe. Remember how we discussed how to describe a college classroom? Describing the environment, the students, and the interactions in words is an example of both *qualitative data and qualitative analysis.* On the other hand, the average grade on the exam is an example of quantitative analysis and—if the exam were multiple choice—quantitative data. However, if the test were an essay test and the professor still reported the average on the exam, this would be an example of qualitative data and quantitative analysis.

Typically, to qualitatively analyze qualitative data, a researcher will use inductive reasoning. Conversely, to quantitatively analyze quantitative data, a researcher will use deductive reasoning. Of course, there are always exceptions to this!

Qualitative research has many strengths and provides deeper understanding to the unknown. However, because it lacks a formal structure, there can be concern regarding whether the research is universally applicable. Also, because it often requires some subjectivity of the researcher, there is certainly concern for how bias plays a role in qualitative research. While qualitative research provides a wealth of information, it is timely and costly. *Quantitative research*, however, is not without its problems. It often does not tell the whole story and leaves you wanting more (and not in a good way!). Imagine reading a novel and having certain parts just left out—this is what it can be like working with quantitative research. It is, however, considered to be less affected by research bias and is typically less costly and timely.

In reality, both qualitative and quantitative research have their strengths and weaknesses, and both have a very prominent place in social science research—there is room at the table for two kings (or queens!). To combat the issues with both, one of the best remedies is to use mixed methods research—meaning bring the best of both worlds! Survey a large group of people and also interview some to provide the missing parts of the novel.

Summing It Up:
Where Do We Go from Here?

We are aware that we have thrown a lot at you in a relatively short chapter. Please do not be overwhelmed—we are just trying to get you started with the gist of research. The goal from here is to have you build more of a foundation and begin to understand research enough that you can start thinking of how to conduct your own research.

This book is divided into two parts: the first part has three sections and provides you with the foundations of research and details about different parts of research, like qualitative and quantitative data, the research process, and what approaches we take to try and make sure our research is valid, ethical, and meaningful. The second part of this book is a "how to" guide that coincides with Part 1. Ideally, each section in the "how to" guide can help you with your own research proposal so that you can understand by doing—while making sure that you understand enough to actually do it!

Part 1 of this book is a bit dense because it deals with foundations of research including theory and ethics. Section 2 begins to focus on really specific parts of research and allows you to get a lot of the terminology down and understand how to design research. Lastly, Section 3 of Part 1 provides more understanding on types of research, including surveys, quantitative and qualitative research, and types of data.

We hope you enjoy—or at the least, do not feel tortured by—reading this book.

Discussion Questions

1. Think of an example of when you have conducted research in your everyday life. Explain the steps of the research process you took in this example.

2. What are the differences in agreement and experiential realities? Why are they important in research?

3. What is empiricism and how does it relate to agreement and experiential realities?

4. Why does context matter in research?

5. Name and explain the five approaches to research.

6. What are the differences between inductive and deductive approaches?

7. How are qualitative and quantitative research different? How are inductive and deductive approaches related to qualitative and quantitative research?

Trying It Out

Your professor may ask you to complete the following companion assignment available from the publisher. Using the supplied worksheet form, find the suggested peer-reviewed sources in Google Scholar and evaluate the goals of the sources' research.

References

Anderson, E. (2000). *Code of the street: Decency, violence, and the moral life of the inner city*. New York, NY: W. W. Norton & Company.

Babbie, E. (2015). *The practice of social research*. Boston, MA: Cengage Learning.

Bachman, R., & Schutt, R. K. (2013). *The practice of research in criminology and criminal justice*. Thousand Oaks, CA: Sage Publications.

The Daily Telegraph. (2009, November 20). One-in-10 believe women who have sex standing up cannot get pregnant. Retrieved from https://www.telegraph.co.uk/news/uknews/6607473/One-in-10-believe-women-who-have-sex-standing-up-cannot-get-pregnant.html.

Gladwell, M. (2007). *Blink: The power of thinking without thinking*. New York, NY: Back Bay Books.

Matson, J. (2007, October 11). Fact or fiction?: Chewing gum takes seven years to digest. *Scientific American*.

Statistic Brain Research Institute. (2017). *Attention span statistics*. Retrieved from http://www.statisticbrain.com/attention-span-statistics\.

Steele, C. M., & Aronson, J. (1995). Stereotype threat and the intellectual test performance of African Americans. *Journal of Personality and Social Psychology*, *69*(5), 797.

Vergano, D. (2018, July 27). A study of guns in Boston shows that restrictive laws drive up prices on the street. Retrieved from: https://www.buzzfeednews.com/article/danvergano/illegal-gun-prices-boston.

Wilson, D. B., Mitchell, O., & MacKenzie, D. L. (2006). A systematic review of drug court effects on recidivism. *Journal of Experimental Criminology*, *2*(4), 459–487.

Chapter 2

You Cannot Make This Stuff Up: Science, Theory, and Knowledge

Learning Objectives

- Describe the differences in possible and plausible
- Define retroduction
- Name and define Ronald Akers' four criteria to evaluate theory
- Apply the meaning of tautology to theory evaluation
- Explain causality in the social sciences
- Describe how social scientists conclude research findings
- Name and define the three elements of causation
- Compare and contrast the four types of causality

Asking to Understand

One of the cutest (and most annoying) traits of young children is their inquisitive nature. They ask why about everything. If you tell them it is bedtime, they will ask why; they will ask why the sky is blue, why they need to eat their peas, why they cannot eat all of their Halloween candy on Halloween night. Kids want to understand what makes the world go 'round, and asking why helps this understanding. Why- and how-type questions allow us to understand motivations of behavior, rationales for rules, and reasons for the existence of something.

As a researcher, you should start to channel your inner child. Make sure you do so at appropriate times, as it is probably not a good idea to start asking your professor or boss "why" every five seconds. Just remember that you have lost some of your kid-like cuteness, so you cannot get away with the same inquisitive nature as you once could.

People theorize to explain why. Theories are different from facts, but they are not necessarily the opposite of facts either; facts are those things we consider truth, because we have made repeated observations and/or the results of experiments have supported these statements. Theories are explanations that often incorporate facts.

In the social sciences, a theory should be more than just *possible*—it should be *plausible*. It also should *make sense*.

Remember though, in the social sciences (and hard sciences!) truth is inconclusive; meaning, what we know as "truth" can change from day to day. The reality is, the truth is the truth—it does not evolve or change, people do. We discover things that (ideally) bring us truth and a better understanding of it, we just often do not know it. Think about things we have thought were true in the past: the earth is flat; margarine is better for you than butter; dinosaurs were taken out by a volcano, not an asteroid; etc.

Why Does My Dog Bark?

My husband and I are proud to be owned by both an older cat (Trouble whom I mentioned in Chapter 1) and a young puppy named Walter. Walter is a Coton de Tulear (yes, I do believe that must be the most pretentious breed name possible for a dog). Considering I am a researcher, it should come as no surprise that I did a lot, I mean *a lot* of research when looking for a dog. One of the many reasons we liked Cotons is that they seemed to be playful but only seldom barkers.

I am not sure if the entire Internet has plotted against me and lied about the breed, or perhaps we just got an outlier, but Walter loves the sound of his own bark. I am serious—he sometimes barks in his sleep. I was curious about how to stop the barking, so we started trying many tactics. One thing we had to realize is that the barking was happening for a reason. Moreover, the barking was happening at different times for different reasons. He barks when he wants something, he barks when he is excited, but he also barks when he gets frightened. If we scolded him for barking when he is frightened, it certainly will not ease his fears, and probably will not make him stop barking! To learn *how* to stop the barking, it is important to understand *why* it is happening in the first place.

So, I read about barking behaviors and methods to stop it, and then I test them out. For instance, if the problem is that they are stress barking at strangers, then you should create a "positive association" with strangers by giving dogs treats when you see someone approaching. Let's just say that this was an epic fail with Walter, and I was that idiot crouching down trying to coax their dog with hot dogs and cheese while people looked at me as though I were insane. At this point, we are still in the experimenting phase of trying not to be "those people" with "that dog."

Why Did I Talk about My Dog?

While I enjoy discussing the adventures of Walter, I brought him up to show you why theory matters. The different tactics I use to try and eliminate his excessive barking are all based on some sort of theory. To change something, we have to try and understand why it is happening in the first place. At times, there is a whole body of research that has asked why and tested proposed reasons for it, so it gives us a better guide on where we should start our research. The one thing you should never do is to start research without seeing what information is already available on your subject. Going back to Walter's barking, I could attempt to use my own methods to change his behavior that are based on nothing. Perhaps I perform an interpretive dance to the barking gods or sing Jason Derulo's "Hush." Do these tactics sound absurd? That's because they are because they are lacking any *theoretical rationale*. Me trying to figure out how to stop my dog's barking without looking for any guidance is no sillier than you trying to propose a research project without looking at what research is out there. For instance, if I go to Google Scholar (see Chapter 14: How to Design a Research Article), and type "dog behavior," Google Scholar produced 1.6 million results; so, there are likely a few things available that can help me with my dog. If you think there is less on crime and criminology, you would be wrong: Google Scholar produced 1.98 million results when searching for "crime." Remember that unless you are conducting research on something where the "why" is basically unknown, you want to start with seeing how others have answered the "why" question on your topic—in other words, what theories have been developed to explain the behavior or existence of whatever you are examining?

Funny enough, the more confusing the answers are to the "why," the more interest and opportunities there are. There is a reason that weight loss is a $20-billion-dollar industry: there is no clear-cut answer and what works for one person does not work for another. In fact, the more research that is done on weight loss, the more confused we become. What once seemed simple—eat fewer calories than you burn, lose weight—is really not so simple. While this is not great news for anyone trying to lose weight, it is great if you have some new, inventive, weight-loss method: you could be rich soon. Conversely, for most people, if you saw a commercial for a new type of headache medicine that is shown to be "just as effective" (not more, not less) as aspirin, I doubt it would peak most people's interests. That is because scientists seem to have a better understanding of why headaches occur and how to stop the pain that they cause.

The good news (or bad news, depending on how you look at it) is that the "why" to crime is just as confusing as weight loss, and we do not have any real answers. We can explain why some people commit crime and use methods to prevent them from committing other crimes, but we have found that crime is not a single "why" and "how" subject. There are a lot of things we should understand about the crime and the people committing before we can ever begin understanding why people commit crime and how we can stop crime. So, why is this good news? It is a big business—crime is not going away anytime soon, so there are plenty of employment opportunities.

Theory and Research:
Inductive and Deductive Approaches

In Chapter 1, we introduced you to inductive and deductive approaches to research. We are bringing them back into this chapter to show you how theory is developed or tested in a research context.

There are times when you might observe something that seems peculiar and perhaps you think there must be an explanation for it. While there are certainly unexplainable events, most often, there are theoretical explanations for why something is occurring or why one thing is related to another (Leary, 2016). This is an inductive approach— you want to make sense of what you are seeing or what the "data" hold, so theory could be an afterthought. In his book *Outliers*, Malcolm Gladwell basically asks why some people are so much more successful than the majority of people (Gladwell, 2011). Gladwell states[1] that there must be a synthesis of opportunity and intelligence with about 10,000 hours of practice. Bill Gates and the Beatles are amazing at their crafts, but it was the opportunities to hone their crafts (access to labs for programming and excessive performances at a German strip club, respectively) that allowed them to become the successes they are. Gladwell observed and then tried to explain, by noticing patterns in various stories.

Let's say you read Gladwell's book and were curious whether his theory (opportunities and 10,000 hours) held true. Perhaps you even found his claims suspect, so you collect data on a large sample of the most successful people in the world to test Gladwell's theory of success. This is a deductive approach to research. You started with a theory and are collecting data to test that theory. His theory has been met with a lot of criticism, so you would likely have a lot of support in testing it (Kakutani, 2008).

The research approach and process are messy and cannot be tied up with a bow. Often researchers are not really taking a purely inductive or purely deductive approach to research, but instead, are doing a little bit of both. This is referred to as *retroduction* (Maddan & Walker, 2011). We observe something in our lives and want to make sense of that observation. If there is literature on the subject, then we want to see how that literature jives with what we have observed. Or it could be that you start a project using a deductive approach to test a theory, but then find that the data do not support the theory. You then want to come up with an explanation to explain why the data you collected are showing something different that contradicts the theory.

Take, for instance, studying and test grades, since we have all had our own experiences and observations with test taking. If a theory shows that studying more increases test grades and I test that theory and find that, even when accounting for things like IQ and how someone studied, those who studied over 10 hours for a test

---

1. This summary is not comprehensive and does not do justice to Gladwell's book *Outliers*.

did worse. Not only does my data not support the studying-test-grade theory, they show something *completely different*. Now I need to start developing my own theory to explain these findings and recommend that, in the future, someone needs to test my theory.

What Makes a Good Theory?

I am going to assume you like ice cream, but I am also going to assume you have had a flavor of ice cream that was not so good. If someone who had never had ice cream asked you how you judged whether ice cream was good, you probably have criteria, even if you have never thought about those criteria. Perhaps things like temperature, texture, whether it is a flavor that should never exist in ice cream (stupid bubblegum), etc. We evaluate food, people, and things by whether they are good or bad. If you remember in Chapter 1, I discussed that you had probably already decided whether you liked this book or your Research Methods class. This is also a form of evaluation. (We talk more about evaluation in Chapter 10, just in case you're curious ...)

We can use criteria to evaluate whether a theory is a good theory or a not-so-good theory. Ronald Akers, a criminologist who developed social learning theory (Burgess & Akers, 1966), identified four important criteria to evaluate theory. These include (1) *Logical Consistency, Scope, and Parsimony*; (2) *Testability*; (3) *Empirical Validity*; and (4) *Usefulness and Policy Implications* (Akers & Sellers, 2009).

A theory has different "parts" or "statements" that are often referred to as propositions. For instance, if you have taken Criminological Theory, you may have learned about differential association theory, which is a theory by Edwin Sutherland (1947/1992). In his theory, Sutherland basically argued that criminal acts are learned behavior. However, to elaborate, he had nine assertions or propositions within his theory. Akers has argued that those propositions must make sense (logic), and must support or build on one another (consistency). If you had a theory that refined sugars lead to obesity, you cannot then have a proposition that focuses on how an increased intake of saturated fats are to blame for the United States' obesity epidemic. Additionally, how much the theory can explain is important (scope). If my refined sugars/obesity theory is only applicable to Hispanic females in their teens, this is only helpful to a small portion of the population. The wider the range of the scope, the better—but it is also important that the theorist recognizes the realistic scope of their theory. Keeping that in mind, a theory should also be parsimonious. If you have ever heard the term KISS (keep it simple stupid), that is what parsimony means. You want to provide the simplest explanation with the least number of assertions (propositions) as possible.

For example, let's say Company X developed a new shampoo, and in their commercials, promise that the shampoo produces a "perfect hair day," but only for those people who have thin, fine hair. If **Bob** has thick, coarse hair, he probably will not buy the product since it was not marketed to his hair type; however, BOB also will not write a scathing review of the shampoo and try to return it. This is because Company X was realistic about their scope. JANE, however, has thin, fine hair and purchases the product. After reading the directions on the shampoo bottle, JANE realizes that the "perfect hair day" takes a lot of work:

Perfect Hair Day:

1. While in the shower use exactly ½ of a cup of water to wet your hair.

2. Wait two minutes.

3. Add two teaspoons of shampoo to your hair.

4. With the shampoo still in your hair, blow dry your hair until it is bone dry.

5. Repeat 1–4.

6. Rinse completely. For best results use Company X's conditioner and styling products!

While it may be effective, the process to a "perfect hair day" is not so parsimonious, making the shampoo seem much less appealing. Similarly, a complicated, messy theory will be less appealing. The more you can explain with less, the better.

Testability and Empirical Validity

Part of what makes a theory a good theory is that someone can test its validity. You may live your life with a "no regrets" type of attitude, but that does not mean that you have not felt a pang of regret at some point in your life. A lot of people probably believe that if they had a chance to do some part of their life over, they might make one or more decisions differently than the first time. While this is interesting, and a researcher could find out whether people do believe they would make different decisions, what we cannot find out is if they actually would. Let's say a researcher hypothesized "Given the chance to go back in time, people will make different decisions." That is all well and good, but it is not testable. Current technology does not include methods of time travel; so, at least at this point, there is no way to test this.

In criminology, it is important to have a theory we can test. While it is likely you dislike class exams, papers, and assignments, wouldn't it be much scarier if professors graded you on feelings? Especially if they had never communicated with you? Imagine in a large lecture class where assignments and tests are the only criteria used to assess your knowledge. Without these assessments, a professor would have no way to say whether you had learned what you needed to learn in the class.

In the social sciences, we assess testability by falsifiability. Karl Popper (1959) argued that social scientists needed to do a better job at using the scientific method (remember science lab?). The idea behind falsifiability is that we cannot prove a theory is true, we can only demonstrate that it is false. The test of a good theory is that we can *test* whether it is false. For instance, if I tell you I am the fastest runner in the world, you can test this. It does not mean that you must go measure how fast every single person in the world runs—you simply need to find just one person who runs faster than I do. You have disproved my theory. However, I cannot prove that my theory is *true*.

If I theorize that aspirin cures headaches, that theory is supported only to the point that someone's headache is not cured by aspirin. If you theorize that your childhood friend is the perfect friend, this is true only until your friend does something that contradicts that, such as talking trash behind your back. In these two scenarios, there was evidence that demonstrated both statements were not true.

Circular Thinking and Tautology

One of the common ways that a theory becomes untestable is when it is tautological, which is like using circular reasoning. Let's go back to the weight loss industry. JANE wants to lose some weight. She goes to a weight loss clinic, and they tell her "we have had great success with our 'yay for exercise!' program. Those who exercised lost an average of ten pounds per month." JANE then asks how they measured exercise, assuming they would have used something like pedometers, Fitbits, or even having their clients report what exercises they completed each day. Instead the weight-loss agent responds, "We know they exercised because they lost weight." You cannot measure exercise by weight loss because it is working backwards.

For example, BOB the criminologist writes a theory proposing that anger is related to crime; specifically, the angrier someone is, the more crime they will commit. If BOB defines anger as physical harm of a person or threat of physical harm to a person (hitting, punching, or other bodily harm) and then defines violent crime as those crimes where there was physical harm or a threat of physical harm he is basically stating that crime influences crime—well, *duh*. While this may seem simple enough, sometimes there is tautological reasoning that is more subtle.

One example of this is the Illinois hearsay law. Hearsay is typically inadmissible during court proceedings.[2] While there are exceptions and exemptions, states generally do not allow it. Hearsay has been a point of contention, considering that someone may be unable to testify in court because of the defendant's wrongdoing (for instance, if the defendant killed the witness!). Presented with a parallel scenario during the Drew Peterson murder trial, Illinois ended up passing a law in 2010 that allowed for hearsay when the unavailability of the witness was attributable to the defendant's misconduct. Playing a wacky attorney in *The Good Wife*, Carrie Preston essentially argued that the law's procedures are tautological.

---

2. The term hearsay refers to any statement that was said out of court and is offered up as evidence.

So, let me get this straight. It allows for hearsay as long as a murder is established. And a murder is established here because there is a hearsay statement that establishes it. Tell me when the snake actually devours its tail, okay? (Toye, 2010).

For a theory to be good, it needs to be tested and come out on top. Generally, tests of the theory should *not* be able to falsify the theory. Ideally, to obtain *empirical validity*, tests of a theory should not reveal evidence demonstrating the falsehood of the theory. For example, JANE decides to marry BOB against the wishes of her father, Jon. JANE has theorized that BOB will be a wonderful husband, but Jon is skeptical. However, he cannot seem to find anything wrong with BOB or anything that contradicts JANE's theory. So, Jon, being a paranoid father, sets up a few scenarios. The first is an opportunity for BOB to cheat on JANE. BOB refuses the woman's advances. The second is an opportunity for BOB to become wealthy if he should leave JANE. Again, BOB refuses. These are both tests of JANE's theory that BOB will be a wonderful husband; and in both tests of the theory, no evidence is revealed that disproves it. Therefore, Jon eventually supports the theory that BOB is a good husband to his daughter; however, if BOB were to suddenly run off with the nanny, then Jon would have his evidence to falsify JANE's theory.

Akers' last criteria is that a theory should be *useful and have real policy implications.* This is incredibly important within criminology and criminal justice. Just because something is interesting does not mean it is useful or helpful to anyone! When developing research questions and studies, it is important to step back and ask why the study will matter and for whom does it matter. (Just a heads up: the role of research in policy and practices will be discussed in the last part of Section 2.)

Science and Logic

Science, regardless of whether we are referring to hard sciences (like biology or chemistry) or social sciences (criminology, sociology, psychology, etc.), has the same general goal: answer questions, and answer questions using logical, planned methods (Bachman & Schutt, 2013). If you remember in the first chapter, I mentioned epistemology, which is the science of knowing. We want to know stuff, and the only way to know anything is to ask, guess, investigate, and cautiously answer. In the social sciences, the one thing we *do not do* is commit. Social scientists are like that flaky friend who will not let you know if they are going to show up to the party on Friday night. They say something like "Yeah, I totally want to go and should be able to go ... but I might be wrong." Social scientists will say something similar: "Yeah, how your parents raise you is related to how likely you are to commit crime, but we could be wrong, and we know there are exceptions." Remember to be that flaky friend when you make any conclusions in social science research. We do not prove, we generally cannot say one thing causes another (more on that soon), and everything we do conclude comes with some sort of caveat.

Figure 2-1: The Aggregate and Outliers

Health Recommendation	George's Lifestyle
Drink in Moderation	Drinks 2–28 beers in one sitting.
Do not drink daily	Drinks daily
Do not smoke cigarettes	Smokes cigarettes daily
Five servings of fruits and vegetables daily	Five servings of fruits and vegetables yearly
Exercise 200 minutes a week	Does not exercise (except for random destination walking)
Eat approximately 2,500 calories daily	Skips meals and/or does not eat for days

One versus Many

Before we even broach the subject of causality, I want to make a clear distinction: causality is referring to everyone, not the individual. Just because something works for you does not mean it works for everyone else; and thus, lacks causality. Sometimes, certain events or certain people are simply unexplainable. For instance, a friend of mine (we will call him George) is *truly* a medical marvel. He is quite healthy and more energetic than almost anyone I know; however, he fails to follow just about any health recommendation that exists (see Figure 2-1).

Besides being an example of what *not* to do, this is the only other time that George should be used as an example. But it *works* for George—he is in his mid-forties and is doing quite well. Another example of this is Elizabeth Sullivan, who in 2015 was 104 years old, which she attributed to her consumption of three Dr. Peppers daily (Grossman, 2015). Obviously, something is working for Elizabeth Sullivan, but it probably has little to do with Dr. Pepper. Regardless, she is an exception to the rule, as is George.

Most people are not like this; otherwise, we would not be so fascinated by them. In research, these cases sometimes throw off what we are finding because they are so "out there" (hence the name outliers)! With social science research, we follow the rule of the many, not the few. What works for most is what we are typically interested in, not what works for "that guy." Therefore, we focus on the **aggregate**; meaning the group of individuals, not each individual him or herself. When referencing causality, we are thinking about the aggregate, not the individual.

Causality

There are three conditions that must be met before causality is established. These include: *correlation*, *temporal ordering*, and *absence of spuriousness*.

Correlation refers to a relationship between two variables. If you play the mirror game with a friend, when they move, you move. You can move the exact same way they do or the exact opposite. There is a correlation between hours studied and test grade, or there is a correlation between the number of drinks I consume and the number of stupid things I say. Just remember that *correlation does NOT equal causation*! Repeat this five times—seriously. While drinking is *related* to the number of stupid things I say, there are many other reasons for my stupidity. Additionally, I say stupid things with no alcohol. A correlation simply means there is some sort of pattern between the changes in two variables. That's it.

If your two variables are moving in the same directions, this is a positive correlation, or a positive relationship. If they are moving in opposite directions, this is a negative relationship. So, a positive relationship would be that the more you read this book and make notes in it, the more you understand. A negative relationship would be that the less you read this book and the less you make notes in it, the more money you will receive when you sell it back to the bookstore. Here's a trick to remember the difference between the two: think of your variables as people playing the mirror game. If they can move together in the same direction, these two people probably have a positive friendship/relationship. Those that are moving in opposite directions are probably less in tune with one another and have more of a negative friendship/relationship.

Another element of causation is *temporal ordering*: we need to know whether X is influencing Y. Have you ever heard the question, "Which came first, the chicken or the egg?" This is the idea here! When it is not clear which variable, the independent or dependent, came first, then you are not meeting the criterion of temporal ordering. The question remains, however, of where those friends learned crime, and how someone would end up associating with peers who were deviant. So, for instance, if **Bob** associates with criminal peers, was **Bob** predisposed to be criminal, and that is what attracted him to those peers? Also, from whom did **Bob**'s peers learn crime?

Remember that correlation does not equal causation? *Spuriousness* is a harsh reminder of that! For us to claim causality we must make sure that there is not another variable that is explaining the correlation between variable one and variable two. One of my favorite examples of this is that ice cream sales are related to crime. Therefore, ice cream consumption causes crime. The reality is, there is another variable. "There is a relationship between ice cream sales and crime." If we took this at face value, we would believe that ice cream is making people violent and more willing to go commit crime. But this is a spurious relationship, because there is a missing variable—summertime/heat! When it is warm outside, we are (a) outside more, (b) eat more ice cream, and (c) are easier to victimize because we are outside more.

Additionally, there are four types of causality:

1) Necessary Causation,

2) Sufficient Causation,

3) Contributory Causation, and

4) Absolute Causation (which is a combination of sufficient and necessary).

While these types may seem complex at first glance, they are quite easy to distinguish between. You might have experienced something like the definitions and/or examples from your SAT or ACT tests, as they are popular types of questions for the logic and reasoning portion of those assessments. First, for *necessary causation* to occur, A must exist before B (necessary cause). That means you will never have B if you do not have A. Specifically, if one thing is a necessary cause of another, then that means that the outcome can never happen without the cause. An example of this might be probable cause for an arrest. You cannot have an arrest (B) without first having probable cause (A), therefore probable cause is a necessary cause of an arrest. However, sometimes the cause occurs without the outcome.

For *sufficient causation* to occur, A is sufficient enough to cause B (sufficient cause), meaning if you have A, you will ALWAYS have B. That is, if something is a sufficient cause, then every time it happens the outcome will follow. The outcome always follows the cause. An example of this would be speeding and breaking the law. Speeding (A) always results in violation of the law; (B) however, like necessary cause, sufficient cause means that the outcome may occur *without* the cause.

Contributory causation occurs when factors not required for being necessary or sufficient (though they can be in some instances) have an impact on the effect. So, A causes the outcome B, but only when additional factors are present between A and B. An example of this is the sanction of the death penalty in the U.S. for the crime of murder. It is possible to murder someone in the U.S. and not receive the death penalty; however, if certain contributory causation factors occur (legally they are called aggravating factors) the death penalty can be given. These factors would include killing for monetary gain, killing in a particularly heinous fashion, and killing in the commission of another felony.

Understanding the different combination of causation is where it can get a little tricky, but if you stick with the basic definitions and examples given, you can make sense of the following:

If A is not necessary nor sufficient for B then sometimes when A happens B will happen. B can also happen without A. The cause sometimes leads to the outcome, and sometimes the outcome can happen without the cause

If A is both sufficient and necessary for B, then B will never happen without A. Additionally, B will ALWAYS happen after A. The cause always leads to the outcome, and the outcome never happens without the cause (Boskey, 2017).

This will generally result in one of the following manifestations for A and B:

> Both necessary and sufficient (Absolute). Probable cause must be met for an arrest to take place.

Summing It Up

One textbook definition of theory is *a set of interconnected statements or propositions that explain how two or more events or factors are related to one another* (Curran & Renzetti, 2001, p. 2). While this may indeed be true, theory can take several more practical forms for researchers and serves a few important roles. It can serve as a model or framework for observation and understanding, allowing researchers to shape both what we see and how we see it. Theory allows the researcher to make links between the abstract and the concrete, the theoretical and the empirical, thought statements and observational statements. Additionally, theory can aid in explaining and predicting relationships between variables while simultaneously guiding and generating new research as theory is empirically relevant and always tentative.

Theory frames what we as researchers examine, how we think, and how we analyze. It provides basic concepts and directs us to the important questions. It suggests ways for us to make sense of research data. Theory enables us to connect a single study to the immense base of knowledge to which other researchers contribute. Theory increases a researcher's awareness of interconnections and of the broader significance of data and it allows researchers to describe, explain, predict, or control human phenomena in a variety of contexts (Neuman, 2013).

Discussion Questions

1. What are the three elements of causality? Name and explain each one.

2. How does tautology relate to theory evaluation?

3. What is an example of spuriousness?

4. What is absolute causality? How does it relate to other types of causality?

5. What degree of certainty do social scientists have when making conclusions from their study? Why do they not have more (or less) certainty?

6. Identify a criminological theory and evaluate it using Ronald Akers' four criteria to evaluate theory.

Trying It Out

Your professor may ask you to complete the following companion assignment available from the publisher. Using the supplied worksheet form, identify a theory that you will use and then evaluate the theory using the metrics of evaluation.

References

Akers, R. L., & Sellers, C. S. (2009). *Criminological theories: Introduction, evaluation, and application.* New York: Oxford University Press.

Bachman, R., & Schutt, R. K. (2013). *The practice of research in criminology and criminal justice.* Thousand Oaks, CA: Sage Publications.

Boskey, E. (2017). Understanding necessary and sufficient causes in science and medicine. *VeryWell Health.* Retrieved from https://www.verywellhealth.com/understanding-causality-necessary-and-sufficient-3133021.

Burgess, R. L., & Akers, R. L. (1966). A differential association-reinforcement theory of criminal behavior. *Social Problems, 14*(2), 128–147.

Curran, D.J. & Renzetti, C.M. (2001). Theories of crime (2nd edition). Boston: Allyn & Bacon.

Gladwell, M. (2011). *Outliers: The story of success.* New York, NY: Back Bay Books.

Grossman, S. (2015, March 20). This 104-year-old woman says Dr. Pepper is what's keeping her alive. *Time Magazine.*

Kakutani, M. (2008). It's true: Success succeeds, and advantages can help. *The New York Times.*

Leary, M. R. (2016). *Introduction to behavioral research methods.* New York, NY: Pearson.

Maddan, S., & Walker, J. (2011). *Criminology and criminal justice: Theory, research methods, and statistics.* Ontario: Jones & Bartlett Learning.

Neuman, W. L. (2013). *Social research methods: Qualitative and quantitative approaches.* New York, NY: Pearson Education.

Popper, K. (1959). *The logic of scientific discovery:* New York: Routledge.

Sutherland, E.H. and Cressey D. (1992). *Principles of Criminology.* (11th ed). Lanham, Md.: AltaMira Press,

Toye, F. (Writer). (2010). Hybristophilia [Television series episode]. In M. King & R. King (Producers), *The Good Wife.* Brooklyn, NY: CBS.

Chapter 3

Ethics and Research

Learning Objectives

- Describe the events in the Tuskegee Syphilis Study
- Describe the events in the Stanford Prison Experiment
- Describe the events in the *Obedience to Authority* study
- Evaluate the ethical issues within the Tuskegee Study, the Stanford Prison Experiment, and the *Obedience to Authority* study
- Name and describe the three guiding principles for researchers conducting studies with human participants
- Discuss the development of institutional review boards
- Discuss the *Belmont Report*
- List and define the rules of research
- Evaluate the role of each rule of research within your own proposed study
- Explain the importance of informed consent
- Report the institutional research board application process for researchers

It may seem odd that we need to provide a whole chapter on ethics and research, especially when taking into consideration that most people conducting research are well-educated. Well-educated people should be able to conduct research that is ethical, right? Just do not treat people badly; be caring; do not lie, cheat, or steal; and make sure you do not do anything illegal.

In my elementary and middle school, we had this code of conduct that drove me nuts. I wasn't the only one. Many of the students would mock it when the teachers were not looking. The teachers and administrators made us repeat it at least once every school day, which only intensified our pure hatred for it. When given a timeout at recess, it was because you violated the code of conduct. It was so ubiquitous that even your family knew it (and—if you have parents like mine—might mock it along with you). Unsurprisingly, I still remember them to this day. Surprisingly—and annoyingly—they truly encompass all you need to do in life to be a decent person, both personally and professionally. The code of conduct includes three statements:

Code of Conduct

1) I will respect myself and others.

2) I will be responsible for my own actions.

3) I will treat people the way I want to be treated.

In my eight years of hearing those statements and having to watch as they were used to assess my classmates' and my own bad behavior, not once did I find them to be inapplicable to a situation. I share this with you because if you can remember these three things (I will not ask you to repeat them aloud), you can probably remember the rules of ethics in research.

Learning from the Past: Studies Gone Wrong

Hopefully, hearing ethics and morals makes you think of good things and good people. There are numerous, possibly countless, examples of ethical research in criminal justice and criminology. However, there are also a much smaller number of past studies that provide exemplary guidelines of how *not* to conduct research ethically. We are going to look at some of these examples and later, examine why they were wrong. Sometimes unethical research studies can show how one can get "caught up" in the moment and likely lack intent to commit harm to others. Other unethical studies reveal that sometimes — there is no excuse for the unethical behavior of researchers — people are just the worst.

The one thing all these studies have in common is that they failed to follow the rules of ethical research. These rules (which we will later discuss) outline violations of at least one of the guidelines in the code of conduct: *respect*, *responsibility*, and/ or *equal treatment of others*.

Tuskegee Syphilis Study

Remember, we said that sometimes, people are the worst. In 1932, some government researchers who worked for the *Public Health Service* (PHS), decided they wanted to see what happens to someone who was infected with syphilis. At the time, this seemed like a worthy goal — there was no treatment, and we really did not understand how syphilis affected an individual throughout their lifetime. Originally, the study was supposed to last about a year; however, it ended up lasting over forty. This study is often referred to as the *Tuskegee Study*.

The researchers teamed up with Tuskegee University, which is a historically black college located in Alabama. Prior to starting this study, there had already been syphilis testing in this area of over 4,000 men and women. The researchers decided to recruit only men who were over the age of 25, and initially, they ended up with a sample of

408 men (Gray, 1998). Later, they added a *control group*—a group of 200 men who were relatively the same demographically as the original sampled group but had not contracted syphilis. For the researchers to recruit and keep the men participating, they offered them free medical treatment, sporadic meals, and transportation. When some of the men died, the researchers wanted to conduct autopsies to further their understanding of the physical effects of syphilis. So, they offered free burial insurance to the families of these men in exchange for allowing them to conduct autopsies.

While this all sounds on the "up and up," here's where the issues start: the men who had syphilis were not told they had syphilis but, instead, were told they had "bad blood," which was treated with iron tonic and aspirin (Reverby, 2009).

While the unethical behavior here is bad enough, there is one key detail omitted: all the participants were black men. Also, it gets worse. Eleven years after the start of the study, a treatment for syphilis was introduced: penicillin. By 1947, it was being widely used to treat syphilis. Yet, the Tuskegee Study continued, the men were still not informed that they had syphilis, and the treatment was withheld from all the men. Instead of seeing Penicillin as a blessing to treat their participants, the researchers saw it as a threat to their study (Christensen, Johnson, & Turner, 2011; Gliner, Morgan, & Leech, 2011). The researchers not only failed to provide the treatment to their participants, they actually made sure others refused to provide it to them. When treatment became available in Birmingham (not too far from Tuskegee) and eventually mobile treatment came to the area, a nurse who worked for the study told those administering the treatment that the syphilis study participants were to be refused treatment (Christensen et al., 2011; Gray, 1998).

What's really perplexing is that the Communicable Disease Center (now the *Centers for Disease Control* and Prevention) reviewed the study in 1969—and said it was fine to continue until all the patients died. Another employee of the Public Health Service (PHS), *Peter Buxtun*, was working in California when he became aware of the study. He attempted to challenge the study with others at PHS, but to no avail. Finally, in 1972, he became a whistleblower and the Associated Press picked up the story, which made the public aware of the study (Christensen et al., 2011). The NAACP filed a lawsuit on behalf of the participants, which was settled in 1975 for ten million dollars. Additionally, the men who had participated, and eventually their immediate families, were provided with lifetime medical benefits (Centers for Disease Control and Prevention, 2017). However, it was not until 1997, 65 years after the study had started, that there was an actual apology, which came from President Clinton, who apologized on behalf of the nation (Centers for Disease Control and Prevention, 1997).

Stanley Milgram

In the 1960s, a Yale psychologist by the name of *Stanly Milgram* became curious about why some people follow orders, even when those orders just seem wrong. This all stemmed from him learning about Nazi war criminals and wondering whether they were independent thinkers who acted on their own accord or if they were, in fact, just obeying authority figures. Thus, he began to develop a study he would later publish as *Obedience to Authority* (Milgram, 1963; Milgram, 1974).

Here is an example of the experiment procedure: Three people were involved in each session of the experiment: the researcher, the teacher, and the student. The "teacher" was a voluntary participant in the study. While the student was in another room, the researcher would instruct the teacher to ask questions. When the student answered incorrectly, the researcher would instruct the teacher to push a button, which would deliver an electric shock to the student. For each subsequent question the student got wrong, the shock would increase by 15 volts, with the maximum being 450 volts. Here's the kicker: the "student" was not a volunteer, but a member of Milgram's research team, and the "student" was *never actually shocked;* it was all a hoax.

After the session was completed, Milgram reported that he debriefed each participant to let them know it was a ruse. Milgram wrote that his goal was to see how far people would go just because an authority figure (the researcher in a lab coat) told them to continue, as it was necessary for the experiment—he found that over 60% continued to "shock" the student to maximum voltage.

Perhaps this does not seem that bad—no one was being physically harmed, which at least gives Milgram a leg up in his study compared to Tuskegee. However, there was concern regarding psychological harm. First, the methods he used for debriefing were quite vague, leading some to wonder what methods he was using to debrief participants (Baumrind, 1964). Milgram argued that in later follow-ups with participants, they were generally thankful and glad they had participated in the study. However, some participants have reported a long-term need for psychological care, as well as high levels of stress and anxiety (Blass, 2004; Perry, 2014).

Later investigations revealed even more issues with what Milgram had reported—or more, what he failed to report. In reviewing Milgram's research, *Gina Perry* (a fellow psychologist), discovered that Milgram had, in fact, failed to debrief the majority of participants—most of them actually believed for almost a year that they had shocked another human being (Brannigan, Nicholson, & Cherry, 2015; Perry, 2014). Perry also uncovered some of Milgram's unpublished work. One experiment that was particularly interesting was an iteration of the study where Milgram decided to use volunteer participants for students and teachers, so he recruited pairs of people who were either blood related or well acquainted. In this version of the study, there was a higher rate of disobedience than obedience: there were more participants who refused to continue with shocks than participants who obliged. Moreover, one of Perry's most interesting findings casts doubt on the whole notion of obedience to authority: Milgram had discovered that many of the participants never bought in to the notion that they were actually shocking someone. And, those who did believe they were actually shocking someone were less likely to continue administering shocks than those who did not believe it (Brannigan et al., 2015; Perry, 2014).

Stanford Prison Experiment

One of Stanley Milgram's high school classmates, *Philip Zimbardo,* was the primary researcher of another infamous study of ethical issues in research. Like Milgram, Zimbardo is a psychologist (a social psychologist, to be exact) who was interested in group behavior and how it related to individual behavior. In the 1970s at Stanford University, Zimbardo and his graduate students recruited male college students to partake in a simulated prison. This project became known as the *Stanford Prison Experiment.* As participants, they were given one of two roles, that of the prisoner or the guard. Zimbardo went all out to make the study seem as real as possible: Palo Alto police actually went and "arrested" the prisoner participants and took them to the "prison" (the basement of the Stanford Psychology Department), which had "the hole" for solitary confinement, an office for the warden (Zimbardo), a visitation room, and a room for parole hearings (Goodman, 2007; Haney & Zimbardo, 2008; Zimbardo, 1972).

What happened was surprising: prisoners started to act like prisoners — by the second day they rioted by barricading themselves in their prison cells. The guards responded forcefully, using fire extinguishers to move the prisoners, making use of solitary confinement, and even taking some of the prisoners' clothes. As each day passed, the participants became more certain of their roles, and it took only 36 hours for a prisoner participant to have a mental breakdown.

What's interesting about this study is that Zimbardo, acting as the warden and the researcher, later reflected that he was caught up in his own role. While he had invited a number of colleagues to come view the prison, it was *Christina Meslach* (a former student who later became Zimbardo's wife!) who criticized Zimbardo's methods and made him "see the light" (McDermott & Zimbardo, 2007). As a result, the study, which was supposed to last for two weeks, was terminated after only six days (Goldie, 2004).

Developing a Code of Conduct in Research

One upside to bad things happening is that they often bring some much-needed attention to a certain issue. Specifically, after the treatment of participants in Tuskegee, Congress enacted the National Research Act. Part of the act was the creation of the National Commission for the Protection of Human Subjects of Biomedical and Behavioral Research (Vollmer & Howard, 2010). While a ridiculously long name, the commission was incredibly important to research ethics, specifically, the commission's *Belmont Report,* which was originally published in 1978 (U.S. Department of Health, Education, and Welfare, 2014).

The *Belmont Report*

In the report were three guiding principles for researchers conducting studies with human participants: *beneficence, autonomy,* and *justice.* The beneficence principle guides researchers to assess what type of effect their research will have on their study's participants and to ensure that the benefits of the study outweigh the risks. Autonomy refers to respecting one's participants—participants should generally know what they are getting themselves into before they choose whether they participate—and it required additional safeguards for those participants who might lack some sort of autonomy—such as prisoners or minors. Justice is the idea of fairness; the benefits and risk of the study should be relatively equal across all involved in the study (U.S. Department of Health, Education, and Welfare, 2014; Graziano & Raulin, 1993; Vollmer & Howard, 2010).

Institutional Review Boards

Let's be honest: just introducing these principles would not stop unethical research. It is not like researchers' minds were blown when these were introduced; we generally know that a guiding principle should be treating people with respect and making sure they are not harmed. No need to worry—these principles were just the start, as the *Department of Health and Human Services,* as well as the *Food and Drug Administration* used these principles to develop their own rules and regulations for research. What came of this was the requirement of *institutional review boards* (IRBs). Organizations such as universities and other agencies should create a board of individuals that review whether research is up to ethical snuff; that way, researchers are not just left to their own devices to conduct research. Moreover, each IRB must answer to the National Institutes of Health or the Food and Drug Administration (if conducting research on drugs) (Gladwell, 2007; Office for Human Research Protections, 2016; Maxfield & Babbie, 2014). So, if you get bored one day, Google your school and institutional review board—there should be one!

Rules of Research Ethics and Putting It All Together

The commission's three principles should sound familiar. Remember that annoying code of conduct from my elementary school? It's true—they are pretty much the same thing, just in a context of research. Beneficence and autonomy both fall under respect: make sure that you and whomever you are interacting with leaves the situation feeling like they got more good out of the process than bad. Treating people in the way you want to be treated is like justice: if you treat all people the way you want to be treated, then the benefits and risks they receive will be relatively equal. While the second statement in the code of conduct, being responsible for your own actions, does not fall directly in line with one of the three guiding principles, it really encompasses all three. You must realize the role you play and how much of an impact (good or bad) you can have on others when conducting research.

The Rules of Research and Other Key Points

By no means is this a comprehensive list of the rules of research, but instead, these provide you with some of the more common rules or specific examples of the three guiding principles. Additionally, these are key things to think about when you are conducting your own research.

Minimize Harm

This first rule, *minimize harm*, is somewhat redundant, since it is directly covered by the *Belmont Report*'s principle of beneficence. However, it is an important rule, so we want to make sure to review it some more. Avoid harming others with your research—it is not a good idea to harm people. However, sometimes harm is inevitable. Like we said before, the harm must be outweighed by the benefits. There are some days I really hate to go to work and would rather lay around on my couch and watch Netflix all day; however, the harm (me having to get my lazy self to work and feeling whiny about it) is certainly outweighed by the fact that I receive a paycheck, which allows me to eat and pay for the Netflix subscription.

This is a silly example, but a serious issue. Sometimes it seems like little harm can come of social science research; it is those medical studies that are dangerous. To some extent that is true, yet psychological harm and other types of physical harm can and have occurred in social science research.

Maintain Confidentiality and Anonymity

Maintain confidentiality and anonymity is just as it sounds: if you can, try allowing your participants to be anonymous, so that you do not know who they are. If you give a paper survey, make sure you do not know who is who and who participated. If your participants cannot be anonymous (for instance, you are interviewing them face-to-face), then make sure that you guarantee confidentiality—let participants know that while you know who they are, you are not going to tell anyone else who they are. Generally, when I am ensuring anonymity for participants, I also like to ensure confidentiality. Even though you shouldn't need confidentiality if you have anonymity, this is a "just in case" sort of tactic. Meaning, "I am trying to not know who you are, but if I happen to find out, I'll keep my mouth shut." Let's say I gave a paper survey to a classroom with 200 students and noticed an elderly gentleman in this class. When I review the paper surveys, I see that one participant's age is 87. I can probably guess that I know who this participant is; however, that does not mean I need to tell anyone who this participant is, and I will do my best to forget it. Besides being ethical, maintaining confidentiality and/or anonymity will yield more valid results. This is because people tend to be more honest under the cloak of anonymity. Imagine filling out course evaluations about professors and having to put your name on it. You would probably have some different thoughts then, especially if you knew you would have to see that professor again!

Honesty

Be *honest*—do not lie to participants, unless you must do so. Generally, we can tell participants what the study is about and what our goals for the study are. However, there are sometimes we need people to be unaware of the goals. Research can still be ethical when using deception, but the deception should not harm the participant. In behavioral sciences, we can often use minor forms of deception. If we wanted to conduct a study that examined attention to detail by measuring how long a participant took to review a question, we probably would not want them to know this *explicitly*, because knowing that would probably lengthen the time they would take to review the question (or in some cases, shorten it). This would affect the validity of the research (validity of research will be reviewed in detail in subsequent chapters).

There are, however, other times that deception is a bit more serious, particularly in qualitative research, when one is using covert tactics. Sometimes, the researcher(s) will not disclose that they are researchers at all. These studies can be necessary but often walk an ethical tightrope. So, while a college student, we recommend sticking to studies where you are honest with participants. Wait for covert research until it is truly necessary and make sure the benefits outweigh the risks—by far! Honesty extends beyond working with your participants. Once you have collected your data, you need to be honest about what you found and what you did not find! Do not fudge numbers or facts—ever!

Voluntary Consent

One really important thing to remember about participating in research is *voluntary consent*. Meaning, it should be voluntary—really, truly voluntary. Additionally, participants should know that just because they volunteer does not mean they cannot change their minds later.

Informed Consent

To make sure that we are recruiting participants who want to be a part of our study, there is something called *informed consent*. Typically, IRBs (reminder: institutional review boards) require that participants sign an informed consent form that lets the participant know what they are signing up for, so that they can prepare themselves and truly consent. Additionally, participants have the right to terminate participation at any time, and the informed consent letter/form usually outlines this right, as well as resources (like counseling services or police) should they need these services after participating. The form also provides participants with a way to contact the researcher(s) and the researcher's institutional review board, should they need to report any negative reactions or experiences that they had when participating in the research.

Special Populations

There are certain groups of people whose consent is not so crystal clear or who may need a bit more research protection. In these cases, IRBs watch out for them more. They are referred to as *special populations* or *protected populations* and include (but are not limited to) children, pregnant women, those who are mentally disabled, and those under correctional supervision (especially those who are imprisoned). Additionally, college students can sometimes fall under the umbrella of needing additional safeguards.

Populations like *pregnant women* are generally concerned with anything that may affect the health of the mother and child. While this is most often associated with medical research, let's not forget that psychological stress can be harmful, too! The other special populations are more concerned with how consent is obtained and how to ensure that consent was given without any sort of coercion. To conduct research on those with mental disabilities, a researcher needs to inform the IRB why it is truly necessary to have participants with certain impairments, and researchers need to be ready to explain how they will seek consent, which usually requires that a person who has been authorized to represent them must also consent to the study.

Minors (those under 18 years of age) are generally unable to consent to pretty much anything, and this extends to research participation. If conducting research with juvenile participants, you typically need the parent's permission *and* the child's permission (there are, of course, exceptions to this). Additionally, the research should pose no more than a minimal risk (meaning, the lowest level of risk a study could pose). If the risk is higher, then the benefits must outweigh the risks and must directly benefit the minors who are participating.

At first glance, classifying prisoners and those under correctional supervision as a protected population may seem odd; however, inmates, probationers, and parolees are more vulnerable to coercions. This is especially true for inmates—if there were not procedural safeguards, inmates could be forced to participate in studies at any time and they would have no place to go if they tried to refuse. While this is an extreme example, coercion can also be subtle. If they are afraid they might lose yard privileges or think they could gain good time for participating, then this may be used as a coercive tactic to increase participation. Even a small amount of monetary compensation could be coercive, since prisoners often do not have access to a lot of funds. So, IRBs are especially stringent when reviewing studies that involve prisoners. They want to make sure that the risk is minimal and that consent is truly voluntary.

College students are not necessarily considered to be a special population, but can be in certain contexts. For instance, if your professor asks you all to volunteer in a study by filling out a paper survey, and then sits there to see if you complete it, that can be coercive. Even providing extra credit could be seen as coercive in some situations, if students are not offered an alternative extra credit assignment (such as writing a paper or completing an extra assignment).

Do Not Initiate Crime

Perhaps this rule seems obvious: *do not initiate crime.* As criminologists, we are obviously interested in crime and offenders. It is important to remember that there is a whole other bucket of issues that arise when conducting research (especially research where you are involved with the participants) that involves crime. If you interview individuals who have been convicted of committing a murder, then you are talking with them after the fact; however, before or during the commission of a crime is tricky. On a federal level, you are protected from legal liability; however, some states provide no such protections. I do not recommend hanging out with a research participant while they are on their way to murder someone—not a good idea; however, the guidelines become less clear when referencing more minor crimes. For instance, two anthropologists, *Philippe Bourgois* and *Jeff Schonbert* (2009) documented the lives of heroin users in their book *Righteous Dopefiend*, which included associating with them during times when they bought, sold, and used heroin. Considering part of their purpose was to understand the social dynamics before, during, and after these illegal acts, it would have been a true detriment to their study if they had left any time heroin was around.

While determining whether sticking around during certain criminal activities can be tricky, there is one hard, steadfast rule when it comes to crime: you do not always have to be a crime stopper, but you cannot be a crime starter. As a researcher, you cannot encourage or start crime. So, Philippe Bourgois and Jeff Schonbert could not encourage their participants to use, buy, or sell heroin. A researcher's presence should not increase any criminal activity.

Where Past Studies Went Wrong: Applying the Rules of Research

The three examples we presented earlier, the Tuskegee Study, the *Obedience to Authority* study, and the Stanford Prison Experiment are all great tools to learn what not to do. We can make a checklist of these rules and guidelines, and use these studies as examples to see where things went wrong (see Table 3-1). Determining what rules were violated is partially subjective, so do not be surprised if you have a different interpretation of a rule.

Of the three studies, Tuskegee really takes the unethical cake: the only rule it did not violate was starting crime (technically), even though nowadays, the study itself would be deemed criminal! There was no concern about the benefits to the participants (beneficence/minimize harm), and there was certainly no respect given to participants (autonomy). Additionally, participants were not treated equally, since

Table 3-1: Applying the Rules and Guidelines of Research

Guideline/Rule	Rules Violated		
	Tuskegee	*Obedience to Authority*	Stanford Prison Experiment
Belmont Report Guidelines			
Beneficence	✓	✓	✓
Autonomy	✓	✓	
Justice	✓		✓
Rules of Research			
Minimize Harm	✓	✓	✓
Maintain Confidentiality (or Anonymity)	✓		
Honesty	✓	✓	
Voluntariness	✓		✓
Do Not Start Crime			

those in the control group were not harmed in the same ways as those who had contracted syphilis (justice). Many who were not a part of the study became aware of the Tuskegee participants, considering the nurse informed other medical staff in the area to not provide syphilis treatment to the study's participants. The researchers certainly were not honest with their participants, considering they were not told they had syphilis, but instead, they were told they had "bad blood." While the subjects may have volunteered, there was no informed consent, and they did not really know for what they were volunteering.

The *Obedience to Authority* study was unethical for several reasons; arguably the key violation was their lack of honesty with participants, which lasted throughout the entire study. While it could be psychologically harmful for someone to believe they were shocking someone for the duration of their participation in the experiment (approximately an hour or so), considering that participants were deceived and were not debriefed afterwards is particularly unethical and psychologically harmful. Thus, they failed to follow at least two of the *Belmont Report*'s principles: autonomy and beneficence. In later iterations of the experiment, when they used participants for both the "student" and "teacher," the principle justice was also violated, considering that the students and teachers were not treated equally.

The Stanford Prison Experiment did not really start veering off the ethical path until after it had begun. While some of this could have certainly been foreseen, many of the problems that arose during the study were likely unintentional. The key rules violated in this study were minimizing harm (or beneficence) and voluntariness. It is not that Zimbardo and his colleagues lied to participants—they informed them of the various conditions of the study—it is that the participants *and* the researchers did not really know what they were getting themselves into. Once immersed, many of the participants who were playing "prisoners" truly did not believe they could leave (even though they could). This changed the voluntary nature of the study. Further, after the guards became out of control in their treatment of the prisoners, the study should have been terminated immediately. The risks at that point certainly outweighed the benefits, and harm was not minimized.

IRB Application:
Process and Procedures

Applying to have your research reviewed by your respective institutional review board can be a stressful process. Ideally, the whole process would be uniform across all agencies and universities, but of course, it is not. Just like you may have some professors who return graded work to you very quickly, you have others who may need a bit more time. This is the same with IRBs, since at a university, they are comprised of a bunch of professors! The time an IRB needs to review one's application will differ, just as the actual forms and process will differ, too. Should you ever embark on your own research, it is good to talk with some of your professors to find out about the IRB process at your university or agency, as the review process can significantly affect your research timeline. Some research does not require IRB approval—get it anyway. It is better to have the IRB approve your study when you did not need it than vice-versa.

While they differ, your IRB will typically require you to explain what your research is, what the purpose is, who your participants are, and what procedures you will use to protect your participants. With that, you will explain how you will keep and store your data and how you will go about reporting your research results. You will also need to provide detail about the benefits of your research, as well as what the foreseeable risks might be and how you will manage any negative outcomes.

Generally, there are three levels of review for research: exempt, expedited, and full committee. Exempt is the least stringent level of review. Research that falls under exempt are typically those that do not require any direct contact with people and pose the most minimal risk possible. In most cases, when you apply to have your research reviewed, you do not decide whether it is exempt. Instead, one or more IRB members determine if it is exempt or should be classified as expedited or full (Office for Human Research Protections, 2016).

Research that falls under expedited review is like exempt but generally requires some sort of contact with participants, or does not guarantee anonymity of participants (an example would be conducting face-to-face interviews with adult participants who are not in a protected population). While exempt requires the least time and degree of review, expedited is a bit more stringent in making sure that the procedures for the study follow guidelines, and that the risk is both minimal and outweighed by the benefits of the study. With expedited review, the approval process will take longer than exempt, but requires only a few members to review the procedures.

The most stringent level is full review, or full board review. There is not a single criterion that makes research in need of full board review, it is simply that it does not fall under the criteria of exempt or expedited review. Most often, it is that there is more than minimal risk and/or there is a special population involved. When this happens, the entire IRB must meet to discuss and review your research. This is where the review process can become lengthy, as the IRB only meets every so often (this again varies from agency to agency) and they can only cover so much at each meeting.

Summing It Up

While the process of obtaining IRB approval for research can be taxing, it is certainly important! Sometimes, we lack foresight into seeing what might go wrong with our research, so it is certainly a good idea to have other people review what could go wrong. Just as we did in reviewing past studies, make sure to use the checklist created to ensure that you are on the right path to conducting ethical research. If you're ever tempted to skip the whole IRB process, just remember that it could be your research that we cite as an unethical study in this book's next edition, and we certainly do not want to do that!

Discussion Questions

1. Of the three main studies discussed in Chapter 3 (the Tuskegee Study, the Stanford Prison Experiment, and the *Obedience to Authority* study), which one do you think had the most ethical issues? Which one do you think had the fewest ethical issues? Explain your answer.

2. What are institutional review boards? How were they developed? Why are they important?

3. How would each rule of research apply to your own research project? Think of a project you might want to do and then explain how each rule would apply.

4. Why does informed consent matter? What is a situation in which researchers would want to avoid informed consent? Is it ever ethical not to have informed consent?

5. What are the ethical challenges for researchers studying crime and criminality?

Trying It Out

Your professor may ask you to complete the following companion assignment available from the publisher. Using the supplied worksheet form, you are going to go investigate your own university's institutional review board.

References

Baumrind, D. (1964). Some thoughts on ethics of research: After reading Milgram's "Behavioral study of obedience." *American Psychologist, 19*(6), 421.

Blass, T. (2004). *The man who shocked the world: The life and legacy of Stanley Milgram.* New York, NY: Basic Books.

Bourgois, P. I., & Schonberg, J. (2009). *Righteous dopefiend* (Vol. 21). Berkeley, CA: University of California Press.

Brannigan, A., Nicholson, I., & Cherry, F. (2015). Introduction to the special issue: Unplugging the Milgram machine. *Theory & Psychology, 25*(5), 551–563.

Centers for Disease Control and Prevention. (1997). *Presidential apology: Tuskegee.* Retrieved from www.cdc.gov/tuskegee/clintonp.htm.

Centers for Disease Control and Prevention. (2017). The Tuskegee timeline. Retrieved from www.cdc.gov/tuskegee/timeline.htm

Christensen, L. B., Johnson, B., & Turner, L. A. (2010). Research methods, design, and analysis (11th ed.). Boston, MA: Allyn & Bacon.

Gladwell, M. (2007). *Blink: The power of thinking without thinking.* New York, NY: Back Bay Books.

Gliner, J. A., Morgan, G. A., & Leech, N. L. (2011). *Research methods in applied settings: An integrated approach to design and analysis.* Abingdon, UK: Routledge.

Goldie, P. (2004). What people will do: Personality and prediction. *Richmond Journal of Philosophy, 7*, 11–18.

Goodman, A. (2007, March 30). Understanding how good people turn evil: Renowned psychologist Philip Zimbardo on his landmark Stanford Prison Experiment, Abu Ghraib and more [Interview transcript]. *Democracy Now.* Retrieved from https://www.democracynow.org/2007/3/30/understanding_how_good_people_turn_evil.

Gray, F. D. (1998). *The Tuskegee Syphilis Study: The real story and beyond*: Montgomery, AL: NewSouth Books.

Graziano, A. M., & Raulin, M. L. (1993). *Research methods: A process of inquiry.* New York, NY: HarperCollins College Publishers.

Haney, C., & Zimbardo, P. G. (2008). Stanford Prison Experiment. In B. L. Cutler (Ed.), *Encyclopedia of Psychology and Law* (pp. 757–758). Thousand Oaks, CA: Sage Publications.

Maxfield, M., & Babbie, E. (2014). *Research methods for criminal justice and criminology.* Boston, MA: Cengage Learning.

McDermott, R., & Zimbardo, P. (2007). *The Lucifer effect: Understanding how good people turn evil.* New York, NY: Random House.

Milgram, S. (1963). Behavioral study of obedience. *The Journal of Abnormal and Social Psychology, 67*(4), 371.

Milgram, S. (1974). *Obedience to authority: An experimental view.* New York, NY: Harper & Row.

Office for Human Research Protections. (2016). IRB organizations (IORGS). Retrieved from https://www.hhs.gov/ohrp/register-irbs-and-obtain-fwas/irb-registration/irb-organizations/index.html.

Perry, G. (2014). *Behind the shock machine: The untold story of the notorious Milgram psychology experiments*. New York, NY: The New Press.

Reverby, S. (2009). *Examining Tuskegee: The infamous syphilis study and its legacy*. Chapel Hill: University of North Carolina Press.

U.S. Department of Health, Education, and Welfare. (2014). The *Belmont Report*. Ethical principles and guidelines for the protection of human subjects of research. *Journal of the American College of Dentists, 81*(3), 4–13.

Vollmer, S. H., & Howard, G. (2010). Statistical power, the *Belmont Report*, and the ethics of clinical trials. *Science & Engineering Ethics, 16*(4), 675–691. doi:10.1007/s11948-010-9244-0.

Zimbardo, P. G. (1972). *The psychology of imprisonment: Privation, power and pathology*. Palo Alto, CA: Stanford University.

Chapter 4

The Nitty Gritty: Technical Terms and Parts of Research

Learning Objectives

- Describe the five steps of research
- Apply the five steps of research to one's own project
- Evaluate a research idea regarding viability and importance
- Apply a theoretical framework to a research proposal
- Differentiate between research and null hypotheses
- Differentiate between directional and nondirectional hypotheses
- Explain the differences between variables of interest and control variables
- Differentiate between independent and dependent variables
- Describe the process of recruiting participants
- Define units of analysis
- Explain the difference between a population and a sample
- Explain the role of generalizability in nonrandom and random sampling techniques
- Describe global research designs
- Explain the parts of a research design
- Compare and contrast cross-sectional and longitudinal designs
- Define reliability
- Define validity
- Define operationalization

The truth is, the research process is long and complicated. Further, the quandary of research methods is that to understand research, you need to do research, and to do research, you need to understand it. One of the challenges a lot of our students have had in the past is understanding everything in context, while also being introduced to a bunch of new technical terms. While there will be additional terms and definitions in chapters to come, our goal is to simply get some of the "nitty gritty" out of the way, in hopes that you understand it *some*, so that way, when the term arises again, you will at least have some familiarity with it.

That being said, this chapter will be kind of choppy, and that is purposeful. While we could attempt to make it flow more, we would have to add a lot more transitional information, and we want to keep this to a bare minimum (with some examples, of course). So, we will go through the research process (up through data collection), and then when necessary, at the end of each step, we will provide more detail on the technical terms we presented.

Looking at Primary Data Collection: Distinctions between Primary and Secondary Data Sources and Secondary Datasets

The point of this chapter is to review the steps of the research process for original collection of data, whether those data are primary or secondary sources. A *primary data source* is when a researcher collects data that would not exist without them collecting it, for example, conducting interviews or distributing a written survey instrument. A *secondary data source* is when the data already exists, but not for the purposes for which a researcher is using it. Examples would be arrest records, newspaper articles, or movies. When using secondary sources, the researchers do not actually make the data, but they still have to collect it and put it together in an original way.

In this chapter, we do not cover the use of *secondary datasets*, which do not require original data collection but are already put together for purposes of data analysis (an example would be the U.S. Census or the General Social Survey).

If this seems confusing, think about the three ways to make a cheesecake:

Primary Data Source: Making everything from scratch (all the way down to churning your own butter).

Secondary Data Source: Buying all the main ingredients, but still *make* the cheesecake.

Secondary Dataset: Buying a cheesecake from the Cheesecake Factory.

It is important to note, however, that at times, a secondary dataset requires a lot of work before it is "ready" for data analysis, even though it is put together for that purpose. Researchers often have to put in a lot of time and effort to "clean" the dataset.

Stage One: Coming Up with an Idea
(Inventing a Recipe for Cheesecake)

At times, research ideas may originate from studying past literature on a topic; however, ideas for research often stem from your own experiences and observations. As you already know, individuals' experiences differ a *lot*. That may have an effect on the utility of these research ideas. If the going motto for a new gadget to make life easier is "there has to be a better way!" then the motto for a research idea is probably "there has to be a reason!"

On the show *Shark Tank*, one of the products presented was "Drop Stop," which is used to prevent things from falling between one's center console and the seat of their car. This product has been incredibly successful, since most people know the pain of having their cellphone or wallet or whatever fall into that open crack. However, one of the Sharks, Robert Herjavec, was perplexed at the utility of this. It seems he had never had a problem with this. It seems he had never *experienced* this. So, when thinking about research ideas within criminology and criminal justice, it is normal to think about your own experiences and your own observations. Just remember that they may not be what most people have experienced, which may have an effect on the utility of your research idea.

Stage Two: Is Your Idea Worth It?
(Is Your Cheesecake Worth It?)

Write It Down and Reassess

There have been times I've had a research idea in the middle of the night. I've written it down, looked at it a couple of days later, and decided that I could not have come up with a worse idea if I had tried. Sometimes, we just have bad ideas, and in those cases, it is important to walk away for a bit, come back, and reassess.

Viability

If you get past the reassess stage and decide your research idea is still a good one, that is great! Now it is time to determine if the idea is worth it. One of the worst parts of our jobs is working with students who are new to research and having to rain on their parades. Sometimes, the research idea is fantastic, but carrying it out is unreasonable. This is typically due to time, money, or access. You want to interview serial killers to understand more about the role of their siblings? Not necessarily a bad idea; however, here comes the rain:

1) This would take a lot of money for purposes of traveling to various prisons, staying in hotels, taking time off work and/or school, etc. You would also need recording equipment, transcription equipment, etc.

2) This would take a lot of time (see #1).

3) You have to convince serial killers to meet with you.

4) You have to convince prison administrators to *let* you meet with serial killers.

5) What about your safety? What about others' safety?

6) You are probably going to have a really, really hard time convincing the institutional review board.

Often, the more valuable the study, the more complicated the study, so the more research experience you are going to want to have. The first time you design a research project and the first time you actually collect your own data, *you are going to make mistakes.* The reason I am so certain about this is because I still make mistakes all the time! I have not taken part in a single study where afterwards, I did not think "I wish I had …" My mistakes and regrets are fewer than they were when I began to conduct research. Thus, I recommend keeping the stakes low and treating some of your first research experiences as valuable processes rather than products.

Does It Matter?

Let's say you have made it past these first two steps in the second stage, and you believe your research idea is feasible in that you will not have huge challenges accessing those people you wish to study, and you believe that you can conduct this research without spending money or time that you do not have. Now it is important to ask if the research idea is worth it. There are a few ways to do this, but one piece of advice to start: just because it is interesting, does not mean it is important. By importance, we mean does it have social and scientific impact? Would the findings of the study likely matter to people? Would it possibly have some effect on individuals' lives? Would the findings of the study matter to those in the criminology field? Would it matter to criminological researchers? So, when you think about your idea, if someone asked you "so what?" or "why should I care?" can you answer it? If not, you *may* need to reassess your idea, or you may need to develop a better understanding of the impact of your research idea.

Step Three: Theory and Literature (Examine Your Cheesecake Recipe in Context of Other Cheesecakes)

Theoretical Framework

If you remember in Chapter 2, we talked a *lot* about theory. It is what helps keep you grounded in your research. You want to use theory to help guide your research or use research to help develop theory (going back to Chapter 1—remember inductive versus deductive research?). In the social sciences, most research uses a deductive approach, so that is what we are going to assume within the traditional research process. Therefore, you want to begin understanding your idea in a theoretical context.

Remember that ideas can pop out of nowhere, but they often arise from your own experiences and observations. One example of my own was when I was pumping gas and saw that the directions for the credit card machine said, "Remove card rapidly." Now, I am sure there is a good reason for saying rapidly instead of quickly or swiftly, but it seemed like more people would recognize quickly than rapidly. As I was pumping gas, I thought about how hard it would be to do *anything* if I were unable to read. I could not follow the directions to pump my own gas, never mind many more complicated life tasks, such as writing this very book! Therefore, my undeveloped research idea might be to ask if there is a relationship between literacy and crime. More specifically, I might ask if being illiterate is related to frustration and anger, and if this relates to crime. If I began to develop this idea without looking at theoretical context, I would miss some very important work. Specifically, the work of **strain theorists**, such as **Emile Durkheim**, **Robert Merton**, and **Robert Agnew**. Specifically, one proposition of strain theories is that the inability to achieve goals through legitimate means results in strain, which can increase the likelihood of criminal involvement. Further, strain can refer to feelings of anger or frustration. In examining strain theorists and past literature that has examined strain, my idea now has context and a framework, which gives it more meaning and helps me to organize how I would develop my idea into an actual study.

Past Literature

It is incredibly, incredibly important that researchers understand and review what past researchers have done. If you do not, it is like driving to a place you have never been with no directions—you may get there, but you could have saved yourself a lot of time and stress if you had just gotten directions or used Google Maps.

We examine past literature to see what other researchers have done in relation to what we are looking at and to make sure that what we are doing is unique and *builds on past literature*. If you want to examine the relationship between caffeine and individuals' alertness, you may find that there are 25,000 studies that all demonstrate the same thing: most people are more alert when they consume caffeine. If there is a strong consensus in a field, then you likely do not need to disrupt that consensus. Unless you have some crazy new take when looking at the relationship between caffeine and alertness, you are simply going to be the author of the 25,001st study on the relationship between the two. Generally, that is boring and a waste of time and money. (There is one caveat to that: if you are developing your own research proposals for your Research Methods class, you are probably going to do something that has been done before, and that is okay! Your research proposal should be practice.)

We also examine past literature to learn about what worked and what did not work for past researchers. You can learn from past researchers' mistakes. If you look in a research article, most will have a section on limitations and a section on future research. The limitations section is where they will tell their reader where their research was restricted, because *all* research has limits. Their future research section is very informative, as it serves as directions for future researchers: they are telling their readers *how to build on literature*. (For more on this, see Chapter 13, Part 2, "How to Read Research.")

Step Four: Refining Your Research Question, Developing Research Hypotheses, and Identifying Variables of Interest (Reexamining Your Cheesecake Recipe)

At this point, you have a good idea of what else is out there, research-wise. You have developed a good frame of reference. Your original research idea likely originated from your own personal observations. Using your developed knowledge on theory and past literature, you can begin to develop your idea from more of an academic perspective and identify your **research problem**. This stems directly from your research idea. Perhaps you have noticed that a lot of students seem to cheat on tests. This can be the beginning of you developing your research problem.

Additionally, you can begin to develop your research question(s) and research hypotheses. A research question is a way to begin transforming your research problem into something with a bit more meaning. You may start with "Why do some students cheat?" As you begin to look at the literature, you might observe that one theory used as a framework to explain student cheating is low self-control theory (Gottfredson & Hirschi, 1990; Tibbetts & Myers, 1999). You may further develop that research question to ask, "What is the relationship between self-control and cheating?" Perhaps you want to look even further and examine how self-control is related to different forms of cheating (Stogner, Miller, & Marcum, 2013). You would then refine your research question again. After developing your research question, you then want to begin working on developing your research hypothesis. A *research hypothesis* (or hypotheses) is an educated guess based on the frame of reference you developed examining past literature, including theory related to your topic. A hypothesis is a statement on what you *expect* you will find with your research: some change, relationship, or effect. For instance, there is a relationship between self-control and cheating. (For more on developing research questions and hypotheses, see Chapter 12, Part 1, "How to Get Started with a Research Idea.")

Terminology Interruption: Hypotheses

When defining a hypothesis, I said that you typically expect to see some difference, relationship, or effect. These three words are important to remember when you develop research hypotheses, as one of them will often be included in your hypothesis statement!

There are different *types* of hypotheses, and it is important to know the difference when developing them and when testing them (if you have to take a statistics course, then you will learn about testing hypotheses).

When you develop a hypothesis, you can decide whether you want to state the direction of the hypothesis. You only want to do this if you have a really good framework and have a pretty good idea of what you expect from your research. For instance, you may guess (based on the literature) that those with low self-control cheat more frequently. If you are confident in this guess, then you may specify the direction (increases and decreases) of your hypothesis: *decreases* in self-control are related to *increases* in cheating. This is called a ***directional hypothesis***, because the direction is specified. If my hypothesis does not specify the direction of self-control or cheating, then it is a **nondirectional** hypothesis: there is a relationship between self-control and cheating.

While we develop the research hypothesis, we actually *test* the null hypothesis. Remember in Chapter 2, we discussed Popper's falsifiability: that we cannot prove something is true, we can only prove it is false. So, our research hypothesis is what we expect to see. (A research hypothesis can also be referred to as an ***alternative hypothesis*** or an ***experimental hypothesis***) (Field & Miles, 2012). When we develop a research hypothesis, we also develop a ***null hypothesis***, which is generally the opposite of what we expect to see. (You can usually just add the word "no" or "not" to your research hypothesis, and it takes care of it.) Your research/alternative hypothesis is denoted as H1, and your null hypothesis is denoted as H0. Using the self-control example:

H1: There is a relationship between self-control and cheating.

H0: There is NO relationship between self-control and cheating.

It is important to realize that a research hypothesis can be directional or nondirectional, but regardless, the null hypothesis typically will not change:

H1: Higher levels of self-control are related to lower frequencies of cheating.

H0: There is no relationship between self-control and cheating.

Researchers do not actually talk about null hypotheses when they write up what they found; so, you do not generally have to tell your reader your null hypothesis. However, it should always be kept in your head, because it is how we test whether what you expected to see in your research is what you saw, and whether what you saw will hold true with other people who *did not* participate in your research (more on that in step five).

Table 4-1: Bob's and Jane's Attributes

Bob:
(1) White
(2) 24 years old
(3) Male
(4) Vanilla
Jane:
(1) Black
(2) 21 years old
(3) Female
(4) Mint Chocolate chip

Identify Variables of Interest (Cheesecake Ingredients)

After you have developed and fine-tuned your hypothesis, you need to identify your **variables** of interest. Remember that variable is similar to vary, which is exactly what we are talking about here: a variable is something that changes in one person or is different from one person to another. For instance, age is a variable. My age is probably different from yours (in most cases, I am older than you), and the ages of your fellow classmates *vary*. Another variable would be favorite flavor of ice cream. For example, imagine I asked fifteen people I know what their favorite ice cream flavor is. Five said mint chocolate chip, four said chocolate, and six said vanilla. These different flavors are referred to as **attributes**, which are just some characteristic or category we use to describe something or someone. Variables are then made up of different attributes.

Going back to **Bob** and **Jane**: **Bob** is a white, 24-year-old male who loves vanilla ice cream. **Jane** is a black, 21-year-old female who loves mint chocolate chip ice cream. For each person, there are four attributes.

In Table 4-1, we can see that for **Bob** and **Jane**, we have attributes that can be categorized or paired together: White and Black, 24 years old and 21 years old, male and female, vanilla ice cream and mint chocolate chip ice cream. The categories that we can place each pair of attributes in are examples of variables: White and Black are *races*, 24 years old and 21 years old are a*ges*, male and female are *genders*, and vanilla and mint chocolate chip are *favorite flavors of ice cream*. We have four variables: race, age, gender, and favorite ice cream flavor.

If you look back to the nondirectional research hypothesis, there are two variables in there: self-control and cheating. These are the variables we are interested in including in our study (see more on variables in Chapter 12, Part 1, "How to Get Started with a Research Idea" and the example research paper in Chapter 14, Part 3, "How to Design a Research Article").

Terminology Interruption: Variables

Control Variables

Although we have variables of interest, we probably want to know some other things too, right? When examining the literature, you may have noticed that even when researchers were examining this relationship between cheating and self-control, they also had other variables, like age, ethnicity, gender, and perhaps, grade point average. There tend to be differences in the frequency of cheating for different groups of people; for instance, those who are older are typically less likely to cheat on exams than those who are younger. These are examples of *control variables*. The simplest explanation of control variables is that we want to know how self-control influences cheating, regardless of one's age, ethnicity, gender, and GPA. If we set up our study correctly and include these variables, then when we test our hypothesis, statistical tests will allow us to hold these control variables constant. Meaning, that we would look at the difference in levels of self-control and how it is related to cheating frequency within participants who are the same age, same race, same gender, and have the same GPA.

For instance, let's look at Lisa and Carmen to understand what "holding constant" means.

Lisa is Latina, 21-years old, female, with a 3.2 GPA.

Carmen is Latina, 21-years-old, female, with a 3.2 GPA.

If we used a score for self-control that ranges from a scale of 0–100 (100 being highest level of self-control and 0 being lowest) ...

Lisa scored 4 points.

Carmen scored 98 points.

If cheating is measured by the number of times one has cheated on an academic test ...

Lisa reported 28 times.

Carmen reported 2 times.

Then, we can say that even though Lisa and Carmen are the same age, the same gender, the same ethnicity, and have the same GPA, it looks like there are major differences in their levels of self-control, as well as the number of times they cheated.

Statisticians are able to use statistical tests to compare our variables of interest to multiple individuals with the same control variables. This gives us a better idea of the *real* relationship between self-control and cheating.

Independent and Dependent Variables

In Chapter 2, we talked about temporal ordering: which came first, the chicken or the egg? In most studies, we want to be able to identify which *does* come first.

For instance, one study looked at gender in relation to favorite comfort foods (Wansink, Cheney, & Chan, 2003). If we wanted to conduct a similar study, we could hypothesize that there is a difference in comfort food preference accounting for gender. We have two variables of interest: gender (male/female/other) and comfort food preference. Our variables of interest can be further categorized as *independent variables* and *dependent variables*. In this example, we want to ask which one *could* have an effect on the other. Food preference should not have an effect on my gender; meaning, if I prefer homemade macaroni and cheese instead of chocolate cake, I will not transform into a man. My gender is *independent* of my comfort food preferences. In the study that actually examined how comfort food preferences varied for males and females, the researchers found that men were more likely to prefer hearty-type foods (steak, salty foods) and women were more likely to prefer snack-type foods (ice cream, cookies). So, *could* gender have an effect on comfort food preference? Yes! Comfort food preference can change based on your gender, so it can be dependent on your gender. In this example, then, *gender is your independent variable* and *comfort food preference is your dependent variable*.

Going back to the self-control cheating example: cheating on a test will not change one's self-control level, but how often someone cheats on a test may *depend on their level of self-control*.

While it is best to understand independent and dependent variables, there is a trick: often (not always!), your independent variable is first in the sentence! This, however, is not always true, so I do not recommend relying on it.

Here are a few more examples of independent and dependent variables. Remember to look for the primary relationship; meaning, do not look for the exception to the rule!

There is a relationship between alcohol consumption and level of drunkenness.

    Independent: alcohol consumption

    Dependent: level of drunkenness

There is a difference in delinquent behavior accounting for gender.

    Independent: gender

    Dependent: delinquent behavior

Age has an effect on criminal activity.

    Independent: age

    Dependent: criminal activity

Designing Your Study (Step-by-Step Directions for Your Cheesecake): What or Whom Are You Studying?

A research project has to have a plan that is based on how you are going to "answer" your question. One of this first things to ask is "what or whom am I studying?" This is your **unit of analysis.** (See Chapter 7 for more detailed coverage of units of analysis.) This is also your **population.** If you are studying individuals residing in the United States who have been arrested at least once, then all individuals in the U.S. who have ever been arrested are your population. A sample is a handful of your population (the size of that "handful" depends on a number of things, which we will discuss in the sampling chapter).

Sample and Population

You then need to determine *how* you are going to collect a handful of individuals from your population. For instance, if your unit of analysis is college students, and your population is college students at the University of Georgia, you could put every student's name in a hat (or use a computer program!) and select 500 individuals who would ideally agree to participate in your study. In this example, your population is the University of Georgia and your sample is those 500 individuals whose names you pulled from a hat. In this case, we used a *random sampling technique.* Random sampling techniques are certainly best (see "Terminology Interruption: Sampling Techniques"). However, in the social sciences this is not always feasible. If you remember from Chapter 3, "Ethics and Research," participating in a research study is voluntary! While this is definitely a good thing, it does decrease your likelihood of recruiting a random sample of individuals. If your unit of analysis is not individuals, but something like newspaper articles, then using a random sampling technique is much more feasible!

Recruiting participants can be challenging, and it often depends a lot on time and money. If you are able to provide an incentive to participants, this can certainly make your recruitment efforts easier, but it may also recruit people who are not really interested in being good participants: they just want to reap the rewards! After you identify your population, it is best to think about how you might contact participants or obtain the data you need. As I stated, this is easier when your unit of analysis is *not* individuals.

For instance, if I want to examine online news coverage of Iran in the last week, I could access my population by using Google News Search. This would give me a better idea of how big my population is, which in this case, is over 35,000 articles! I could then use a random sampling technique to select a sample of articles to examine.

Terminology Interruption: Sampling Techniques

Random sampling techniques (or probability sampling techniques) are best because we can *generalize* to our population. The way you know if it is random is if *each and every individual in the population has an equal chance of being selected.* If we use a *nonrandom (or nonprobability) sampling technique*, we cannot say that our sample is *generalizable* to our population, because it may not be *representative.* Going back to the University of Georgia example: if you were a student at the University of Georgia and your professor told you to go select 500 students, you would probably select your friends and associates. Perhaps if you are in a sorority or fraternity, you would select others in that organization. You might know a lot of people in your major, so there may be a number of criminal justice/criminology majors in those 500 people that you select. What we can almost be certain of is that your 500 people will not represent the **polation** of the University of Georgia, by race, gender, major, political preference, etc. That is because your friends are not random—they have certain things in common with you. If you then asked those 100 people how much alcohol they drink, this probably would not be the same as the entire population: I cannot *generalize* what I found in my sample of 500 friends and associates to all students at the University of Georgia. A random sample of 500 students at the University of Georgia would be more likely to be representative, and thus, more generalizable.

Setting Up the Research Study

You then want to ask, "*How am I going to set up this research study?*" This is referred to as your research design. Additionally, this is where you want to identify your research procedure, particularly the steps you will take to collect data and the steps you will take to analyze the data. (See more on designing research in Chapter 14, Part 3, "How to Design a Research Article.")

How one's research is set up is often dependent on how much time and money the researcher has. Therefore, it is important to develop and reassess your *budget* and *timeline* throughout your research process. The time and money your research will take is dependent on how difficult or easy a researcher foresees collecting their data will be: if using a secondary data source, such as articles from a Google search, a researcher can have their data at their fingertips in an instant. If using a primary data source, such as interviews or survey responses from individuals, collecting data will take much longer!

However long you believe it will take to collect primary data: double that! The logistics of recruiting and accessing participants can be very timely and costly. For instance, if Professor **JANE** wishes to conduct interviews with female police officers in New York City about their stress levels, the professor will need to think about how she will access police officers. She would first need to establish her population (female

Table 4-2: Example of a Study's Cost

Cost of Recruitment of Female NYPD Officers Using Mailed Recruitment Letters and Reminder Letters			
Product	Count	Cost per unit	Total Cost
Printing	12,000 sheets	10¢/sheet	$1,200
Paper	12,000	1.2¢/sheet	$144
Envelopes	12,000	.03¢/each	$360
Stamps	12,000	.49¢/each	$5,880
Total			$7,584

NYPD officers), which is over 6,000! (Federal Bureau of Investigation, 2014). Professor JANE has also decided that a lot of female officers will probably *not* want to participate in her study, so she is not going to take a sample of female officers but instead, is simply going to interview any of those who volunteer to be interviewed.

Professor JANE would need to first contact all the precinct captains (there are 76 precincts) to gain their permission to simply *ask* whether she may try and recruit female officers to participate in her study. She may want to do this in person or through a written request (both of these are ideal), but may need to resort to other means of contact, such as telephone calls and/or emails. After receiving permission, she would then need to work on recruiting female officers within each precinct. Again, determining how to contact them really depends on what will be most effective and easiest on the officers. Seeing an officer on the street and walking up to them randomly will *not* do the trick. You will likely want to start with a letter and then provide your contact information. You may need to follow that up with a phone call, a reminder letter, or an email. Within this study, the recruitment process alone could take months — and Professor JANE has not even started data collection!

Regarding the cost at this point: if Professor JANE mailed request letters and reminder request letters to precinct captains and then both request and reminder request letters to all female officers in the NYPD, then she would have to mail over 12,000 letters. This would be the most *formal* but also the most expensive method of recruitment. In Table 4-2, you can see the foreseeable costs, *just for recruitment into the study*.

Besides the monetary cost, it can also take a lot of time. Many researchers have a research team to help with these sorts of tasks. As a student, you would (in my experience), not be expected to handle something like this on your own! You surely would not be expected to come up with $8,000 to recruit participants! This simply serves as an example of why it is important to think about time and money *prior* to delving into your research study! Better to prevent disaster then to get stuck in it.

Terminology Interruption: Research Designs

There are a number of possible *parts* to a *research design*, including groups for your research participants (such as *experimental group[s]* and *control group[s]*), tests (*pretests* and *posttests*), *treatments*, and *random assignment*.

There are three global (main) categories of research designs: experimental, quasi-experimental, and nonexperimental (including ex-post facto research designs).

An experimental design is most commonly associated with medical studies and includes all the parts to a research design. A common experimental design is called the *classical experimental design* or the *pretest posttest control group design*. In the classical experimental design, you have participants who are randomly assigned (R) to one of two groups: the experimental (E_1) or control group (C_1). Both groups are given a pretest (O_1), then the experimental group is given a treatment (X_1), then both groups are given a posttest (O_2). The design looks like this:

$$R \quad E_1 \quad O_1 \quad X_1 \quad O_2$$
$$R \quad C_1 \quad O_1 \qquad\quad O_2$$

Here's an example: Dr. Bob and Dr. Jane have developed a new drug for treating migraines. They hypothesize that their drug will decrease the pain symptoms associated with migraines. Their population is those within the U.S. who suffer from migraines. They recruit a random sample of 100 people from their population, and then they *randomly assign* their 100 participants to either the experimental group or the control group, making sure there are 50 in each. Dr. Bob and Dr. Jane could easily put their 100 participants' names in a hat, with the first name they pull going to the control group, the second to the experimental group, the third to the control group, etc. The control group (C_1) is the group that will not receive the treatment, which in this case is the drug for treating migraines. The experimental group (E_1), however, will receive the treatment. Dr. Bob and Dr. Jane used random assignment in an effort to make both groups relatively equal. They can then use their pretest (O_1) to ensure that members in both groups seem similar, particularly in relation to their migraine pain. So, if Dr. Bob and Dr. Jane were to ask patients to rate their migraine pain on a scale of 1 to 10, and the participants in the control group averaged a 7.3, we would hope that the participants in the experimental group would be right around a 7.3, as well. Dr. Bob and Dr. Jane would then give the experimental group the treatment, over a period of time. Then, they give a posttest. Now, the doctors no longer want the groups to be equal: they hope that the experimental group reports much lower pain on average than the original 7.3.

While most often associated with medical studies, experimental designs can be used in many criminological/criminal justice studies. For instance, if Professor Bob and Professor Jane worked at a university where students were required to take Introduction to Criminal Justice in their core curriculum, they could use an experimental design to determine whether taking Introduction to Criminal Justice has any effect on perceptions of the death penalty. If, during freshmen orientation, they were able to randomly assign 100 students to take Introduction to Criminal Justice and another 100 *not* to take the course in their first semester, then they have randomly assigned participants to both an experimental (Introduction to Criminal Justice) and control (those *not* in Introduction to Criminal Justice) groups. They could then give all 200 students a survey asking about their perceptions of the death penalty (which would be the pretest). The treatment is the actual criminal justice course! After the course was completed, the researchers could then give all 200 students the same survey on their perceptions of the death penalty (this would be the posttest).

While experimental designs are ideal, because they get us closer to being able to claim a causal relationship (remember elements of causality from Chapter 2?), researchers in the social sciences are not always able to set these up, often because of the types of *treatment* we are examining. For instance, if we want to know how a drug rehabilitation program works for cocaine users who *have* been arrested and see how it compares to drug users who *have not* been arrested, we cannot have random assignment, because our control group (cocaine users who have not been arrested) would be assigned by a characteristic—in this case, not being arrested. Those in the experimental group would also have a certain characteristic: having been arrested. Therefore, if we put everyone's name in a hat to assign randomly, our arrestees and non-arrestees would get all jumbled. This is an example of a **quasi-experimental design**. Quasi means *almost*. In this case, a quasi-experimental design is trying really hard to be an experimental design but just cannot meet the mark. So, in this case, our research design would look the exact same, just without the randomization: E_1 is the arrestee cocaine user group; C_1 is the non-arrestee cocaine user group. Both groups are given a pretest to determine their current use of cocaine (O_1), then E_1 is given the treatment, and then both groups are tested again (O_2).

$$
\begin{array}{cccc}
E_1 & O_1 & X_1 & O_2 \\
C_1 & O_1 & & O_2
\end{array}
$$

The other type of **main (or global) design** is nonexperimental designs, which often include ex-post facto designs as well. In nonexperimental designs, we are missing more than randomization; researchers are really just looking to see how something is related to something else. Remember the example that we have continued to use is examining the relationship between self-control and cheating. Do either of those seem like they are a treatment that researchers can give to their participants? They should not, because they are not! In fact, what has happened is that the *treatment has already occurred*. This is what we mean by ex-post facto; the treatment has already happened. In this case, we cannot *give* different levels of self-control to individuals—it simply is what it is. Therefore, we are not randomly assigning individuals and then pretesting them, providing a treatment, and then providing a posttest. We would likely just use one "test" that is neither pre- nor post-, such as distributing a survey to our recruited participants. This is an example of when we would want to use control variables. Since we are not able to randomly assign and see how our participants are alike within an experimental design, we can instead (using statistical tests that we will not discuss in this book) group individuals by similarities (age, ethnicity, gender, etc.) to see how the treatment (self-control) influences the outcome (cheating). When making observations about a group of people at just one point in time (like a survey instrument given to college students just once), this is referred to as a ***cross-sectional design***. Cross-sectional research designs tend to be substantially less powerful than ***longitudinal designs***, which are those that have multiple observations using the same group of subjects. Longitudinal studies allow researchers to be more certain that an independent variable had an effect on a dependent variable, than if the researcher had just looked at the relationship after the fact.

As stated, experimental designs are ideal because they get closer to causal explanations. This is because the researchers know when the treatment started and when it ended. If Professor **Bob**'s Introduction to Criminal Justice course starts on August 1st and ends on December 1st, then Professor **Bob** knows his treatment lasted from August 1st to December 1st. Moreover, because Professor **Bob** conducted a pretest and a posttest, he is more certain about how his treatment influenced his outcome than if he had simply conducted a nonexperimental study. Specifically, if Professor **Bob** just surveyed students and asked their views on the death penalty and asked if they had taken Introduction to Criminal Justice, it would be harder for him to pinpoint whether the class had *truly* influenced their beliefs on the death penalty, because Professor **Bob** has no measure for their perceptions *before* they took the course—only after (because the treatment has already occurred).

Reliability and Validity

When a study is *closer* to providing a causal explanation, this demonstrates that the study has more ***validity***. There are multiple types of validity, none of which we will discuss in this chapter (for more on validity see Chapter 5). However, when conducting a study, researchers are aiming for their study to be both reliable and valid. ***Reliability*** refers to *consistency* while validity refers to *correctness*. Here's something that is confusing: If something is reliable, it may or may not be valid; however, if something is valid, it *has* to be reliable.

Example:

I had a friend in graduate school who was *always* late—I literally never witnessed her on time for anything. She was *consistently* late, so she was never *right* on time. It was so bad, that I would actually tell her a different time than what I intended; so, if we were going to meet at 6pm, I would tell her 5:45pm and she would then show up at 6pm.

Her always being late made her timing invalid (because it was the wrong time), but she was *reliably wrong*. If her timing was valid, it would mean that she showed up at the right time, *every single time*. To be right, something has to be *consistently* right.

Another Example:

I used to have a tracking bracelet (like a Fitbit, only not a Fitbit) that would give me two steps for every one step I took. While this was annoying, it always did this consistently. So, I knew that if it told me I had 20,000 steps, I had actually taken 10,000—it was easy to figure out. Now, imagine if it were *sometimes* accurate in counting steps and *sometimes* inaccurate. It would be neither valid nor reliable. This is the worst-case scenario: I would not have any clue about how many steps I had actually taken!

So, in a study, researchers' goals are to *at least* have reliability, and then work towards validity. It is important to know, however, that *validity is always a goal, but one that is never attained. A study (especially in the social sciences) is never perfectly valid.*

Developing Your Instrumentation

Regardless of what type of data you are collecting, you will need some sort of instrumentation to organize it. This may be within your data collection (for example, a survey instrument used to survey college students about their levels of self-control and cheating), or it may be used *after* you have completed your first stage of data collection of a secondary data source (for example, an instrument used to examine news coverage of marijuana in 2010).

An instrument is an incredibly important tool. When collecting a primary data source, the instrument cannot typically be modified once it has been distributed to your participants (there are exceptions to this)! When collecting data from a secondary data source, the instrument can sometimes be modified, but it typically means starting over at the beginning (see "Terminology Interruption: Survey Instruments").

When a researcher develops an instrument, s/he wants it to be **reliable** and **valid**. One way to do this is to create it and have others review it, ideally other researchers who are experienced in what you are researching. Additionally, (when possible) you would want to **pilot** the study: in other words, distribute it to a small sample of people who are like those whom you aim to be your participants and see where things go right and where they go wrong. (For more on survey development, see Chapter 8.)

Terminology Interruption: Survey Instruments

An instrument is a guide to information you need that includes items and questions aimed at collecting that information for you. If you provide a written survey instrument to college students asking their age and student classification, your survey instrument could have two questions to gather the information you seek.

1. What is your age in years?

    _____ years.

2. What is your student classification?
    - Freshman
    - Sophomore
    - Junior
    - Senior

When collecting a secondary data source, you may be interested in knowing how many words each article was that referenced marijuana, and how many people were quoted, up to five people. You could create an instrument for yourself (as the researcher) to collect the information you seek.

1. Article Words: _____words

2. How many people are quoted in the article?
    - 0
    - 1
    - 2
    - 3
    - 4
    - 5 or more

One of the hardest parts about developing an instrument is identifying *concepts* and defining them. Defining concepts in a measurable way is called *operationalization*. A concept is something that is not directly observed and cannot be directly measured. For instance, a therapist would not ask a client "Are you depressed?" to measure depression. Instead, the therapist would try to find out information about the client's behaviors, which *are* measurable. The therapist would first need to know how we operationalize depression. One operational definition of depression is "the persistent feeling of sadness or loss of interest … that can lead to a range of behavioral and physical symptoms" (Mayo Clinic, 2017). An operational definition should provide a description that allows the reader to almost "see" the concept in their head. We can take that operational definition and dive further

---

into what those physical and behavioral symptoms are, like sleeping a lot (or sleeping a little), loss of appetite, crying a lot, etc. If we ask someone about whether, and how often, they've experienced these symptoms, we can then "add them up" and determine if they are likely to have depression.

You can also think that the example we have been using (cheating and self-control) has two concepts that should be defined: cheating and self-control! Sometimes the researcher will need to define and develop ways to measure concepts; however, often other theorists and researchers have operationalized these concepts. For instance, when developing the theory of low self-control, Gottfredson and Hirschi identified six concepts that, together, comprise one's level of control: impulsivity, self-centeredness, preference for simple tasks, risk-seeking, preference for physical activities, and temper. While these provide a deeper understanding of self-control, these are not necessarily an operational definition (they do provide one, but that is going down another rabbit hole). In reality, these six concepts are just that: concepts! As a result, other researchers have tried to figure out ways to measure all six of these concepts, with the most popular being the Grasmick scale (Grasmick, Tittle, Bursik, & Arneklev, 1993). They use 24 questions (statements) about an individual's behavior. For instance, one of the statements for impulsivity is "I am more concerned about what happens to me in the long run rather than the short run." Other researchers have attempted to look at more specific behaviors to measure these concepts, such as whether someone has skydived as a behavior indicative of risk-seeking.

Behavior is not always used to measure concepts. For instance, when you take a Research Methods test, your professor will be attempting to measure your understanding of different concepts. Possibly, your professor may also want to assess your ability to explain those concepts or critically evaluate them. Your final exam, ideally, should measure your overall understanding and knowledge of information in the course—this is a concept that is measured by items (test questions). (For more on operationalization and conceptualization, see Chapter 12, part 1, "How to Get Started with a Research Idea" and the example paper in Chapter 14, part 3, "How to Design a Research Article.")

Step Five: Institutional Review Board Approval

The last part of the research process that takes place before actual data collection is obtaining approval from your institutional review board! (See Chapter 3 for more detail on IRBs.) This requires you to complete various forms and assess the risks and benefits of your research. To find out what your IRB requires, you can typically search your school website for the institutional review board.

Reviewing the Five Steps of Research: Easy as Pie (or Cheesecake)!

This is a dense chapter that has a lot of terminology. The idea was to present it in context of the research process and the steps you would take to actually design a study and collect data. While the terminology was emphasized throughout, these concepts are also discussed in later chapters.

One fear is that by introducing all the terminology, we have made the research process hard to understand. So, we want to review those five steps by using the example we used about primary and secondary data sources: cheesecake. In Table 4-3, I am going with the parallel of collecting a secondary data source, because I certainly will not be making most of this stuff from scratch.

Discussion Questions

1. What are the differences in directional and nondirectional research?

2. Imagine you were going to survey students in your major at your university or college. Using the five steps of research, create an informal proposal. Identify which steps would be most challenging for you.

3. Explain the difference between independent and dependent variables. Then explain how you can recognize which is which in a research study.

4. What is the role of generalizability in random versus nonrandom sampling techniques?

5. Are longitudinal or cross-sectional studies considered to be more powerful? Why?

6. Can a research instrument be both valid and reliable? Can it be reliable and not valid? Can it be valid, but not reliable? Explain your answer.

7. What are the parts of a classical experimental research design?

8. Describe how you might use a classical research design to study something of interest in the social sciences.

9. Do you think it is challenging to operationalize a concept? Why or why not? Provide an example.

Trying It Out

Your professor may ask you to complete the following companion assignment available from the publisher. Using the supplied worksheet form, you are going to identify five terms that you learned about in this chapter, and then write multiple-choice test questions for each.

Table 4-3: Examining the Five Steps of Research in Context of Cheesecake

Step #	Step Description	Cheesecake Parallel	Explanation
1	Coming up with an idea	Inventing a recipe for cheesecake	Many people love Nutella. A lot of people love coconut crème pie. Why don't we make a coconut crème Nutella cheesecake?
2	Is your idea worth It?	Is the cheesecake worth it?	I have to think about the time and money I will spend creating this cheesecake—is it worth it? Considering that I just have to buy the ingredients once, and may spend just a few hours figuring it out, I can assess that it is. However, if after I try it, the only thing that I can conclude is that it is "interesting tasting," then it probably is not worth creating again!
3	Theory and literature	Examining the new cheesecake idea in context of other cheesecakes	What if my idea already exists? What if there is something similar and it has bad reviews? What if there is something about the actual construction of the cheesecake and crème pie combo that makes it likely to fail? I need to make sure to check past "literature" (in this case, recipes) to make sure that my idea is a good one. Also, I can begin to figure out how I will actually go about *making* the cheesecake.
4	Designing your study	Developing your recipe	At this point, I have a strong framework of *how* to make a cheesecake and what ingredients I will need. I then need to create my procedure: where I will go to buy my ingredients, what kitchen equipment I need (like bowls, spring form pan, mixer, etc.), and so on. These are important things to plan for—I know I do not want to be in the middle of making my cheesecake and realize I forgot five things at the store! That may mess up my recipe. My actual recipe is my instrumentation, as following its steps will provide me with the "data" I aim to collect: a ready-to-eat cheesecake.
5	Institutional review board approval	Selling others on your cheesecake	This is the poorest parallel; however, if my cheesecake was awesome, and I opened a restaurant to sell it, I would need to follow the health department's standards, and the way in which I created my cheesecake would be assessed.

References

Federal Bureau of Investigation. (2014). *Uniform crime reporting program data: Police employee (LEOKA) data, 2012.*

Field, A., & Miles, J. (2012). *Discovering statistics using r.* Thousand Oaks, CA: Sage Publications.

Gottfredson, M., & Hirschi, T. (1990). *A general theory of crime.* Palo Alto, CA: Stanford University Press.

Grasmick, H. G., Tittle, C. R., Bursik, R. J., Jr., & Arneklev, B. J. (1993). Testing the core empirical implications of Gottfredson and Hirschi's general theory of crime. *Journal of Research in Crime and Delinquency, 30*(1), 5–29.

Mayo Clinic. (2017). Depression: Major depressive disorder. Retrieved from https://www.mayoclinic.org/diseases-conditions/depression/symptoms-causes/syc-20356007.

Stogner, J. M., Miller, B. L., & Marcum, C. D. (2013). Learning to e-cheat: A criminological test of internet-facilitated academic cheating. *Journal of Criminal Justice Education, 24*(2), 175–199.

Tibbetts, S. G., & Myers, D. L. (1999). Low self-control, rational choice, and student test cheating. *American Journal of Criminal Justice, 23*(2), 179–200.

Wansink, B., Cheney, M. M., & Chan, N. (2003). Exploring comfort food preferences across age and gender. *Physiology & Behavior, 79*(4), 739–747.

Section II

Designing Research in Criminology and Criminal Justice (Chapters 5–7)

The fact that you are still reading this book after Chapter 4 and have not yet sold this book on Amazon—major props to you. This next part goes over three chapters (5–7). The first four chapters (especially Chapters 1–3) are all a bit more abstract. These three chapters are (hopefully) a bit more concrete. This is where you learn how research is designed and how you would design your research. Once again, think back to that middle school science procedure—same idea here! These chapters will help you with how you go about designing your own research project. You will first learn about how research should be designed so that it is as valid and reliable as it can be. This is really so you can (hopefully) say "the results of my research matter!" And no one else can say "Nope, they really do not." Just a quick example: say you have created a new toothpaste and your spouse is a dentist. You give your spouse and four of their dentist friends $1,000 to say they'd choose your research. Besides being just a bit shady, this also does not give very valid results! For one, you would want to make sure that people actually *use* the toothpaste for some period of time, and you'd want another group of people who did *not* use the toothpaste for some period of time. Ideally, you'd want to then show how much more of an improvement there was for the "using your toothpaste" group as compared to the group that did not use your toothpaste. Another reason that "bribing dentists" study is not so valid is because of how you chose participants for your "study." It is vital to consider how people get selected in your study, which is why Chapter 7 on sampling is especially important. You want to know whether the people you choose for your study can represent other people.

After these three chapters, you should have a much better idea of how you could *start* to write your own methods section and design your own research project. Do not worry, though! There is still plenty to learn.

Trying It Out

Your professor may ask you to complete the following companion assignment available from the publisher. Using the supplied worksheet form, you are going to identify the parts of a journal article with the examples provided.

Chapter 5

Validity and Reliability

Learning Objectives

- Distinguish between validity and reliability
- Identify the four methods of assessing reliability
- Explain the procedures for each method of assessing reliability
- Identify and define the four types of validity
- Distinguish between statistical conclusion validity, population validity, and construct validity
- Identify each threat to external validity
- Apply each threat of external validity to a research scenario
- Identify each threat to internal validity
- Identify and explain the four types of issues that can arise with treatment
- Explain how additive and interactive effects of threats to internal validity differ from other threats to internal validity
- Identify and define each threat to construct validity

Atlanta, Georgia, is well known for many things, but it is infamous for its traffic. My university (University of West Georgia) is relatively close to Atlanta, and I have developed a deep sense of dread anytime I have to drive through or to Atlanta. Once in a while, it is a pleasant surprise: I am able to get right where I need to go with no major traffic jams or issues. Other times, it is a bit heavy, with a few issues, and I am delayed around 10–15 minutes. Yet, other times, it is a *disaster*, and it has delayed me for an hour or more. Generally, Atlanta traffic is unpredictable, and so you plan for the worst, which can result in you arriving at your destination extremely early.

Some of my colleagues live in Atlanta and have found it best to leave absurdly early in the morning and arrive at work around seven. That is the trick to navigating Atlanta traffic: one must simply avoid it all together. When they leave this early, there are typically no significant traffic issues; so, they know when to leave to arrive on time— not too early, not too late.

What is so annoying about Atlanta traffic is its unpredictability—it lacks **reliability**, and the design of the city is certainly not sufficient to meet its traffic needs, meaning that traffic never flows perfectly smooth—it lacks **validity**. While I despise Atlanta traffic regardless, I would be more accepting of it if I knew it was going to delay me 30 minutes or an hour each time, because then I could plan for it. If this were the case, it would be **reliable**, because it is *consistent*, but it would *not* be **valid**, because it is not "right" (it causes a significant delay). In a perfect world, Atlanta traffic would flow smoothly and it would *always* flow smoothly. In such a scenario, it would be both **valid** and **reliable**.

One of the most common ways to think about reliability and validity is a target. Imagine you were in the police academy being evaluated on your firearms training. You would certainly want to be *both* reliable and valid. You would want to hit as close to the bullseye as possible, and you would want to do that *consistently*. Hitting the bullseye is representative of validity, and hitting the bullseye (or very, very close to it) consistently is representative of reliability. If you shot to the right of the entire silhouette every single time, then your shooting would be demonstrable of reliability, not validity, and that would be *bad*. It would be even worse if your aim were completely unpredictable! One time you shoot someone else's silhouette, another time you shoot the floor, etc. In this scenario, your shooting would lack reliability and validity. So, if you had to pick a shooter to shoot apples off your head, which one would you pick? The one who is reliable *and* valid, the one who is only reliable, or the one who is neither reliable nor valid?

Another example for sports fans: Imagine you are an NBA team owner, and you are looking for an excellent free throw shooter. You do not need someone who has fancy free throws and makes it once in a while, nor do you need someone who misses more than they make it, you want someone who consistently makes the shot. When given the choice between Ben Wallace, who has a free throw percentage of a little over 40%, or Steve Nash, whose free throw percentage is above 90%, the choice should be pretty easy (Neuharth-Keusch, 2016; Chalk, 2016)!

Reliability

We have discussed examples of reliability being consistent, and this holds true in research. We think about reliability most often in what we measure and how we measure it. So, it is particularly important within our instrumentation (see Chapter 4, "The Nitty Gritty"). If Dr. Bob is conducting a medical trial that requires me to take someone's weight daily, there are a few different ways in which he would want to ensure his study is reliable. Some of his concerns are that the recorded weight could be unreliable if someone was weighed in the morning or weighed in the evening. Further, if participants were not consistent with how much they ate before the daily weigh in, this could certainly show differences in weight that are not real. Lastly, if the scale (this is his instrumentation for the study) is wonky and changes due to temperature, then it could report someone at 140 pounds one day and 145 pounds the next, when there was actually no weight difference. So, first, he would want to do weigh-ins at the same time every day. Second, he would want to make sure that relatively the same amount of food and liquid had been consumed before each weigh in. Third, he would want to make sure whatever scale he is using is dependable. These three provisions are methods to ensure that the study is consistently measuring weight.

If you remember in Chapter 4 ("The Nitty Gritty"), we talked about *operationalization* and *conceptualization*. Specifically, we discussed how you might measure depression by using the sum of different behaviors, such as sleeping a lot (or a little), eating a lot (or a little), not wanting to participate in activities that were once enjoyable, etc. We could sum these up in a fancy way to determine if someone meets the criteria to establish if they are depressed (but you can only do this if you are trained in it!).

Researchers use behaviors as indicators for depression, because depression is an abstract construct—we cannot see it. We want to use measurable *items/questions* that collectively can make the abstract concrete. For instance, if you wanted to determine if you are ADHD, you can take a self-administered online test (Schweitzer, Cummins, and Kant, 2001), which asks about your behaviors. The table below provides some of these questions.

---

(1) I often fidget
(2) I avoid or delay tasks that require a lot of thought
(3) I talk too much in social situations
(4) I have a hard time remembering my obligations and appointments

Modified from part of the Adult ADHD Self-Report Scale. This modification is for example purposes only, is not comprehensive, and should not be used for any diagnostic purposes (Schweitzer, Cummins, & Kant, 2001).

The highest one could score on each item is 10, so the highest sum one could receive would be 40. The higher the score, the more one is reporting behaviors that are indicative of ADHD. Do remember that this is only an example—do not take this to be a true indicator of ADHD on its own! The lower the score, the less one is reporting behaviors that are indicative of ADHD. Therefore, if one's rankings were the following:

1. 8

2. 9

3. 10

4. 9

Then their value on an ADHD index would be 36 (10 + 9 + 9 + 8 = 36).

The more items in a scale or index, the more reliable it tends to be (as long as it is consistent!). Sometimes, one item may not hold true for a participant. If there are only four items, that can throw the reliability way off. Conversely, if there are 20 items, it will not have such a big effect on the score. So, imagine that **Bob** took the questionnaire and provided rankings to the four items on ADHD, and rated the first three statements (items/questions) as 10, but the last statement as a one—he has no issue remembering his appointments. Their sum would be only 31, and their average would be 7.75. Now, imagine if we had replaced "I have a hard time remembering my obligations and appointments" with "I interrupt others when they are in the middle of things," which **Bob** does frequently, so he rates this statement a 10. There is a 22.5% difference in these scores: sums of 31 vs. 40 and averages of 7.75 vs. 10; conversely, if that one item were included in a list of 20 items, it would not have such a big impact, as there would only be 4.5%. The index would still be a 9-point difference, but out of 200: sums of 191 vs. 200 and averages of 9.55 and 10. This is why we often like longer tests, because missing one question has little impact on a 100-question test, but a huge impact on a 2-question test!

If we say that the scale or index of some construct is reliable, that simply means it is consistent. For instance, **Jane**, who is concerned that she may be an alcoholic, decides to take the alcoholic self-test. While answering the questions, which included behaviors about alcohol and alcohol tolerance, **Jane** is then asked, "do you love puppies?" This should seem way off the mark, because it is. If you ever played the game "which one of these is not like the other," the answer in this scenario is "do you love puppies?"! If **Jane**'s answer to "do you love puppies" is included in the sum of items to measure possible alcoholism, this would certainly decrease the reliability. We want the items/questions to be consistent, meaning that they follow a similar pattern and make sense together.

Here is an important point about reliability of constructs: even if the measure of a construct is reliable, that does not mean it is valid. Meaning, it may or may not be measuring the construct it aims to measure. For instance, **Bob** goes to the doctor. In the waiting room, the receptionist requests him to fill out a form about his medical history. At the top, the form indeed says, "medical history." However, it has only these five questions:

(1) How many television shows do you watch?

(2) Do you watch television daily?

(3) How many hours of television do you watch a day?

(4) Is there a set time that you watch television?

(5) Has your television watching increased or decreased recently?

Assessing Reliability

This seems to be a questionnaire that has items aimed at measuring television viewing habits—not medical history. While this is not a valid measure of medical history, it is plausibly reliable. The questions follow a consistent pattern—they just do not measure what they aim to measure.

Although the questions in the last example about television watching appear to be consistent, it is important to make sure, which is why we can use tests to assess reliability. Specifically, there are four tests to determine the reliability of whatever we are measuring: (1) test-retest methods, (2) parallel forms of the same test, (3) split-half method, and (3) inter-rater reliability.

Split-Half Method

The split-half method (also referred to as intra-test reliability) assesses reliability by seeing if items/questions are related if they split into two. Think literally about the saying "two peas in a pod" (Ellis, Hartley, & Walsh, 2010). Would we know that the two peas were once in the same "pod" if we separated them?

If Teacher JANE wanted to know if her math test was reliable, she could take the 50 questions on the exam and split them randomly (like odd numbers in one and even numbers in the other) and could then see whether the two halves were strongly and positively correlated, which would indicate that they were reliable. This method, while a good indicator of reliability, requires the researcher to split the sample and split their measure. Second, it does not specify *how* the items are split. Third, because the items to measure the construct are decreased by half, the reliability will probably be underestimated for each measure (just like we discussed in the example of four vs. twenty items).

So, in an attempt to remedy these issues, Lee J. Cronbach, an educational psychologist at the University of Illinois (Shavelson, 2002), created **Cronbach's Alpha** (a), which essentially is a statistical test that imitates the split-half method, by calculating the correlation of every scenario, splitting the items evenly, and then averaging them (Field & Miles, 2012; Gliner et al., 2011). (No need to worry—at least not in this class—you do not need to hand calculate Cronbach's Alpha—statistical software can calculate this for us.) Unsurprisingly, this is a much more common way to assess reliability than the split-half method.

Parallel Forms of the Same Test

Since one of the issues with the split-half method is that each half is underestimating reliability, one way to overcome this is by using the second method of assessing reliability: parallel forms, which is also referred to as cross-testing (Frankfort-Nachmias & Nachmias, 2015).

The idea here is to create two tests (or scales or indexes) that both measure the same construct. Therefore, you could have twenty items measuring depression and twenty *different* items that still measure depression (Shadish, Cook, & Campbell, 2002). So, item one in the first test could be a statement that one could rate their agreement/disagreement with: *Most days, I oversleep*. On the second test, a different item could be used: *I often sleep more than I intend to sleep*. Each item is different, yet collectively measuring the same thing.

This biggest issue with this form of assessing reliability is how to ensure that both forms are truly equal, so it is important that the researcher keep this in mind when examining the results. Think about if your Research Methods professor gave half of you one test and half of you another, and each had different questions on it (Frankfort-Nachmias & Nachmias, 2015). You would likely wonder if they were *really* equal or if you would have done better on the other test form (or even worse)!

Test-Retest

The third method to assess reliability is test-retest, which is exactly how it sounds: give a test, then give it again. Ideally, the scores should be the same, so they should be very strongly correlated. However, this method also has its issues. For instance, if you took a Research Methods test and then were allowed to take it again, your score would likely improve, regardless of whether you studied after the first test. This is because you became more familiar with the questions (this is referred to as a testing effect, which is referenced in this chapter again under "Threats to Internal Validity"). If you took the ACT or SAT more than once, your score likely improved for this reason.

Another issue with the test-retest method can be memory. For example, on January 8th, 2016, BOB asks JANE how many beers she consumed in the last week (so from January 1st to January 7th), and she answers seven. Two months later, on March 8th, BOB asks JANE again how many beers she consumed from January 1st to January 7th. Her answer may be different, because she does not remember how many beers she consumed during a week that occurred two months ago. I do not know about you, but I barely remember what I had to drink this morning, never mind two months ago. Therefore, if she does not remember, her answer may be different, resulting in two tests that are not strongly correlated.

Inter-Rater Reliability

The last method of assessing reliability is used when there are possibly subjective judgments or ratings being made about something. So, if Researchers BOB, JANE, and Lisa are examining the violence of video games, they may each give a rating to represent how violent each video game is. To make sure that there was consistency among the three researchers, they could use inter-rater reliability if their ratings are strongly correlated. Think about a show like *Dancing with the Stars*, which uses judges to provide a numeric score for a dance. These numbers tend to be consistent, but at times might be noticeably different. If one judge gives a four, and the other two give eights, there is probably something wrong that needs to be assessed. Therefore, this method aims to ensure that even in more subjective measurements, reliability can still be assessed (Gliner et al., 2011).

Validity

Validity can be understood as truth, the correctness of what we are saying. In research, we can think of validity as a goal, but never a product, just like causation. In fact, the two are very, very related: without validity, there is certainly no causal relationship that a researcher can claim! The more valid our research is, the more our conclusions can be deemed as fact (but never actually are) rather than merely opinion. Again, I want to emphasize: conclusions in social science research *are not fact and they do not prove anything.* Our conclusions are only used to support or not support a theory and/or hypothesis. Following the guidance of Shadish, Cook, and Campbell (2002), when we say something is valid or that we believe something to be true, this is not equal to absolute certitude. If you remember in Chapter 2, I encouraged you to be a "flaky friend" type as a social science researcher, and I would emphasize that again.

Reminder: Repeat from "The Nitty Gritty"

There are three global (main) categories of research designs: experimental, quasi-experimental, and nonexperimental (including ex-post facto research designs).

An experimental design is most commonly associated with medical studies and includes all the parts to a research design. A common experimental design is called the ***classical experimental design*** or the ***pretest posttest control group design***. In the classical experimental design, you have participants who are randomly assigned (R) to one of two groups: the experimental (E_1) or control group (C_1). Both groups are given a pretest (O_1), then the experimental group is given a treatment (X_1), and then both groups are given a posttest (O_2). The design looks like this:

R	E_1	O_1	X_1	O_2
R	C_1	O_1		O_2

If you can think back to Chapter 4 ("The Nitty Gritty"), we reviewed the types of global research designs (experimental, quasi-experimental, and nonexperimental). If you have forgotten this, we have provided you with the explanation from Chapter 4 (see "Reminder: Repeat from 'The Nitty Gritty'"). If you also recall, using experimental designs tends to be more *valid* because it allows for other possible causes or other factors to be ruled out as causal explanations of our dependent variable, so there is a greater likelihood that our statement of causality is valid.

The reason validity is a goal is because there are always threats to that validity. These threats can be thought of like a toxic friend, in that their presence indicates a loss in validity, or more specifically in research, why your statement might be wrong or invalid. It is also important to remember that there are a number of different ways someone can be wrong about something: they could have missed something, they could be lying, they could be failing to see the big picture, or they could have misunderstood something. Keeping that in mind, there are four aspects or components of validity: ***internal validity***, ***external validity***, ***statistical conclusion validity***, and ***construct validity***. To understand these four types of validity, we are going to use the same statement: A course in Research Methods is detrimental to its students' mental health.

Internal Validity

Internal validity refers to the validity of the statement you are making. Remember that in the beginning of us discussing what validity is, I said that validity and causation are highly related. Internal validity is examining whether our observed statement (what we conclude from our study) is causal, or if the change in an independent variable is the absolute cause of the dependent variable, or if there are other factors that influence change in our dependent variable, which are known as *confounding variables* or *extraneous variables* (Christensen, Johnson, & Turner, 2011; Passer, 2017). For instance, I know my dog will wag his tail when he sees a treat, but is that the *only* time he wags his tail? No. Are there other causes of his tail wagging? Yes! Have there been a few times that he is distracted and therefore does not wag his tail? Yes! Therefore, there are other factors that have an effect on my dependent variable (tail wagging) other than my independent variable (letting my dog see a treat), and while the independent variable *typically creates* the change in the dependent variable (treat presence typically makes dog's tail wag), it does not *always* occur.

With our specific statement, the question then becomes, does taking Research Methods *cause* students to have poor mental health or is it merely a factor of one's insanity? If we conduct a study and conclude that our statement is *likely* correct, then we want to see if what we observed in the study is causally valid and not due to error, including failure to account for other causes (think back to spuriousness from Chapter 2). Internal validity is dependent on things that are both in the researcher's control and uncontrollable. One of the ways that a researcher may be able to control it is the research design. Since experimental designs tend to be more valid, a type of experimental design would be ideal (more on that in Chapter 6, "Research Designs") particularly because of random sampling and random assignment.

> *Students from two classes (one Research Methods course and one World History course), each with 100 students, were given a questionnaire to complete after their respective course concluded. The questionnaire included a demographic form (questions on age, race, sex, student status, etc.) and questions to measure their current state of mental health (scored from zero = severe detriments to mental health to 100 = excellent mental health). The findings revealed that students in Research Methods had a mental health score of 60, while students in World History had a mental health score of 90. After running statistical tests, the researchers concluded that yes—a course in Research Methods causes poor mental health.*

If Researcher **BOB** and Researcher **JANE** conduct a study to test the hypothesis that a Research Methods class harms mental health and their observations lead them to conclude that they support this hypothesis, then it would be important to assess why their observations could be invalid. Here are the details of their study:

So, what is wrong with this picture? Here are some of the key issues (however, this list certainly is by no means exhaustive!).

- One, we always aim for causality, but never reach it. So, I would recommend avoiding the word cause!

- Two, what were the other variables for which the researchers accounted? Demographics, and only demographics! The researchers did not include what other classes students were taking, or if there were other events that had occurred during the semester that may have harmed their mental health (a breakup, a family death or conflict, etc.).

- Three, the difference observed between World History students and Research Methods students may *have been there beforehand.* The researchers did not issue a pretest, and therefore, we do not know what the mental state for students in either class was before this.

- Four, we do not know *why* students were taking Research Methods and *why* students were taking World History. Perhaps World History is an elective and Research Methods is a required class for every major. That alone could cause stress and mental health issues—students needing to pass a course to graduate are likely more stressed about their grade in a course than students taking a class that—should they not pass—can be replaced with another course.

- Five, ideally, the researchers should have *randomly sampled* and *randomly assigned* students to take Research Methods and to *not* take Research Methods.

- Six, the researchers may want to examine groups of students taking many *other* types of classes and make sure to account for these. Perhaps World History is good for mental health, but Organic Chemistry might have a different effect and might be even *more* detrimental than Research Methods. Specifically, another issue with the researchers' research design is that they did not have a *control* group—they had two groups receiving different treatments: one treatment was Research Methods and one treatment was World History.

Many of these issues were in the researcher's control. Therefore, the less sound the research design, the poorer the validity. When the researchers are able to make the research process and the research design better, then they should. There are, however, a number of issues that would not be. What if the researchers *did* ask about other life events that had occurred, but the participant chose not to report that a family member had died? In this sort of study, due to anonymity and confidentiality, there would likely be no way to verify the validity of the self-report data. Therefore, this is an issue that is inevitably possible, with no way of verifying if the issue is even an actual issue in a certain study!

External Validity

The second main category of validity is external validity. Internal validity focused on what was going on inside the study to effect whether conclusions were valid. External validity focuses on whether the conclusion from a study would hold true on different populations, specifically, generalizability (see Chapter 4, "The Nitty Gritty," for a reminder). The idea being that if Researcher **Bob** conducts a study on a random sample of students from Stanford University, would the conclusions he made in his study be the same if he sampled a random group of students from a college class in a state prison? Probably not! This is why it is important to not only use random sampling, but to identify both your population and your sample, so that you know to whom you can generalize. The larger the scope of generalizability, the greater the external validity of the study.

You have probably heard the statement "What happens in Vegas stays in Vegas." This statement refers to the wild things that can happen in a city like Las Vegas — people do some crazy, impulsive things, such as get married. It is not shocking that Nevada has the highest rate of marriage of any state in the United States. While some couples first decide to get married, and then decide to do so in Las Vegas, others' nuptials are more spur-of-the-moment. If one were to observe a wedding chapel in Vegas at night (depending on the chapel), they may observe that alcohol use causes people to marry. While this is an understandable observation in the context of Vegas, this is definitely not true everywhere! If we can overlook the issues with the research design, we can understand that what happens in Vegas does *not* necessarily happen in the rest of the United States.

Similarly, if, through the results of their study, researchers **Bob** and **Jane** observe a relationship between taking a Research Methods course and deteriorating mental health, this may only hold true for students at their university.

There are two keys to demonstrating external validity: the first is random sampling, to ensure generalizability to the specified population, and the second is repetition, repetition, repetition! Regarding the first, researchers must establish their population, then use a representative sample from that population to be able to generalize the observations of that study to the population. This is referred to as *population validity* (Christensen et al., 2011).

A study should be replicated over and over again within different populations, different climates, different times, etc. If the results show the same observed effect repeatedly, then this provides support for external validity, because there is evidence of *ecological validity*, which is when the results of repeated studies demonstrate that the observations hold true regardless of different contexts and cultures. Considering the culture of Vegas is very different than the culture in Salt Lake City, if the observation made in a study on a sample of Las Vegas also was observed in the same study on a sample in Salt Lake City, this would begin to lend support for external validity (Christensen et al., 2011). For instance, if a study on social learning theory and drug use that finds a significant relationship between friends' drug use and an individual's drug use, and another study replicating the original study, but using a different population, finds a significant relationship, and another, and another — this would begin to be demonstrable of external validity (Christensen et al., 2011; Shadish et al., 2002).

Statistical Conclusion Validity

Another category of validity is *statistical conclusion validity*, which is concerned with whether the appropriate statistical tests were used to make conclusions about whether there is a relationship, difference, or effect that is *real* and not by chance or error. If you remember from Chapter 4 ("The Nitty Gritty"), when we reviewed different types of hypotheses, that there are two hypotheses we use in a study: research (or alternative) hypothesis and the null hypothesis. Additionally, remember that we actually *test* the null hypothesis, because of falsifiability (Popper, 2005). I did not get into too much detail in Chapter 4 about what conclusions we make regarding the null hypothesis—but do not worry, we will go over that now!

Also remember that we do not find the null hypothesis true or false. In Chapter 4, we discussed that we either find support or do not find support for our research hypothesis, which is usually one of difference, relationship, or effect.

When we conclude whether or not we found support for our research hypothesis, we most often do this by using statistical tests, which reveal how "sure" we are that what we are seeing is a real relationship, difference, or effect, and not due to chance or error. When we reach a certain likelihood that what we are seeing is *probably not* due to chance or error, then we say that this is *a [statistically] significant relationship, difference, or effect.* Most often, we want to see that the chance of error is less than .05, meaning that if the study were repeated on another similar sample, the relationship would *not* exist 5 times out of 100. However, we work in probabilistic terms, because we are that flaky friend.

You reject the null if you conclude:
 There is a real relationship, difference, or effect.
 That your research/alternative hypothesis is *probably true.*
 That there is a statistically significant relationship, difference, or effect.
You fail to reject the null if you conclude:
 There is no real relationship, difference, or effect.
 That your research/alternative hypothesis is *probably* false.
 That there is no statistically significant relationship, difference, or effect.

When we find support for our research/alternative hypothesis, we *reject* our null hypothesis. When we do *not* find support for our research/alternative hypothesis, we *fail to reject* our null hypothesis. What fail to reject essentially means is "keep," but we never say keep! Again, because we are using probabilistic terms, just like a flaky friend (I'll *probably* come to the party, but I *might* not be able to make it; or, I'll *probably not* be able to make it, but I *might*). Other ways to think about this:

Even when the correct statistical test has been used, there is still a chance of error, which is why we speak in probabilistic terms. Researchers can observe that there is a significant relationship when, in fact, there is not. Additionally, researchers can observe that there is not a significant relationship when, in fact, there is. When we conclude that there *is* a difference, and in reality, there is not, then we have a ***type I error.*** Conversely, when we conclude there is *not* a difference, and in reality, there is, then we have a ***type II error.*** It is also important to note that anytime the null is rejected, there is a chance of a type I error. Anytime the null fails to be rejected, there is a chance of a type II error.

Imagine that you hear a rumor that your best friend has been talking trash (throwing shade) about you. Once you assess the evidence (perhaps asking other people, asking your best friend, or by other creative means), you are going to make a decision that will result in you either forgiving your best friend (or believing their denials) and maintaining your friendship, or dropping them as a friend for good. In this example, if you conclude that your friend talked about you, then you would reject them; meaning, you concluded that the gossip was *real* and you *rejected* your friend. If you decide that your friend gossiping about you is probably *not* true, then you would maintain your friendship, or *fail to reject* them.

Using our statement: if we conclude that the relationship between Research Methods and mental health is significant, then we would reject our null hypothesis and have a chance of a type I error. If we conclude that the relationship between Research Methods and mental health is not significant, then we would fail to reject our null hypothesis and have chance of a type II error.

Construct Validity

Another component of validity is construct validity, which deals with how something is measured. Like we talked about with operationalization and conceptualization, if we are attempting to transform observations into some measure or construct, it must be measuring what we aim to measure. One common example of this is recidivism, which obviously is an important topic in the field of criminal justice. Upon first glance, recidivism seems like a pretty self-explanatory construct: an individual committing another crime. However, when thinking about how to measure it, things can get complicated. For instance, does recidivism refer to simply committing another crime? If so, how do we account for all those individuals who were not caught committing another crime? If we are referring to being arrested again, how do we account for arrests in another state? A construct that seems so simple to measure is actually quite complicated.

Going back to our statement, we have two concepts: mental health and Research Methods course. It may seem that the only challenge to achieving construct validity is mental health. However, measuring "Research Methods course" is also quite complex. There are many aspects of a Research Methods course that could change the outcome if not accounted for in the measure. For instance, what *time* was the class period? How long did each class last? Who was the teacher? Was the course on campus or an online class? What was the average grade in the class? Were there extra credit opportunities? What was each student's grade in the class? Also, *what if a student was enrolled in Research Methods but never actually attended the course?* If Research Methods course was measured only by "currently enrolled in Research Methods," then the researchers' study is lacking construct validity. A lack of construct validity can be dangerous, because researchers can make conclusions from a study that are false simply because they are not measuring what they claim to be measuring.

We certainly would not tolerate a lack of construct validity with other things in our lives—at the least, we expect specificity. If a weight-loss drug company said you would lose 10 in a week's time, and another weight loss drug company claimed 15 in a week's time, it would be important to know that company one is referring to 10 pounds, while company two is referring to 15 kilograms—see why specificity matters?

If recidivism in study one is defined as rearrests in a state, and in study two, recidivism is defined as reconviction, it is important that both studies specify *how* they define and measured recidivism, because the two studies are not comparable! In all likelihood, the recidivism rate in the first study would be much higher than the second, since there are more arrests than convictions. If there was no accounting for the difference in how recidivism was measured, and study one examined how effective rehabilitation was on reducing recidivism, while study two examined how effective long prison terms were at reducing recidivism, we could end up concluding that prison terms are likely more effective at reducing recidivism—while this may be true, we certainly could not make that conclusion based off of these two studies; it is like comparing apples to oranges.

Threats to Validity

As we have already mentioned, to a certain extent, there are always challenges to validity; but specifically, there are challenges to each *type* of validity. Most often, there are ways to combat each threat, but sometimes combatting one threat only strengthens another threat. Further, sometimes the threats can work together to create a whole new threat.

If you have ever seen the movie *Taken*, or even the trailer for the movie, Liam Neeson's daughter has been kidnapped in France. He ends up on the phone with one of the kidnappers and informs them that he has a "particular set of skills" and will find them and his daughter. In this context, you, the researcher, are Liam Neeson, and validity is your kidnapped daughter. The individuals whom you will fight or kill are your threats to validity: at times when you beat up one "bad guy" a bigger, scarier, more skilled bad guy arises, or sometimes, the bad guys work together, and are much, much stronger together than separate. And, just when you think that you are done fighting the enemy, another one arises. While Liam Neeson (Spoiler Alert!) eventually finds his daughter, you will forever be in search (sometimes very close search) of a perfectly valid study.

There are numerous, numerous threats to each type of validity. To simplify this, we are going to spend the most time going over the threats to internal validity, and then addressing many of the major threats within external and construct validity. We will not go over many of the threats of statistical conclusion validity because many of them require a baseline understanding of statistics, which many of you probably have, but some of you may not! We will, however, address only a couple of major threats to statistical conclusion validity.

Types of External Validity

It is important to note that when a study is replicated, the characteristics of the study are held constant with the exception of one difference. There are five types of external validity: population, treatment variation, ecological, outcome, and temporal (Christensen et al., 2011; Shadish et al., 2002; White & McBurney, 2012). Each one is important to consider when determining to whom, what, where, and when results can be generalized.

(1) **Population validity** is how the results can be applied to different populations: if the results of a study on college students at one university are generalizable to students at another university.

(2) **Treatment variation validity** refers to whether the results of a study can be generalized from one treatment to another, as there may be differences in the administration of treatment. Think of police use-of-force, for example. The way in which one police officer uses a subduing tactic will differ—even if only slightly—from another police officer. Can the findings from one police officer's use of force be generalized to another police officer's use of force?

(3) **Ecological validity** refers to whether the outcome of a study would be generalizable in a different place. Different places can have an effect on how something effects a person; for instance, the environment one is in can have an effect on their drug tolerance. This is because of social cues, among other things (Siegel, 1983)!

(4) **Temporal validity** refers to whether the outcome of a study would be generalizable across time. This may refer to different times of day, different seasons (climates), or even different centuries. For instance, you would not want to test the popularity of an outdoor running app in Fargo, North Dakota, and Key West, Florida, during December, considering that the average temperature in Key West is much, much warmer! If you did this, then it could appear as though the app is more popular for Key West residents, when in fact, for residents in Fargo, it might just be colder than cold with two feet of snow on the ground, making it almost impossible to run outdoors. Similarly, you would not want to test the running app in Atlanta, Georgia, during the day and Detroit, Michigan, at night.

(5) **Outcome validity** refers to whether the findings of a study would be generalizable across slightly different outcomes. If Professor JANE finds that studying in groups increases test grades in Research Methods, would group studying also increase test grades in Criminological Theory? If a drug helps reduce anxiety, would it also reduce stress levels?

Threats to Internal Validity

Ambiguous Temporal Ordering

The first threat to internal validity is *ambiguous temporal ordering*. Sometimes, there is not a clear understanding of whether X (independent variable) came before Y (dependent variable). This should sound familiar from Chapter 2 (on theory and research), when we discussed temporal ordering as an element of causation. For instance, Researcher Bob surveys students who have and who have not taken a death penalty course and asks them their perceptions of the death penalty. He finds that those who have taken a death penalty course are significantly less likely to support the death penalty. While this is an important finding, Bob cannot be sure that the death penalty course had any effect on perceptions of the death penalty, because he did not pretest either group of students, nor did he randomly assign students to either group. He can only claim that there is a significant relationship between the two. The best bet to being able to claim causal ordering (X causes Y) is to use an experimental design.

Selection Bias

If a researcher does not use a random sampling and assignment technique, there is a chance of *selection bias*. Consider the challenges of random sampling techniques, it can often be easiest to rely on those participants who are easily available (see Chapter 7, "Units of Analysis, Samples, and Sampling," for more on this). If Dr. Bob wants to try out a new risky surgery to treat Alzheimer's, he would need volunteers for a treatment group, which may also leave him with a group of participants who have Alzheimer's, but do *not* want the surgery. There may be significant differences in these groups before any treatment is given, which is referred to as *nonequivalent groups*. Therefore, when feasible, random assignment is the best bet. In this example, Dr. Bob should (at the least) pretest both groups to determine any differences between the two.

History

Sometimes, there is an event occurring *outside* your study that has an effect on the results of your study. This is referred to as *history*. For instance, Researcher Jane conducted a study on how learning about different cultures affected fear of terrorism. She used an experimental design, random sampling, and randomly assigning participants to two groups, with the treatment group receiving the "treatment" of learning about different cultures. While Jane hypothesized that learning about cultures would *decrease* fear of terrorism, she actually found that both groups' fear increased significantly. This is likely due to the timing of the study: she started the study in August of 2001, and finished it in August 2002 — her start date was a bit more than five weeks prior to September 11th. At times, it may be less extreme circumstances; perhaps Researcher Jane examines how a caffeine-free herbal supplement affects sleep. Her research participants all live in a small town. During the time of the study, the first Starbucks opens in that small town. It is likely that the amount of caffeine her participants consume will increase, which could also have an effect on sleep! While many of these outside effects are not controllable, we can account for them using survey instruments so that we can control for them. Researcher JANE could use a pretest and ask about caffeine consumption and also include the same question in the posttest.

Maturation

Over time, people change. Remember, the only constant *is* change. **Maturation** is easiest to think about as individuals maturing over time; however, it can be any sort of natural change. For instance, if Researcher **BOB** is interested in seeing how participation in sports affects the behavior of middle-school-aged children over a three-year period, he better account for the substantial changes in personality that occur in middle school. If Researcher **BOB** did not use an experimental design, he will have a very hard time showing that sports participation makes children calmer and more mature! With an experimental design, he would, at the least, have a control group to which he could compare the treatment group (those who participated in sports). If those who did not participate in sports were significantly more hyperactive and less mature, then he would have a much easier time making the argument that it is likely that sports participation had an effect on behavior. It is important to think about some of the absurd claims we could make if we did not account for naturally occurring changes. Using the previous example, if Researcher **BOB** did not use a control group, he could try and claim that sports make children taller!

Regression

One of the reasons that random sampling, in addition to random assignment, is so important is because of *regression*. People are often in the mood for self-improvement when they've hit their lowest. Moreover, researchers often want to study the worst of the worst and/or the best of the best. For instance, a first-time offender (Sally-Sue) is arrested for buying cocaine. Prior to her first appearance, Sally-Sue is required to fill out assessment measures of drug use, depression, and anxiety. At the time, Sally-Sue is stressed out, mad at herself for committing a stupid crime, worried about money, and upset by her drug use. She reports that her drug use is a huge problem, and is found to be depressed and have a high degree of anxiety. Upon meeting with the judge, Sally-Sue is given the option of going through the traditional system (and possibly receiving jail time), or instead, she can participate in a pretrial diversion program, which requires her to participate in three-month psychotherapy/ drug rehabilitation. Further, should she choose the rehabilitation path, her record will be wiped clean once she completes the program. At the end of the three months, even if Sally-Sue had not participated in any treatment, simply having her record wiped clean and being no longer in the heat of crisis (from being arrested), Sally-Sue would likely report less depression, less anxiety, and perceive her drug use (regardless of whether the frequency of use has changed) as being *less* of a problem than before. Over time, people (and things) tend to regress to the mean. People join a weight loss program when they are feeling the *worst* about their weight and are likely at their heaviest weight. On the other hand, people may decide to train for a marathon when they are already in great shape. If we recruit those who are at their highest or lowest, they will naturally progress closer to the mean over a period of time, regardless of the "treatment." If a researcher does not account for this (usually by using a control group), then the researcher could attribute this change to their treatment.

Attrition

I imagine the first day of your Research Methods class will look very different from the last day of the course. While students can often add a course late, some students will drop a course. Typically, you end up with fewer classmates than you had the first day. Students drop a course for various reasons, but the result is the same: *attrition*. When conducting a study, it is natural to lose participants, especially in a study takes place over a long period of time. Some may not want to participate any longer, some may move to a place where the study is not being conducted, and in unfortunate cases, someone may pass away. While losing participants is bad regardless, the reason this is a threat to *internal* validity is because it may make your randomly selected and randomly assigned groups *different*. If you started with a pretest and made sure there were no significant differences between the two groups, that may no longer hold true. Imagine Teacher JANE wants to know how individual tutoring affects test scores. She randomly samples ten students (this is too small of a sample—I am only using this for purposes of this example!), and randomly assigns them to a treatment and control group. She gives them a pretest: the control group has test scores of 70, 75, 80, 85, and 100 and the treatment group has scores of 95, 90, 90, 85, and 50, then both groups have pretest scores that are equal, as they both have a mean of 82. However, say that one student drops out of each group: the control group loses the student who made a 100, and the treatment group loses the student who made a 50. Now, the average of the control group is 77.5 and the average of the treatment group is 90. Losing participants can create group differences that were not there in the beginning.

Testing

If you remember from earlier in this chapter, test-retest was discussed as a method to assess reliability, but that there can be an issue called *testing effect*, which is a threat to internal validity. A testing effect occurs when being exposed to the test (such as the pretest), naturally improves one's scores: retaking the ACT or SAT likely improved your score, even if you did not study more for it. For example, Fitness Researcher BOB wants to see how continuous use of caffeine can have an effect on the time it takes a non-runner to run a mile. BOB wants to see this effect over time, so each week, he tests his participants to see how fast they are running. Imagine if you are a non-runner, and now you are required to run a mile at least once a week. The simple act of testing (running once a week) would improve your running time, regardless of the amount of caffeine you consumed.

Instrumentation

When conducting a study, *instrumentation,* meaning the instrument you are using to measure something, might change, which could have an effect on the results. Imagine that Psychologist **Bob** wants to determine whether physical force is an effective method to subdue suspects. After recruiting 100 police officers, they all go through a training and learn the degree of force to use. Now imagine that some of the police officers increase their weight training significantly—the degree of force may increase. In this case, the instrument used to deliver the treatment (the police officer) changed over a period of time. Or, imagine that Researcher **Jane** is interested in measuring young children's ability by timing how fast they can put together a puzzle. The first child would have access to a crisp, new, clean, puzzle; while the last would be using a very different instrument: it might be sticky with folded soft edges, making it harder to put together, and thus, increasing the time needed to put together that puzzle. In this case, too, the instrument changed over time.

Issues with Treatment

At times, there may be *issues with the treatment* in your study. Specifically, changes in outcome may be attributed to the treatment, when in fact, it was more attributable to the grouping of subjects. Specifically, how one group may be effected by what they and/or the other group is or is not receiving, or what they perceive they are (or are not) perceiving. A study is in danger of these threats when the participants know whether they are in the control or experimental group, but also if they know who else is in both groups. To combat these threats, researchers will often use either a single-blind study (where the subjects do not know whether they are in the control or treatment group), or even better, a double-blind study (where neither the researchers nor the subjects know who is in which group). Treatment grouping actually encompasses four different threats (Maxfield & Babbie, 2014).

- *Diffusion/imitation of treatment* can occur when the experimental group and control group discuss the study and the treatment. For instance, if a group of prisoners were randomly assigned to a treatment and control group to determine how an anger management class can reduce prison violence, those in the treatment group may share the tactics of managing anger with the control group participants, allowing the treatment to also have an effect on the control group.

- *Compensatory treatment* can occur when the control group knows what treatment the experimental/treatment group is receiving and believe they are being deprived. For instance, say that your professor was interested in seeing how extra time on a test would affect grades. S/he randomly assigns your class into two groups: treatment and control group, and you are in the control group. You would probably believe this to be unfair, as you were being robbed of that extra test time, which could be very valuable to you. This may have an effect on how well you do on the test, and how well other participants do. The *way* that it affects the control group can vary. The control group might experience *compensatory rivalry*, thus working harder and harder to do better on the tests than the treatment group. Or, the control group may experience *demoralization*, believing that they have been robbed of the treatment and thus, retreat or give up, resulting in lower test grades than if they had never been involved in the experiment (Maxfield & Babbie, 2014).

- *A placebo effect* can occur when those in the control group believe they are receiving the treatment and therefore start feeling the benefits of that treatment. For instance, if **Bob** the medical researcher is studying a drug that is supposed to reduce the side effects of heroin withdrawal, he may observe minimized side effects in the treatment group, if the subjects in the treatment group *know* they are receiving the treatment. The best way to minimize the threat of a placebo effect is to use a double-blind study (Ellis et al., 2010; Maxfield & Babbie, 2014).

- *Hawthorne Effect:* If you have ever been employed, you probably know that you act differently when the boss is around, and you also act differently when customers are around. Generally, when being watched by someone, behavior changes. When being observed in a research capacity, behavior can often change, too. Imagine wanting to study whether diversity training will decrease racial profiling among police officers. Let's assume that in reality, the department you are observing *does* racially profile. If they are aware that this is the purpose of your research, they may be less likely to racially profile if you are riding along and observing them, regardless of whether they received the treatment (diversity training). The act of being observed can also bring about positive feelings. For instance, if a Research Methods professor wanted to see whether one-on-one tutoring with the professor would help improve students' test scores, some students might be impressed that a professor is giving up so much of their time to work one-on-one with students, that those same students start studying harder, showing up for class more often, and generally putting in more effort. In turn, their test grades improve. This improvement is due simply to research efforts, not the treatment itself (Adams & Lawrence, 2014; Ellis et al., 2010).

Additive and Interactive Effects of Threats to Internal Validity

The bad news is that a researcher can try their best to control and prevent threats to internal validity, but there is only so much one can do. For one, it is important to realize that a study will have multiple threats, and they often combine to form a super threat where there are differences in the treatment and control group due to selection bias that are then aggravated by another threat. For instance, a researcher could have both selection bias and maturation in one study: the groups are not equal and one is changing at a much faster rate than the other. Another example could be selection and instrumentation: When measuring intelligence as the time taken to complete a puzzle, the researcher assigns participants to two groups which are nonequivalent; the treatment group is a first-period class and the control group is a second-period class.

Threats to Statistical Conclusion Validity

Using the correct statistical test is beyond the scope of this book, but know that a statistical test must be appropriate to use to test the null hypothesis in your study, and the test must be appropriate for the type of data you have. More specifically, different statistical tests have rules (called assumptions), and if the data do not follow those assumptions, then using the test is a threat to statistical conclusion validity.

Threats to Construct Validity

There are a number of threats to construct validity that generally focus on how the construct is defined, understood, explained, and measured. Two of the main threats include inadequate explanation and construct confounding.

- *Inadequate explanation* of the construct occurs when there is not in-depth understanding and a comprehensive description of the construct. The items used to measure the construct may not wholly represent the construct.

- *Construct confounding* occurs when the items used to measure a construct are representative of more than one construct. For instance, in previous chapters, I have referenced Gottfredson and Hirschi's (1990) self-control theory, which is often measured using the Grasmick scale, which includes questions about preferring physical activities to mental ones, or giving up on a project if it is too hard. If I also wanted to measure an individual's symptoms of ADHD, I might have some items that are indicative of *both* ADHD and self-control. This creates a confounding construct!

In addition to these two threats, some of the threats to external and internal validity are also threats to construct validity, including **grouping treatments** and **ecological validity**. The best methods to combat threats to construct validity is to make sure there is a clear, comprehensive understanding of the theory, the construct, and the methods used to measure. Additionally, any new index or scale used to measure a construct should be piloted (tested with a small group of participants) as well as reviewed by a panel of experts, including experts in research methods and statistics, as well as experts in the theory/construct you aim to measure.

Summing It Up

One of the most important things to remember is that research is never perfect, and there will be mistakes made. It is important to recognize those mistakes, and control for those that you can. One of the best ways to do this is to plan your research, then plan again! Careful planning will ideally result in a strong study design, which should minimize the threats to internal validity and, ideally, construct validity. Just always remember that you will forever be seeking validity and never perfectly achieving it!

Discussion Questions

1. What would be an example of something that is reliable but not valid? Explain your answer.

2. Name all threats to internal validity, then choose four and provide examples of them in research scenarios.

3. What is construct validity and how is it different from internal validity?

4. What is external validity and how is it different from internal validity?

5. Design a research proposal and identify the threats to each type of validity to which you think your study would be most vulnerable.

6. What are additive and interactive effects of threats to internal validity? How are they related to other threats to internal validity?

7. What are the four issues that can arise with treatment? Provide examples of each.

8. What are the threats of construct validity? Name and explain each.

Trying It Out

Your professor may ask you to complete the following companion assignment available from the publisher. Using the supplied worksheet form, you are going to attempt to determine what 24 questions/statements are trying to measure.

References

Adams, K. A., & Lawrence, E. K. (2014). *Research methods, statistics, and applications.* Thousand Oaks, CA: Sage Publications.

Chalk, T. (2016, October 20). Top NBA free throw shooters of all-time. *Fox Sports.* Retrieved from https://www.foxsports.com/nba/gallery/top-free-throw-shooters--stephen-curry-steve-nash-ray-allen-reggie-miller-020816.

Christensen, L. B., Johnson, B., & Turner, L. A. (2010). Research methods, design, and analysis (11th ed.). Boston, MA: Allyn & Bacon.

Ellis, L., Hartley, R. D., & Walsh, A. (2010). *Research methods in criminal justice and criminology: An interdisciplinary approach.* Lanham, MD: Rowman & Littlefield.

Field, A., & Miles, J. (2012). *Discovering statistics using r.* Thousand Oaks, CA: Sage Publications.

Frankfort-Nachmias, C., & Nachmias, D. (2015). *Research methods in the social sciences* (8th ed.). New York, NY: Worth Publishers.

Gliner, J. A., Morgan, G. A., & Leech, N. L. (2011). *Research methods in applied settings: An integrated approach to design and analysis.* Abingdon, UK: Routledge.

Johnson, K. K. (1995). Attributions about date rape: Impact of clothing, sex, money spent, date type, and perceived similarity. *Family and Consumer Sciences Research Journal, 23*(3), 292–310.

Maxfield, M., & Babbie, E. (2014). *Research methods for criminal justice and criminology*. Boston, MA: Cengage Learning.

Neuharth-Keusch, A. J. (2016, January 23). Ranking the NBA's worst free throw shooters of all time. *USA Today*. Retrieved from https://www.usatoday.com/story/sports/nba/2016/01/23/nba-worst-free-throw-shooters-ben-wallace-shaquille-oneal-andre-drummond/79174958/.

Passer, M. (2017). *Research methods: Concepts and connections*. Basingstoke, UK: Macmillan Higher Education.

Popper, K. (2005). *The logic of scientific discovery*. Routledge.

Schweitzer, J. B., Cummins, T. K., & Kant, C. A. (2001). Attention-deficit/hyperactivity disorder. *Medical Clinics of North America, 85*(3), 757–777.

Shadish, W. R., Cook, T. D., & Campbell, D. T. (2002). *Experimental and quasi-experimental designs for generalized causal inference*. Boston, MA: Houghton Mifflin.

Shavelson, R. J. (2002). Lee J. Cronbach, 1916–2001. *Educational Researcher, 31*(2), 37–39.

Siegel, S. (1983). Classical conditioning, drug tolerance, and drug dependence. *Research Advances in Alcohol and Drug Problems, 7*, 207–246.

White, T. L., & McBurney, D. H. (2012). *Research methods*. Boston, MA: Cengage Learning.

Chapter 6

Research Designs

Learning Objectives

- Describe the relationship between validity and research designs
- Explain the importance of random assignment
- Distinguish between experimental, quasi-experimental, and nonexperimental research designs
- Identify the parts of each specific experimental design
- Identify the parts of each specific quasi-experimental design
- Identify and explain the parts and process of factorial research designs
- Apply research designs within different research proposals
- Evaluate the feasibility of experimental designs within different research proposals

My dog, Walter, whom I mentioned in previous chapters, is a terribly behaved dog—partly because he is quite intelligent (really, he is). However, one of the things that I find perplexing is his ability to smell something he wants, but cannot have, from a mile away. Yet, when I try to play games with him like "find the treat," I start doubting his intelligence. He was not very good at this game. I found, however, that making sure I used the same type of treat each time we played the game seemed to help, and he is quickly becoming a master at it.

Assuming you are an undergraduate criminal justice or criminology major (or at least some sort of social science major), my dog's sniffing skills probably seem off topic, or at the least, inapplicable to you. However, should you become (or already are) a police officer or a park ranger, you may find yourself in an emergency situation where a dog's sniffing skills are particularly important: perhaps trying to find a crime scene or perhaps during a search and rescue mission.

Imagine that you are a police chief in a small, rural town, and a mother has reported that her child has been missing for a little more than an hour. You believe the child to still be alive. Since you are in such a small town, your agency does not have a K9 unit. A larger agency has offered one of their search and rescue dogs; however, they want to know if you want a dog that can search for both cadavers and live bodies, a dog that can only search for cadavers, or a dog that can only search for live bodies. It may seem obvious that you would want a "crossover dog," one that can smell out for both cadavers and live bodies; however, researchers of one study (Lit & Crawford, 2006) showed that dogs trained only in searching for live bodies have far better accuracy than crossover dogs. They made these conclusions by using a *quasi-experimental research design.*

If you remember from Chapter 4, "The Nitty Gritty," we discussed three types of research designs: experimental, quasi-experimental, and nonexperimental. Here's the bad news: these are broad categories or global designs, and there are *specific types* of each one of these global designs (which we will call specific research designs). Here's the good news: we will go through a number of different specific designs; however, we will not review *all* possible designs.

Nonexperimental Designs

Unfortunately, many times researchers in criminal justice and criminology end up having to use *nonexperimental designs*. More specifically, these researchers use ex-post-facto designs (which were mentioned in Chapter 4, "The Nitty Gritty"), which means *after the fact*, and are used when the treatment has already occurred. For instance, if JANE the psychologist wants to understand how gender (male or female) affects aggression, she cannot *assign* the treatment; meaning, she cannot randomly assign subjects to be male or female — because she has no control over assigning sex; the treatment has already occurred. Nonexperimental designs tend to be *cross-sectional designs*, which mean that observations were made at one single point in time with a group of subjects (such as a survey given to customers at a restaurant asking about their experience). Cross-sectional research designs tend to be substantially less powerful than *longitudinal designs*, which are those that have *multiple* observations using the same group of subjects. Think about course evaluations: you evaluate one course and its professor only once — you do not complete the course evaluation multiple times over the semester. Or, imagine that your grade in a course was based on one single paper instead of multiple assignments. Now imagine that your professor is in a *really* bad mood when they grade that one paper — yikes!

Going back to the example about JANE the psychologist wondering whether sex affected aggression, JANE knows the time order of these variables: someone being born male or female likely came before their current level of aggression. More so, while sex can affect aggression, aggression cannot change someone from being male or female. However, since nonexperimental research tends to use cross-sectional designs, we often do not know the time order of our treatment variable and our outcome variable. When this occurs, it is called **correlational research**. If, instead of sex, JANE the psychologist wanted to look at how alcohol affected aggression, she could only establish whether there was a relationship between the two. Alcohol use could affect aggression, but levels of aggression could also affect alcohol use. Since she only collected data at one point in time (a cross-sectional design), she cannot say which one is affecting which.

Experimental Research Designs

If you remember from earlier discussions of experimental designs (see Chapter 4, "The Nitty Gritty," and Chapter 5, "Validity and Reliability"), they tend to be valuable when they are feasible. Experimental designs are the most powerful of designs because they get researchers closer to being able to claim a cause-and-effect relationship. This is because experimental designs allow researchers to establish not only a relationship, but also temporal ordering and most often, an absence of spuriousness (to review the elements of causation, see Chapter 2 on theory and philosophy).

In the social sciences, experimental designs can often be challenging to implement. This is because the researchers (in some way or another) have to *give* the treatment. Since criminologists are most often looking at crime, we cannot *make* people commit crime and call it a treatment! That would be unethical! Further, it is particularly challenging to always randomly assign subjects to either a control group or an experimental group. For instance, imagine designing a study where the research question is "Does the addition of drug treatment for probationers with a history of substance abuse significantly reduce recidivism rates?" To recruit participants, a researcher would have to find those who are about to start probation who are willing to participate in the drug treatment program—and then *not* provide it to half of them (the control group). This may be feasible, but what if the research goal was to examine drug treatment *versus* traditional probation? That would require random assignment to each group— which would require the cooperation and participation of the court system. This also has real-world implications on the offenders, as there would be different expectations for probation and drug treatment. The lesson here is that when it is feasible to implement an experimental design, it should be done—but not at the expense of any other part of research integrity. Remember that the first goal of ethical research should be to ensure that the benefits outweigh the risks.

So, even though social scientists' researchers often cannot implement an experimental design, it is really important to understand these designs, as they are the goal—when we do not use this type of design, the research has a lot of limitations, and moves much farther away from being able to claim a causal relationship. An important note is that social science research *not* using an experimental design is still valuable—it is incredibly valuable! It is just important to realize how the research design changes the claims we can make from research. Further, there are other designs that we can use that can get us closer again to a causal relationship.

Parts of the Research Design

In an experimental design, there are a few staple components (though sometimes these are modified). These include groups of subjects, typically a *control group* and *experimental group, a treatment, a pretest*, and *a posttest*. In previous chapters, we discussed experimental designs as looking at a treatment and how it affects an outcome. To put this in a familiar framework, a treatment is simply an independent variable and the outcome is the dependent variable. If you asked, "How does reading the Research Methods textbook affect Research Methods test grades?" your treatment or independent variable would be reading the textbook, and your dependent variable would be Research Methods test grades. If you remember when developing hypotheses, we typically examine a relationship, difference, or effect. If the research design cannot account for temporal ordering (which came first, the chicken or the egg?), then we typically are only able to conclude whether there is a relationship or a difference. We avoid using language like "effect/affect," unless we know the timing of the independent and dependent variable. For instance, I would not hypothesize that alcohol use affects bullying behavior if I do not know which came first: the alcohol use or the bullying.

An experimental design typically includes a pretest and a posttest. The word "test" can throw some people off—it is really a "measurement" of some sort *before* the treatment (pretest) and a measurement of some sort *after* the treatment (posttest). Pretests are useful as they provide time ordering (so we know which came first—the treatment or the outcome). Pretests allow researchers to establish a baseline. Polygraph examiners ask their subjects baseline questions to establish their "normal" heartbeat, skin temperature, and breathing rate. The importance of a pretest and posttest is to see how the pretest is *different* from the posttest for those subjects who received the treatment. For instance, think about this in an individual case: if you claim that your friend's Southern accent becomes much more prominent when they drink alcohol, they may not believe you. You would probably want to establish a baseline or the pretest: record them with your phone when they are sober. You would then want them to have the treatment, which you would then follow with a posttest: recording your friend again after a few drinks, when they are saying things like "y'all are runnin' around like a chicken with its head cut off!"

The reason that researchers use a control group is to make sure that any change in the treatment group from pretest to posttest is due to the treatment, and not some other cause. If you think back to our internal threats to validity, there are other possible explanations that can explain a change in the treatment group (maturation or history, for example—see Chapter 5, "Validity and Reliability"); however, those outside influences should have the same effect on the control group as well, as long as the groups are *equal*. Group equivalence is achieved through randomization (or matching, which we will discuss later in this chapter).

When reviewing the different specific designs, I would recommend comparing each one to the classical design—what is different—is it missing something that the classical design has and/or does it have something that the classical design does not have? In addition to presenting an explanation of each design, I am going to provide an example of each. Instead of using a bunch of different study examples, we are going to just use one, and continue to modify it, in hopes that it is easy to differentiate between the study designs.

Example: Have you ever seen those cellphone cases that also work as lighters? As an ex-smoker, I've wondered whether that would have been a good thing to have

Figure 6-1: Classical Experimental Design

R	E_1	O_1	X_1	O_2
R	C_1	O_1		O_2

in my younger years, as I was *always* losing my lighter. The question then becomes whether I would have smoked a lot more because I always had a lighter. So, the research question for this example is: Does possession of a cellphone lighter case effect the frequency of smoking? Another important note is that my population would *only* be those people who smoked and who have never used a cellphone lighter case.

Types of Experimental Designs

Classical Experimental Design

The classical experimental design (also referred to as the pretest posttest control group design) is "classic" because it has all the parts but nothing extra. There are two groups—a control group, and an experimental group (or treatment group)—a pretest, a posttest, and a treatment. Figure 6-1 is a diagram that models a classical experimental design. R is used to denote random assignment, E for experimental group and C for control group. O_1 is the pretest and O_2 is the posttest. In the classical experimental design, the researchers randomly assign subjects to one of two groups, experimental or treatment, and then give them a pretest as a baseline measure. The pretest is also used to establish equivalence—there should be no real difference in the two groups on the outcome (dependent variable).

Classical Experimental Design: Cellphone Lighter Case Example

I would randomly assign subjects (whom I selected from my population of smokers who have never used a cellphone lighter case) to the experimental group and the control group. For my pretest, I would give each individual five cartons of cigarettes (50 packs) and have them report how many they smoked during a two-week period (which they can tell by determining how many cigarettes remain in the carton[s]). I would also have them report how often they use their phone (considering some people do not use it very often!). I would then use the results of the pretest to ensure that my groups are equivalent. Following this, my treatment group subjects would each receive a cellphone lighter case that fit their phone. After ensuring that they knew how to use it, I would give both groups additional cartons of cigarettes and have them report back how many cigarettes they smoked in another two-week period.

Figure 6-2: Posttest Only Control Group Design

R	E_1		X_1	O_1
R	C_1			O_1

Posttest Only Control Group Design

A *posttest only control group design* (also called an *after-only experimental design*) is the exact same as the classical design, except that it is missing a pretest (hence the name—posttest only). The design is still considered an experimental design, because there is still random assignment, and therefore, the groups are likely equivalent. The rationale for using a posttest only control group design may vary, but it would typically be due to some circumstance regarding the participants or a need to get the results of the study as fast as possible (Ellis et al., 2010). So, as seen in Figure 6-2, the researcher randomly assigns (R) subjects to the experimental group (E_1) and the control group (C_1), then gives the experimental group (E_1) the treatment, which is followed by a posttest (O_1) for both the experimental and control groups.

Posttest Only with Cellphone Case Example

I would randomly assign subjects (whom I selected from my population of smokers who have never used a cellphone lighter case) to the experimental group and the control group. Following this, my treatment group subjects would each receive a cellphone lighter case that fit their phone. After ensuring that they knew how to use it, I would give both groups five cartons of cigarettes and have them report back how many cigarettes they smoked in a two-week period.

Solomon Four-Group Design

While the posttest only design has something missing when comparing it to the classical experimental design, the *Solomon four-group design* has some components that the classical design does not. For starters—it has four groups—two control groups and two treatment groups. While the classical design helps to combat some of the threats to internal validity, like maturation and history, there are still issues regarding testing effects. So, a Solomon four-group design takes the classical design one step further, and provides an extra set of experimental and control groups that *do not receive the pretest.* Now, we have two groups receiving a treatment, two groups *not* receiving the treatment, and they were all randomly assigned. What is even better about the Solomon four-group design is that the effects can be measured and compared amongst the four groups. A Solomon four-group design is the most powerful design when it comes to protecting the validity of the research from internal threats.

Figure 6-3: Solomon Four-Group Design

R	E_1	O_1	X	O_2
R	C_1	O_1		O_2
R	E_2		X	O_1
R	C_2			O_1

The design is illustrated in Figure 6-3: subjects are randomly assigned to one of four groups (R): experimental group 1 (E_1), control group 1 (C_1), experimental group 2 (E_2), or control group 2 (C_2). Experimental group 1 (E_1) and control group 1 (C_1) are given the pretest (O_1), and then both experimental groups (E_1 and E_2) are given the treatment (X), which is then followed by a posttest, which is given to all four groups. This serves as the second test for experimental group 1 and control group 1 (O_2) and the first test for experimental group 2 and control group 2 (O_1).

Solomon Four-Group Design with Cellphone Lighter Case Example

I would randomly assign subjects (whom I selected from my population of smokers who have never used a cellphone lighter case) to the experimental group and the control group. For my pretest, I would give each subject in my "one groups" (experimental group 1 and control group 1) five cartons of cigarettes (50 packs) and have them report how many they smoked during a two-week period (which they can tell by determining how many cigarettes remain in the carton[s]). I would also have them report how often they use their phone. I would then use the results of the pretest to ensure that my groups are equivalent. Following this, subjects in my treatment groups (experimental group 1 and experimental group 2) would each receive a cellphone lighter case that fit their phone. After ensuring that they knew how to use it, I would give all four groups (both experimental groups and both control groups) additional cartons of cigarettes and have them report back how many cigarettes they smoked in another two-week period.

Factorial Designs

Factorial designs can be used when there is more than one treatment. If a researcher wants to stick with using an experimental design, but also has multiple treatments, then the classical experimental design can be modified. Factorial designs allow for researchers to look at the differences between and within groups; meaning, in the control group, a researcher can look at the difference within each participant from the pretest to the posttest, as well as look at differences between participants in the control group and the experimental group.

Figure 6-4: Factorial Design with Two Treatments

R	E_1	O_1	X_1	O_2
R	E_2	O_1	X_2	O_2
R	C_1	O_1		O_2

Factorial Designs with Two Treatments

One way that a factorial design could be used when there are two or more treatments is by simply adding a second treatment group. There would then be three groups that were randomly assigned to either experimental group 1, (E_1), experimental group 2 (E_2), or the control group (C_1). This factorial design is illustrated in Figure 6-4. All three groups would still receive the pretest, and then experimental group 1 (E_1) would receive the first treatment and experimental group 2 (E_2) would receive the second treatment, while the control group would receive no treatment.

Factorial Design with Two Treatments: Cellphone Case Example

I would randomly assign subjects (whom I selected from my population of smokers who have never used a cellphone lighter case) to experimental group 1, experimental group 2, and the control group. For my pretest, I would give each individual in all three groups five cartons of cigarettes (50 packs) and have them report how many they smoked during a two-week period (which they can tell by determining how many cigarettes remain in the carton[s]). I would also have them report how often they use their phone (considering some people do not use it very often). I would then use the results of the pretest to ensure that my groups are equivalent. Following this, my experimental group 1 subjects would each receive a cellphone lighter case that fit their phone, and my experimental group 2 subjects would receive a keychain lighter to attach to their keys. After ensuring that they knew how to use it, I would give all three groups additional cartons of cigarettes and have them report back how many cigarettes they smoked in another two-week period. I can then examine the difference in smoking frequency for subjects smoking before and after using a cellphone lighter case (using the pretest and posttest of experimental group 1). I can also examine differences within my subjects in each group: first, I can examine differences in smoking frequency for subjects smoking before and after using a keychain lighter (using the pretest and posttest of experimental group 2), and I can examine if there were any differences in smoking frequency from one week to another week for my control group. I can also examine the differences of the posttests in each group to determine whether cellphone cases or keychain lighters increased smoking frequency as compared to the control group, and if they *did*, I can also determine if cellphone lighter cases increased smoking *more or less* than keychain lighters.

Figure 6-5: Factorial Counterbalanced Design with Three Treatments

R	E_1	O_1	$X_1X_2X_3$	O_2
R	E_2	O_1	$X_1X_3X_2$	O_2
R	E_3	O_1	$X_2X_1X_3$	O_2
R	E_4	O_1	$X_2X_3X_1$	O_2
R	E_5	O_1	$X_3X_1X_2$	O_2
R	E_6	O_1	$X_3X_2X_1$	O_2
R	C_1	O_1		O_2

Factorial Designs and Counterbalancing

Factorial designs can also be used when you have multiple treatments and want to know whether the *order* in which subjects receive treatment matters. For instance, if you run and then use weights, is that better than using weights and then running? Or, what if you have a cold? Is it better to take cold medicine, then have chicken soup, and then take a nap — or vice-versa? When we are interested in the order of multiple treatments, we use counterbalancing. If we are interested in all possible orders, then for each different order, we will need an additional experimental group. Using counterbalancing can make things complicated, and quickly! Imagine if you had eight treatments. If you wanted to know how any possible order would affect the outcome, you would need 40,320 treatment groups (8 x 7 x 6 x 5 x 4 x 3 x 2 x 1 = 40,320) — that is not going to happen (Leary, 2016; Passer, 2017; White & McBurney, 2012)!

Figure 6-5 illustrates a counterbalanced factorial design with all possible orders for three treatments. There are six experimental groups (E_1, E_2, E_3, E_4, E_5, & E_6) and one control group (C_1). Each group receives a pretest (O_1) and then each experimental group receives a different order of treatments. The first one receives the first, then the second, then the third, the second experimental group receives the first, then the third, then the second, etc. After the treatments are given, all groups are given the posttest (O_2).

Example of Factorial Counterbalanced Design with Three Treatments

Unfortunately, I lied — for this one, I am not using the cellphone case design, because it would be a bit of a stretch to figure out why the order of lighters would matter. Have you ever heard the saying "liquor before beer, you're clear; beer before liquor, never sicker"? This is a motto many college students will repeat and some will abide by — for some, it seems to hold true, for others, not so much! Another common guideline with preventing sickness from alcohol is food. However, some people say

Figure 6-6: All Possible Orders of Treatment for a
Factorial Counterbalanced Design

Design with Three Treatments
Beer, Liquor, Food
Beer, Food, Liquor
Liquor, Beer, Food
Liquor, Food, Beer
Food, Beer, Liquor
Food, Liquor, Beer

it is best to eat before you drink, some people say after you drink, and some even say *while* you drink. Therefore, using an experimental design, a researcher could examine whether the order of these three treatments (liquor, beer, food) affects the outcome: sickness (see Figure 6-6). One note: it is important that the treatment *amounts* are the same (i.e., same amount of liquor for each group, same amount of food, same amount of beer). Just like in Figure 6-5, we will need six experimental groups since we have three different treatments (3 x 2 x 1). Therefore, I would randomly assign subjects to one of the seven groups (six experimental groups and one control group). I would first give a pretest to all the experimental groups and the control group to measure their current level of sickness. Following that, I would give the treatments in different orders to each treatment group. (See the possible combinations in Figure 6-5.) I would then give the posttest to all seven groups, which would measure their level of sickness.

Quasi-Experimental Designs

Have you ever heard someone say, "kind of, sort of, but not really…," and think it was a total contradiction? Basically, this is what quasi-experimental designs are. They are kind of, sort of experimental designs … but not really! They are missing key elements and therefore are less powerful, and are further away from being able to claim a causal relationship. As we have previously discussed, while less than ideal, *quasi-experimental designs* are often what social scientists use, because of ethical issues or research constraints, since we are most often researching human behavior of some sort. The main issue with quasi-experimental designs is that they are missing randomization; meaning, they are missing random assignment into control and experimental groups.

While quasi-experimental designs certainly have their disadvantages, oftentimes, conducting experimental studies would put the researcher at just as much, if not more of a disadvantage—even when not accounting for the ethical implications. Imagine attempting to determine whether social interaction has an effect on likelihood of psychopathic tendencies (spoiler—it has a great effect). To design a study, it would

Figure 6-7: Nonequivalent Control Group Design

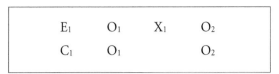

be necessary to lock one group of individuals up in separate rooms from the time of infancy and only provide them with bare necessities, and little-to-no talking to ensure minimal social interaction. Locking a child in a room by themselves is more than just failing to provide no more than minimal social interaction. Being indoors for years at a time, coupled with no physical touch, would undoubtedly contribute to any psychopathic tendencies just as much as the minimal social interaction.

For these study designs, I will use the cellphone lighter case example when I can; however, it gets a bit more challenging to do so! Therefore, I will also use other examples to help explain these studies.

Nonequivalent Control Group Design

Considering that criminologists and criminal justice researchers are often dealing with those involved in the criminal justice system, it may be impossible to use an experimental design. One of the biggest challenges is random assignment. Typically, if we are looking at the effectiveness of treatments or punishments, researchers do not get to randomly assign some to one type of punishment and other subjects to a different punishment. When random assignment is not possible, researchers can use a *nonequivalent control group design* (see Figure 6-7). This design lacks group equivalence but has all the other parts of an experimental design: an experimental group, a control group, a pretest, a treatment, and a posttest. For instance, if **Bob** the researcher wanted to see whether a group counseling was effective at reducing levels of anger for inmates, **Bob** likely would be unable to randomly assign inmates to either an experimental or control group—it would have to be those who were eligible and/ or volunteered to be a part of group counseling. This obviously makes the groups nonequivalent, which opens the study to the threat of selection bias. However, **Bob** could measure their anger levels before the group counseling, and again after the group counseling to see if there was observable change in anger. If there were, then this would *likely* be due to the treatment (group counseling); however, it is *possible* that any changes would be due to an interaction of validity threats: perhaps because the groups are unequal (selection bias) each group is maturing (maturation), but the treatment group is maturing at a faster rate.

One way that a researcher can make a nonequivalent control group design more powerful is by using *matching*. Using the previous example, while **Bob** would be unable to pick who would participate in group counseling, he could possibly be pickier about who is in his control group and use *individual matching*, meaning, he finds require that individuals match other individuals in the treatment group. He could do this on an individual level; so perhaps he would want to match on demographics and anger level (which we will say is measured on a scale of 1 to 10). If subject #1 in the treatment group is a 30-year-old white male with an anger score of 7, he would want to find someone who matched those characteristics for the control group: a 30-year-old white male with an anger score of 7. If it is not possible to match subject to subject, BOB could try to use *aggregate matching*, which would have the groups matched by demographics and anger level. If the treatment group has 40 participants, with an average age of 35, all male, with 50% white, 30% black and 20% other race(s), then BOB would want his control group to match on an aggregate (group) level: a control group with an average of 35, all male, with 50% white, 30% black, and 20% other race(s).

One type of control group design that is common in criminal justice research is *cohort designs* (Maxfield & Babbie, 2014). A cohort is a group of people who are grouped together for one reason or another. A sorority or fraternity would be an example of a cohort, or even all freshmen at your college would be a cohort. Researchers cannot randomly assign students to be in a sorority or a fraternity, so if a cohort were used as a treatment group, it would not be randomly assigned. For instance, a researcher may want to determine if sexual assault awareness training would reduce beliefs in rape myths. Perhaps the researcher would use a cohort, like freshmen on campus, and provide the training during orientation. The researcher could also provide the pretest to other students (sophomores, for instance) and then give both cohorts the posttest. Should the researcher find that there is a significant reduction in beliefs in rape myths for freshmen, then the training was likely effective.

Nonequivalent Control Group Design with Cellphone Lighter Case Example

After sampling from my population of smokers, I assign participants to one of two groups: the treatment group, which includes only those who use a smartphone for more than two hours a day, and the control group, which are those who use their phone less frequently and/or have a traditional cellphone. For my pretest, I would give each individual five cartons of cigarettes (50 packs) and have them report how many they smoked during a two-week period (which they can tell by determining how many cigarettes remain in the carton[s]). I would also have them report how often they use their phone. I would then use the results of the pretest to ensure that my groups are equivalent. Following this, my treatment group subjects would each receive a cellphone lighter case that fit their phone. After ensuring that they knew how to use it, I would give both groups additional cartons of cigarettes and have them report back how many cigarettes they smoked in another two-week period.

Before-and-After Group Designs

When a control group is unfeasible for a study, researchers may use a time-series design that looks at either one group or multiple groups, and may include several or one observation (pretest[s]) before the treatment and several or one observation (posttests[s]) after the treatment.

Of course, there are different types of time series designs. If a researcher is sticking with one pretest and one posttest, then this is a before-and-after design. One of the distinctions between types is whether there is one group or more than one group. When the researcher uses just one group, these are **one-group before-and-after designs.** When there are multiple groups—you guessed it—the design is referred to **multiple-group before-and-after designs.** When using multiple groups, it is important to realize there is no control group—each group is receiving the treatment(s).

Interrupted Time-Series Designs

Another type of time-series design is **interrupted time-series designs.** In these designs, researchers use a series of observations (pretests) before a treatment and then multiple observations (posttests) after a treatment. Interrupted time-series designs are often beneficial in criminal justice research when examining the effects of a new policy or law. For example, if a researcher were to collect monthly data on marijuana use in teens in Colorado for five years *prior* to Colorado legalizing it, the researcher could then collect monthly data over a five-year period *after* its legalization. For instance, JANE has begun developing a program that works with neighborhoods to increase cohesion. Specifically, JANE provides a three-hour training on making a neighborhood a better place by implementing block parties, getting to know your neighbors, and watching out for their homes. JANE wants to know whether the program has a real effect on crime within the community. Therefore, six months prior to providing the training in a community, she hires BOB the researcher to collect data on crime rates in the community (these are the pretests). Once JANE provides the treatment (the neighbor training), BOB then collects data on crime rates in the community for another six months to see if crime decreases. This will allow JANE to see whether the program *may* be having a significant effect on reducing crime.

Cellphone Lighter Case Example with Interrupted Time-Series Design

Using a group of smokers who used smartphones, I would make weekly observations about the frequency of their smoking over a one-year period. I would then provide all the subjects with a cellphone lighter case and then make weekly observations about the frequency of their smoking over the following year.

Types of Nonexperimental Designs

Panel Designs

Often, as social science researchers, the treatments we are observing are out of our hands. We cannot provide high- or low-quality education, good or bad neighborhoods, good or bad parents, etc. These are things that are out of the researchers' control. If we cannot control whether they are good or bad, then we certainly cannot keep them from happening, so a control group becomes out of the question. For instance, if **Bob** wanted to see how bad parenting affected grades in school, **Bob** cannot randomly assign people to good parents (the control group) and bad parents (the treatment group). Therefore, researchers have one of two choices: they can conduct research after the fact and see how these things are *related* to behavior, or they can follow people over a period of time and attempt to observe how these treatments *appear* to affect behavior. While interrupted time-series designs may make observations about the same or different people, *panel designs* are focused on making observations with the same sample of people over a long period of time. Since they collect data on the same group of people over a long period of time, these are also known as *longitudinal studies*, which I mentioned in the beginning of this chapter when discussing nonexperimental research designs. Longitudinal studies are just as they sound — those that take place over a period of time and have multiple observations (more than two!). When making observations about a group of people at just one point in time (like a survey instrument given to college students just once), this is referred to as a *cross-sectional* study. This can be challenging, considering you want to recruit a representative sample of individuals who will agree to be a part of a study for years! An example of a panel study that is popular in criminal justice and criminology research is the National Longitudinal Study of Adolescent Health, which is run by the University of North Carolina-Chapel Hill. In this study, researchers using a nationally representative sample of youth in the United States has made a series of observations since 1994–1995 (Harris & Udry, 2017)! In fact, the data are *still* being collected. This study did not focus solely on one treatment or independent variable but collected multiple variables, so that researchers could look at correlations and be more confident in the time order of things.

Longitudinal studies allow researchers to be more certain that an independent variable had an effect on a dependent variable, than if the researcher had just looked at the relationship after the fact. If **Bob** the researcher is curious how changes in family structure relate to grades in school, he may use a panel study design, or he may examine relationships after the fact, with a cross-sectional design. When using the cross-sectional design, **Bob** may observe that many of his participants have a low GPA and have divorced parents. While **Bob** can conclude that there is a relationship between these two, he cannot claim that parents divorcing affected grade point averages in his subjects. However, if he uses a panel design, he may observe a significant reduction in GPA *after* subjects' parents are divorced. This allows **Bob** to start saying that one thing may have an effect on another: having to deal with parents getting divorced may negatively affect grades.

Case Studies

We have mostly been discussing how one independent variable (a treatment) affects the outcome (one dependent variable). As we know, social science research is complex. If I asked you why people commit crime, I imagine you could come up with multiple reasons—and probably *all* of them contribute to criminality in some way. Humans are complex, so our motives to do something are also complex. Therefore, researchers often want to look at multiple variables (or treatments); however, these are often treatments that researchers cannot *give*, and they cannot control when these treatments are implemented. To gain a deep understanding of how multiple treatments influence an outcome, it may be necessary to observe a few people very, very closely. These are referred to as *case studies*. If JANE wants to understand the motivating factors for joining a gang, she could conduct case studies, where she makes multiple observations with a small group of individuals who may be susceptible to joining gangs, in an effort to identify motivating factors and begin to determine each of their influences on joining a gang. Case studies can use qualitative or quantitative data collection; however, because they require so many observations, it is best to start smaller to build a foundation of understanding.

Summing It Up

In addition to determining what type of research design one can use to answer a question, it is also important to determine what kind of research design other researchers are using. As I discussed in the beginning of this chapter, one of the easiest ways to identify types of experimental and quasi-experimental designs are to see what is different about it, as compared to the classical experimental design. You can answer these questions to serve as a tool in identifying these specific designs:

1) How many treatment groups are there?

2) How many control groups are there?

3) How many pretests are there?

4) How many posttests are there?

5) How many treatments are there? (If there are multiple treatments, are they given separately or in different orders?)

6) Is there random assignment?

For example, if I answered these questions for a study description as one treatment group, one control group, zero pretests, one posttest, one treatment, and yes, there is random assignment, this would be a description of a posttest only design. If I answered these questions as three treatment groups, one control group, one pretest, one posttest, three treatments given in different orders to each group, and yes, then this would probably be an example of a *factorial counterbalanced design with three treatments*.

The truth is, research is hard! While it may seem like social science research should be easier, it can be just as challenging as any other research—if not more! When considering what type of research design to use, it is important to think through all the implications: the research design is important, but so too are the legal and ethical implications. When an experimental research design is feasible to answer a research question, then it should be used. If not feasible, it is important to determine *why* it is not feasible and then examine the next best alternative. If a researcher cannot use random assignment but can implement the treatment, then using a nonequivalent control group design might work. If a researcher cannot use random assignment or a control group, s/he may want to see if it is possible to use multiple groups in a before-and-after design.

Discussion Questions

1. What type of specific research design is the best to combat against threats to internal validity? Why?

2. Why are experimental research designs not used more often in social science research?

3. What are case studies? How do these differ from other types of research designs?

4. What are ex-post-facto research designs? Provide two examples of ex-post-facto research designs.

5. What is the importance of random assignment? Explain in context of validity.

6. Why is random assignment not always possible?

7. What is the primary difference between quasi-experimental and experimental research designs?

8. What specific quasi-experimental design (nonequivalent, before-and-after group designs, or interrupted time series) is the most similar to a posttest only design (in experimental designs)? Explain why they are similar and what makes them different.

Trying It Out

Your professor may ask you to complete the following companion assignment available from the publisher. Using the supplied worksheet form, you are going to identify the research design in each research scenario.

References

Ellis, L., Hartley, R. D., & Walsh, A. (2010). *Research methods in criminal justice and criminology: An interdisciplinary approach.* Lanham, MD: Rowman & Littlefield.

Harris, K. M., & Udry, J. R. (2017). National longitudinal study of adolescent to adult health. Retrieved from http://www.cpc.unc.edu/projects/addhealth/about.

Leary, M. R. (2016). *Introduction to behavioral research methods*. New York, NY: Pearson.

Lit, L., & Crawford, C. A. (2006). Effects of training paradigms on search dog performance. *Applied Animal Behaviour Science, 98*(3), 277–292.

Maxfield, M., & Babbie, E. (2014). *Research methods for criminal justice and criminology*. Boston, MA: Cengage Learning.

Passer, M. (2017). *Research methods: Concepts and connections*. Basingstoke, UK: Macmillan Higher Education.

White, T. L., & McBurney, D. H. (2012). *Research methods*. Boston, MA: Cengage Learning.

Chapter 7

Units of Analysis, Samples, and Sampling

Learning Objectives

- Identify the four types of units of analysis
- Identify the unit of analysis within research studies
- Explain the importance of units of analysis in sampling
- Compare and contrast nonprobability and probability sampling techniques
- Identify specific probability and nonprobability sampling techniques within research studies
- Explain the differences between populations and samples
- Explain the relationship between sampling techniques and generalizability
- Define replication
- Define sampling frames
- Explain the events of the Monty Hall Problem
- Define population parameters
- Calculate confidence intervals
- Define sampling distributions

I'll admit it—I am not a huge fan of Rate My Professor.[1] While I see some value in it, I think that the ratings should be interpreted with some caution. As an undergraduate, I really loved it and saw it as a great tool. Before I would go and sign up for classes, I would search for the professors on the website and see how they were rated. To me, it was a roadmap to taking the right professors: I did not mind challenging but wanted fair teachers who were respectful and knowledgeable in the subject.

I started to see the problems with it, however, when I wrote a couple of ratings of my own professors. I only felt motivated to write reviews for two professors—one of

---

1. www.ratemyprofessor.com.

whom I loved and one of whom I hated—it was one extreme or the other! There were many professors I had enjoyed but did not see a need to make a rating in that regard. It was only those life-changing professors—in a good or bad way—that made the cut.

It made me realize that ratings had to be taken with a grain of salt. For instance, maybe the professor had a number of ratings that were bad, but only in a short period of time. Meaning that perhaps that professor was going through a tough time, or they taught a class that was not in their normal expertise. It does not necessarily indicate that the professor is a bad teacher (but it definitely *could*).

As a professor, I know that I (along with other professors) might be critical of the site, because it may not really represent how our students view us. For instance, when filling out university-official course evaluations a professor may have a rating of 4.5 on a 5-point scale. However, their Rate My Professor score may be substantially lower, such as a 2.9 on a 5-point-scale! Assuming that the questions asked on Rate My Professor were the same questions asked on the university course evaluations, why would there be such a difference? For one, the number of ratings may differ vastly: there may only be five ratings on Rate My Professor and hundreds of students on the course evaluation.

The other reason that the numbers are different (and the reason that I used this example) is that *the sample is not representative.* Rate My Professor did not seek out students whom each professor has taught; only those students who *wanted* to rate the professor did so. Even if Rate My Professor *had* sought out students who took that professor, they would need to do so randomly—meaning that each student who took that professor at some point or another would need to have the exact same chance of being selected to write a review as any other student who took that professor.

It may seem that it is easy to collect a random sample of people from a population. However, this is incredibly challenging! Therefore, just like there are various experimental research designs and quasi-experimental research designs, there are various probability (random) sampling techniques, and various nonprobability (nonrandom) sampling techniques. Just like social scientists aim to use probability sampling techniques, this is not always feasible. When a researcher is unable to use this type of technique, their sample is likely not representative of the population.

Before we begin to look at these different sampling techniques, it is important that we understand whom or what it is we are sampling, to make sure it corresponds to our unit of analysis. This may seem easy: I am analyzing people! I am analyzing newspaper articles! However, the unit of data collection may differ from the unit of analysis. Additionally, with some studies, the unit of analysis can get a little unclear, so it is important that you can refer to classifications of these units to figure out how it applies to your own study. Do not worry—I will provide examples of this and explain it in more detail.

Units of Analysis

There are four types of units that we can analyze: *individuals*, *groups*, *organizations*, and *social artifacts* (Maxfield, 2015). The distinction between them is not necessarily how the units are sampled, but instead, how they are analyzed or compared. The unit of analysis is individual, when we are describing and comparing individual characteristics. When we are describing or comparing a collection of people to another collection of people, the unit of analysis is either a group or an organization. However, to compare one group to another, we often have collected data from individuals. The way to determine each is to ask, *whom am I sampling?* And then to ask *whom/what am I analyzing?*

Individuals

For instance, the unit of analysis is individuals when we are comparing or describing individual characteristics. If we are discussing students in your Research Methods course, we may be able to say that students in your Research Methods class (just guessing) are, on average, 20 years old, and 60% of the individuals in your class are male and 40% are female. When we start comparing individuals in your class, this is *still* an example of individuals. So, if I observed that over half (58%) of the students scored 80% or higher on their Research Methods midterm, the unit of analysis is still individuals. Generally, the *sampling unit* (whom/what we sample) would actually be individuals when our unit of analysis is individuals.

Groups

When, for analysis purposes, we compare one collection of individuals to another, the unit of analysis is not individuals, but groups. Consider that we may want to look at the rate of drinking in different social cliques at a high school. We would compare the mean (average) rate of drinking between one clique and another. We may say that "The rate of drinking of clique A was twice as high as the rate of drinking of clique B." When we are examining a grouping to another grouping, this is often referred to as an aggregate. In this case, however, the individuals may be the sampling unit, while the unit of analysis would be groups. Groups are informal collections of individuals, such as social groups, gangs, cities, neighborhoods—if a collection of people are clustered together because of its place (like neighborhoods, streets, and census tracts), and one collection is compared to another, similar, collection, then the unit of analysis is a group.

Organizations

Organizations are collections of individuals that are together for a formal reason. Think about your group of friends versus your coworkers: your coworkers and you could be an organization (since it is a formalized collection of people), while you and your friends would be a group. Sometimes these overlap: for instance, if you belong to a sorority or fraternity, you belong to an organization—but if you have a few close friends within that sorority or fraternity, these would be a group. Similar to groups, our sampling unit is often individuals, but the way in which we analyze the data we collect may make the unit of analysis organizations. Imagine **Bob** the researcher wanting to determine whether the rate of drinking differs among members of Greek organizations at one university. He would collect data on individuals who belong to each Greek organization, but then he would analyze the data by comparing one organization to another. It may be hard to distinguish between groups and organizations as the unit of analysis. If the people collected together are formally clustered, then it is typically an organization. If they are collected together because of the location or because they simply want to be together, it is typically a group.

Social Artifacts

The last unit of analysis is social artifacts. These are the "things" that exist because of humans and their actions. Things like newspapers, paintings, blogs, Tweets, Facebook posts, magazines, pictures, movies, television shows, etc. The easiest way to distinguish a social artifact from another unit of analysis is to ask whether you could have a conversation with what you are comparing. Perhaps you want to analyze the violence in different movies. You (generally) cannot have a conversation with a movie. If it is not alive or comprised of individuals who are or who were once alive, it is a social artifact. Most often, the sampling unit is also a social artifact. If you remember in Chapter 4, we discussed collecting secondary data. Secondary data collection is when a researcher collects social artifacts. The content would be analyzed, which would also make the unit of analysis social artifacts.

Why Do Units of Analysis Matter?

Units of analysis matter because they help a researcher keep their head on straight. If you are conducting research and do not continually consider your unit of analysis, you can have a disconnection between your research questions, your data collection/ sampling, and your analysis, as well as between your analysis and your conclusion. If your unit of analysis is individuals, you cannot make conclusions about groups. Conversely, if your unit of analysis is groups, you cannot make conclusions about individuals.

As I mentioned, the data collection methods do not necessarily indicate the unit of analysis. In fact, data collected can sometimes be used for multiple analyses with multiple units of analysis. One great example of this is the National Incident-Based Reporting System (NIBRS). NIBRS collects data from police agencies across the U.S. that includes detailed information about each *incident* of serious crime, and also includes incidents of disorderly crimes when there was an arrest. When examining NIBRS data, it is key to know your unit of analysis. In fact, one of the first recommendations about looking at the data is to identify your unit of analysis. Typically, you can identify your unit of analysis by looking at your research question. Perhaps you want to determine which cities have the highest rates of crime (specifically, the number of violent crimes per 1,000 people). This could be answered using NIBRS, if the data were aggregated—meaning, you would sum the crimes for a year within one city and then divide by the population by 1,000. (For instance, a city with a population of 20,000 who had 250 violent crimes would have a violent crime rate of 12.5 per 1,000 people.) In this example, you would be comparing cities' crime rates, and therefore, would be using groups as your unit of analysis. However, you may wish to examine how the place of homicide incidents differed between attempted and completed homicides. In this example, your unit of analysis would be social artifacts, specifically, incidents of crime. You can also use individuals as your unit of analysis when analyzing NIBRS data. However, you would need to go even further than that: there are three types of individuals that can be your unit of analysis within NIBRS: victims, offenders, or arrestees.

If we make conclusions about individuals when our unit of analysis was groups, then we have committed an *ecological fallacy*. One example might be that if Researcher JANE examined rates of alcohol consumption at five different high schools. JANE finds that the high school (High School A) with the highest rate of alcohol consumption also has the highest mean grade point average of any other high school. Based on this finding, JANE concluded that individuals with higher grade point averages drink at a higher rate than other individuals. *This conclusion is made in error.* From the study, JANE cannot conclude whether this is true, and there are multiple reasons why.

1. While High School A has the highest grade point average, it may be that the students with low GPAs at High School A are drinking at an exceptionally high rate.

2. Making such a conclusion would assume that students at the other high schools who had high GPAs also drank at high rates, which may or may not be true.

3. Making such a conclusion would assume that students at the other high schools who had low GPAs drank less than those with high GPAs.

4. It may be that the students at High School A who have high GPAs are not drinking *at all*.

However, researchers can also commit another fallacy, referred to as the *reductionist fallacy*, which is simply the opposite of an ecological fallacy: making conclusions about groups/organizations when the unit of analysis was individuals. This is also an example of overgeneralizing. The public is quite guilty of committing reductionist fallacies when it comes to crime. When a high-profile crime occurs, members of society may become concerned that there is a crisis—and sometimes there is! One example of this may be police officers' unnecessary use of force. Even though this has reached crisis level, we cannot overgeneralize—all police officers are not using force unnecessarily. In fact, *most* of them are not. Imagine the rudest, laziest, most egotistical person you know. Now imagine them representing your university—you certainly would not want others generalizing their thoughts on this rude, lazy, egotistical person to all students at your university!

Populations and Samples

You have probably heard the results of polls throughout your life — especially when viewing the news. One recent example of a poll would be that President Trump has a low approval rating, and something like less than 40% of Americans approve of Donald Trump (Gallup Poll, 2019). As a child, I was often confused when I heard the results of polls — *I did not vote in that poll, so how could they say this was true for all people?* I am not sure when that "Ohhh, now I get it!" moment occurred, but I now understand that polls are not actually surveying *everyone*. Researchers who are running polls use a *sample* of individuals that — ideally — are representative of the nation.

Why would someone use a sample instead of surveying *everyone*? There are three main reasons: time, money, and complications. In the United States, there is only one poll conducted that attempts to survey *every household in the nation* — that is the United States Census, and the U.S. government only attempts it every ten years! Let's consider the three main reasons in context of the U.S. Census:

- Time: The 2010 U. S. Census was started in January of 2010. Even though it is illegal to *not* fill out the census, there are some who forget. So, by summer of 2010, those who had not filled it out were then visited by census workers. This leads to the particularly complicated part (Press, 2010).

- Complications: Even though 74% completed the census by mail, 26% did not complete it initially, and were visited by census workers. Might not sound like a big deal — but that is 47 million households! To achieve this, there were more than 600,000 temporary employees! This, obviously, leads to the *money* part (Economics and Statistics Administration, 2010).

- Money: The census in 2010 cost 13 billion dollars, which is approximately $42 per person (*The Economist*, 2011).

I do not know about you, but I do not have the time, money, or know-how to conduct a census. Let's be honest — as a college professor, I certainly do not have 13 billion dollars lying around — or even 13 thousand! This is true for most people. The good news is that we do not have to survey everyone to get a pretty good idea of what is going on in the world. We just need to have a *sample* of our population that is representative.

So, what is a **population**? Is it everyone in the nation? Well, it can be; however, most often, it is not! A population is whatever a researcher makes it, or a **target population**. The **target population** is comprised of all those individuals about whom (or what) we hope to make generalizations. For instance, **JANE** the professor may want to know what students think about open carry on college campuses. Is she interested in what *every* college student thinks? Probably not. In fact, she is particularly interested in her university (The University of Nada), since the state is considering passing a law that allows open carry on campus. If she wants to know *What are students' opinions of open carry on campus at the University of Nada?*, in this example, her primary research question has revealed her target population: The University of Nada. What Professor **Jane** can do is take a representative sample of students from her university and make conclusions about how students at the University of Nada *probably* perceive open carry laws.

To obtain a representative sample, it is important to know who or what, is in your population. Specifically, you would want some sort of list of all the people or things in your target population. This is referred to as a *sampling frame*. In the previous example about Professor **Jane** and open carry, she would want to obtain a list of all current students at the University of Nada.

Representative Samples: Generalization

For years, I have been convinced that Wrigley purposefully makes more of the gross flavors—who really wants a lemon over a cherry? (If you are one of those people, then my apologies.) I mean, really—I cannot tell you how many times I have excitedly opened a pack of Starbursts only to be severely disappointed at the prospect of half of the package tasting like chewy lemon Pledge. I am not the only one who thinks there is a conspiracy going on—just search the Internet for "Starburst conspiracy."

In reality, I've opened Starburst packages that have more cherry and strawberry Starbursts than lemon and orange, but I tend to remember those that were *not* packaged that way. However, anytime I have received a large pack of Starbursts, I find they are much more equal in flavors. So, the question is: does Wrigley make more orange and lemon Starbursts than cherry and strawberry? Probably not. In truth, Starbursts probably makes equal numbers of each, and then *randomly* takes a sample from their total Starbursts, which is their population. When there is an adequate sample size (like a large bag), the numbers are relatively equal. While there are times that the small packages are also relatively equal (four of each flavor), other times they have ten lemon Starbursts or, if I am particularly lucky, ten cherry Starbursts.

The point of this example is to say: if you want your sample to look like your population, it has to be big enough, and it has to be random. When Wrigley randomly selects from its population of Starbursts for its large bags of candy, they tend to be pretty representative. So, if the population consists of 25% orange, 25% cherry, 25% strawberry, and 25% lemon, then, ideally, our sample would look very similar.

When a researcher obtains a random sample from a population, they are taking individuals from the population that ideally should represent the characteristics of that population. For instance, if you look at Figure 7-1, you should see a sample and population. The sample is comprised of 8 people, and the population 80. In

Figure 7-1: Representative Sample from Population

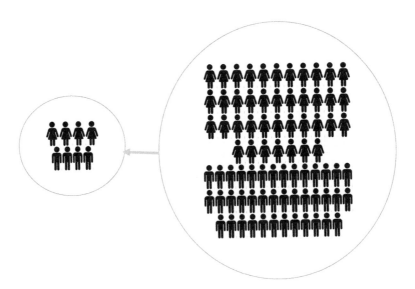

this example, the researcher obtained a 10% sample from the population. The sample appears to be representative, since both are 50% male and 50% female.

In reality, *obtaining* a representative sample that is generalizable to the target population is quite challenging, particularly in the social sciences where your most common sampling unit is individuals. Remember that people do not have to participate in a study, so there are most often issues with **nonresponse**, meaning that even when individuals are randomly selected, they may choose not to participate or may be absent at time of data collection. The reason this is so problematic is that more often than not, those who do not respond hold distinct characteristics from those who do respond; therefore, the sample is not representative of the population.

One example I've used in a few chapters is Gottfredson and Hirschi's theory of low self-control (1990). Imagine you are attempting to see the relationship between self-control and delinquency in high school students. Your target population is high school students in one county. You are attempting to give a paper-and-pencil questionnaire during homeroom during the school week. There are five high schools, and you want to randomly sample students from each school. However, when you go to distribute the survey a number of the students whom you had sampled are absent from homeroom: meaning, they are absent from school or are late! It is likely that a big chunk of those who are absent are skipping school, and they, along with the students who are late, probably have lower self-control than students who were on time and present for the school day! You can no longer say that your sample is representative of the population, because you are missing a big and important chunk from your sample, due to nonresponse.

When we do not use random sampling techniques, there can also be issues of *selection bias*, both conscious and unconscious. For instance, when I was in college, one of my professors had each one of us create a short survey questionnaire and distribute that survey to twenty people. I cannot, for the life of me, remember the purpose of this (it was an English course), but I do remember to whom I gave the survey instrument: my friends! Let me tell you—they were not a representative sample of the college population. Friends, or those around you (like coworkers or classmates), tend to be a lot like you, and you typically miss out on a whole group of other people. I imagine that if Kyle (the other author of your book) and I were each asked to find twenty people to fill out a questionnaire, his sample would be more similar to him, while mine would be more similar to me, and neither would be generalizable to any population.

Generalizability

In talking about representativeness so much, it is important to realize why researchers would care about a representative sample. We want to be able to say that whatever we find within our study, using our sample, is *generalizable* to our target population. Meaning, if Researcher **Bob** finds there is a relationship between alcohol use and cheating on exams, he wants to say that relationship holds true for his target population. Thus, if he surveyed a representative sample of students at the University of Nada, that relationship *probably* exists within the population of students at the University of Nada.

If you remember from Chapter 5, "Validity and Reliability," we discussed generalizability in the context of external validity. External validity is concerned with whether the findings in a study could hold true for the target population of the study. Additionally, external validity is concerned about whether the findings would hold true on another population. Having a representative sample of your target population does not answer the question of whether the same would be found for *another* target population. For instance, going back to Professor **Bob** and his finding that alcohol use and cheating on exams are related; if he used a representative sample, then he can say that his findings *likely* hold true to his target population: students currently attending The University of Nada. However, he cannot conclude whether the same relationship would exist for students at the University of Todo. To do that, someone (either Researcher **Bob** or another researcher) would need to *replicate* the study. Meaning, the same study (in every which way possible) would need to be conducted on a representative sample of students at the University of Todo. Repeated replication (conducting the study on a representative sample of students at many different universities) is the only way to begin to evaluate the external validity of a study.

So, researchers like to use random sampling techniques, because they can obtain a *representative* sample, which, in turn, allows them to generalize the findings of the study to their target population. However, I have emphasized throughout that the findings of the study are *likely* to exist in the population, or that they *probably* exist

Figure 7-2: Dice Combinations of Eight

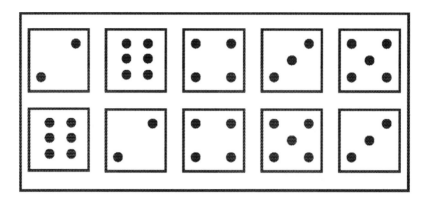

in the population. This is because there is always, always error! As discussed in the reliability and validity chapter, there are ways that researchers can decrease threats to validity; however, some may be out of their control. Further, there is *always* a chance that even though a sample was selected at random, that they are not actually representative of the population. For instance, if Researcher **Bob** took a random sample of students from the University of Nada and asked about cheating and alcohol use, is it possible that he would just randomly select (think about pulling names from a hat) the biggest partiers and alcoholics on campus. Sure—it is possible! It is not likely that would occur, but it *could*. So, researchers always need to say that they are only so sure that their findings would exist or be "real" in our target population. What is nice about using random sampling techniques is that it allows researchers to know *how* certain they are that their findings would exist in their target population. Meaning, researchers can calculate the ***probability*** that something is real.

Before we begin to understand probability in context of samples and sampling, it is important to look at probability in context of one single event occurring. For instance, if you guessed my height, how likely is it that you are right, and how likely is it that you are wrong? I imagine you are probably getting bored about now, but probability should (ideally) perk you up a bit, particularly if you are—at all—a gambler. Being able to calculate how likely something is to occur is a good tool for gambling! If you are shooting craps, it is good to know dice probability—because *they are being thrown randomly*. There are 36 possible combinations of rolling two dice. Think about how likely you are to get a total of eight versus a total of twelve. There are five ways to roll an eight, which are shown in Figure 7-2: two and six, six and two, four and four, three and five; and lastly, five and three. So, of thirty-six possible combinations, five of those will result in a total of eight. Meaning, there is almost a fourteen percent chance that, with two dice, someone would roll an eight. However, if you were looking to see how likely it is that someone would throw a twelve, the probability is *much lower*, because there is only one combination that results in a total of twelve with two dice: six and six. The middle number totals (five to nine) are the best bet! In fact, if you bet a friend that you would throw anywhere from a five to nine, you have almost a seventy percent chance of being right. And you can bet this over and over again—each and every time, the likelihood that the dice you throw will total anywhere from five to nine remains at almost seventy percent.

It is decently easy to calculate probability from throwing dice because we know all possible combinations, and we can identify these specifics. However, we want to examine probability as something that we do not have access to—it is not available in our study, but we can provide an estimate of how likely something is. Specifically, we need to begin to understand the probability that what we found in a representative sample is what we would find in the population.

Probability Theory

The reason probability is so important is that we want to be able to be fortune tellers: how likely is it that something is going to occur? We like to be able to predict the outcomes of random processes, which are those processes that occur where the outcome is not known. For instance, rolling dice: no one can know the exact outcome. To understand how we can begin estimating the likelihood of different outcomes, we need to understand what probability is, and what it means. First, is that probability is a number that ranges from 0–1 and tells us how often an event would occur from a random process if that random process was completed an infinite number of times. If your eyes are crossing right now, that is certainly understandable! So, I will attempt to explain the characteristics of probability so that we can come back to this idea of probability and infinite number of times.

Specifically, what I mean by this is that if you rolled two dice an infinite number of times, you could determine the proportion that you would score an eight. If you remember from earlier, we said that the probability of throwing two die that total eight was almost 14% (specifically, 13.8%). Since probability is a proportion (not a percentage), this would mean that the probability of landing an eight was 0.138.

Another rule of probability is that something must actually occur. We know that a random process will result in something—not nothing. If I roll dice, the outcome will be *some* number! So, there is a probability of 1 (or 100% chance) that I will roll two dice and get a number. You can flip that around and also say that there is a 0% chance that I will roll two dice and *not* get a number.

A third characteristic of probability is that the likelihood (the proportion) of all possible outcomes will, together, sum up to one. This actually provides us with some important information. What if you were unaware of the probability of throwing two dice and the total being eight? What if I only told you the likelihood of *not getting an eight*, which is .8611, meaning an 86.111% chance of obtaining any other total number *other* than eight. If you remember that probability cannot be greater than one (meaning 100%), then it is easy to determine that the probability *of* obtaining an eight is 13.8%! Meaning, the likelihood that a student is going to read this is 1 (or 100%) minus the likelihood that a student is *not* going to read this. So, if 60% of students read this, 40% do not.

Probability also does not change from one process to another—it is isolated to each process. If I throw two dice ten times and every single time I roll an eight, the likelihood that I will roll an eight an eleventh time is still 13.8%. *Even if I roll an "8" 500 times in a row, the chance of me rolling an eight again is the exact same as that first time. The first 500 random processes (throwing the dice) have absolutely no effect on probability.*

Another characteristic of probability is that when one event (event 2) occurring is dependent on another event (event 1), then the second event will be more likely to occur than the first. For instance, what is the probability of being sentenced to an all-male prison? For that to occur, someone must first be or identify as a male. There are more men (event 1) than there are people who have been imprisoned at an all-male facility (event 2). Similarly, the probability of someone being arrested for driving under the influence (DUI) is dependent on two things: that a person has consumed alcohol, and that a person has driven. A person is more likely to have consumed alcohol than received a DUI, and further, a person is more likely to have driven a car before than received a DUI.

Another characteristic of probability is that we can figure out the likelihood of more than one event occurring, as long as both those events cannot occur at the same time. Meaning, they are mutually exclusive: I cannot roll two dice and get an eight *and* a seven. I can only get one or another. Just like a student could not take a test and score a 50% and a 90%—you only score one or another. However, during different processes, the outcomes can change—a student could earn a score of 50% on one test and a 90% on another. I could roll two dice once and roll an eight; I could roll two dice again and roll a seven. So, we already know that the probability of throwing two dice that total 8 is almost 14%. The probability of rolling a "7" is even higher— 17%. That is because there are six different combinations of the two die that result in a total of 7 (1 + 6, 6 + 1, 2 + 5, 5 + 2, 3 + 4, 4 + 3). We can sum these two probabilities to then determine how likely someone is to roll a 7 or an 8: 31%.

So, what does probability mean in the real world? If you roll 2 dice 100 times, will you roll a "7" 17 times and an "8" 14 times? No—things are never that simple! It means that if you rolled a set of dice an infinite number of times, 17% of those rolls would total "7" and 13.8% would total "8."

To make this simpler, think about flipping a coin. We know that there is a 50/50 probability that you will get heads or that you will get tails—this is why referees use a coin toss for football games to see who gets the ball first: it is a fair shot for both teams, as neither team has an advantage over another.

However, if you decided to flip a coin ten times, do you think it would come out equally? It may—but what if you do it again, will it come out equally again? *If you*

Figure 7-3: The Monty Hall Problem

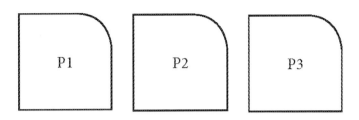

want to try this out, you can either use a coin, or Google has a coin flip (just Google "coin flip" and it will pop right up. When I flipped a coin ten times, I flipped only three heads! However, if I flipped a coin a thousand times, it is likely that it would be much closer to 50% for heads and 50% for tails.

Let's look at one more example to understand probability: The Monty Hall Problem, which is named after the game show host of *Let's Make a Deal.* Suppose that your Research Methods professor gives you the opportunity to select your grade on your next test: but there is some definite risk! If you select wrong, you will end up with a 0% on the test! Specifically, s/he writes a score of 100 on one piece of paper and folds it, a score of 0 on another piece of paper and folds it, and a score of 0 on a third piece of paper (see Figure 7-3). Say you select the first piece of folded paper (P1). S/he then unfolds P3—it says 0! S/he then asks you if you want to switch your selection from P1 to P2. Should you do it?

I imagine that your first instinct is to say, it does not matter, the likelihood will not change regardless of whether you switch! However, it does. Recall that probability does not change from event to event, and the same can be said here. Go back to the three pieces of paper, before your teacher unfolded one. What was the likelihood that you would select the sheet with 100%? If there are three choices, and only one says 100%, then the likelihood is one-third, or 33%, that you would select 100%. Also recall within the characteristics of probability that the sum of the probability of one event (the selection of 100%) and the opposite (you selecting a sheet of paper that does not have 100%, i.e., 0%) is equal to one, or 100%. Therefore, the likelihood that you would select the paper with a score of "100%" is one-third, and the likelihood that you would *not* select that paper with a score of "100%" is two-thirds.

This means that you were more likely to be wrong, than to be right. If you did not switch papers, the likelihood that you would select the paper with a score of 100 is 33.3%. If you do switch, the likelihood that you would select the paper with a score of 100% is two-thirds or over 66%! To a lot of people this is really mind boggling. The point of it is that the probability does not change after your teacher unfolds the third piece of paper—you made your selection based off of three pieces of paper, and the probability remains constant, because it is isolated from each event.

Sampling and Probability

Getting back to sampling and probability, we need to understand how likely it is that a sample will produce outcomes that would match the population. The way that we can start to understand this is to take the idea of flipping a coin, but draw a *sample* of coin flips. So, with the previous example, I flipped a coin ten times, and seven of those times, the coin landed on tails. Now, imagine that I flipped a coin another ten times: this time, the coin landed on heads six times and tails four times. Imagine that I did this over and over again, for an infinite number of times. The average of each of those infinite series or samples of ten coin flips would be five and five.

Sample Distributions and Sampling Distributions

There are two types of distributions that are important in understanding the role of generalizing: sample distributions and sampling distributions. I realize they are ridiculously similar, but they are two very different things. A sample distribution is used to say how each unit (usually people) in one sample "scored" on an outcome. If you see in Table 7-1, we can use an example in which the target population is a class of 25 students. (Side note: *Typically, you would have a population greater than 25, and if your target population was this small, there would be no reason not to survey all of them. However, I am attempting to keep it simple for purposes of the example!*)

Let's say we want to know the number of siblings someone has. In this population, we can identify the mean number of siblings for our population, which is an example of a population parameter. Specifically, a ***population parameter*** is the numeric measurement or information of a variable for our population. (Another example would be average national ACT scores.) Table 7-1 also provides our ***sampling frame***: we have twenty-five individuals that comprise our population from which to sample.

Getting back to our example, the ***mean or average*** number of siblings in the target population is two. We can calculate the mean by summing the number of siblings for all students (50) and then dividing by the number of students (25). Let's say that we took five random samples of five individuals in hope that this would give us representative samples of our population. To randomly sample, we can use a computer program or, when we have so few cases, we could draw numbers out of a hat. You can see in Table 7-2 that the means for each sample of five were somewhat close to the actual mean of the population (being 2); however, there were some that were closer than others! That range of the means—3.4 being the highest and 1.4 being the lowest—matters! However, what happens if we calculate the mean of the means? Meaning, we take the mean from each sample and see what the average is of those

Table 7-1: Individuals' Number of Siblings in Population

Student #	Number of Siblings
1	2
2	0
3	3
4	4
5	2
6	1
7	2
8	2
9	3
10	1
11	2
12	0
13	3
14	4
15	2
16	1
17	2
18	2
19	3
20	1
21	2
22	0
23	2
24	4
25	6

five samples? (3.4 + 1.8 + 1.4 + 2.6 + 1.4/5 = 2.1). Remember that our population mean is two, which is *incredibly close* to the mean of our means (2.1). When we take multiple samples from the population and then examine the distribution of all the sample means, we can get much closer to the true value for the population. If we were to increase our number of samples to ten, twenty, or thirty, we would get even closer to the true value of the mean for the population. The more samples you have, the more they will cluster (get close to) the true mean of the population.

Table 7-2: Five Random Samples of Five from Population of 25

Sample 1		Sample 2		Sample 3		Sample 4		Sample 5	
ID	Siblings	ID	Siblings	ID	Siblings	ID	Siblings	ID	Siblings
4	4	11	2	6	1	13	3	5	2
23	2	2	0	7	2	3	3	10	1
7	2	10	1	16	1	19	3	12	0
21	2	24	4	22	0	18	2	21	2
3	3	1	2	9	3	26	6	18	2
Mean = 2.6		Mean = 1.8		Mean = 1.4		Mean = 3.4		Mean = 1.4	

Now, this worked within this example because we had such a small population (only 25). However, in "real life" our populations are typically much larger, which requires much larger samples! Even though we were *closer* to the real population mean, it was still not "right on target." Now, imagine if we took samples from the population ten times instead of five—we would be more accurate. The more random samples we take and distribute, the closer we get to the true value in the population. Here is the bad news: not only are populations much larger in real life, but we also generally do not *know* the true value in the population, which is why we use *sampling distributions*. As mentioned earlier, these provide a distribution of an infinite number of random samples. Do not worry—there is not someone selecting random samples from the population over and over and over again! They are theoretical or mathematically derived.

What is cool (yes, I used the word cool here) about random sampling techniques is that they give us what we hope is a representative sample of the population—but there is always a chance that they really are not representative. By using sampling distribution, we have a pretty good idea of how likely it is that we are right in assuming our sample is an accurate representation of the population.

Offenders' Ages and Sampling Distributions

So, what if we were to look at a much larger population? For instance, we could look at the average age of offenders in Virginia within offenses that occurred in 2013. These data are derived from the National Incident-Based Reporting System. I used Virginia, because it is a state where all agencies participate, so we can view this as a population. There are over 290,000 offenders whose ages were known. The mean age of offenders is 29.5. With such a large population, we can increase our sample size to 100. So, what if we took *thousands* of samples of 100 offenders and looked at their ages? Figure 7-4 provides an example of what that distribution would look like.

If you remember that the mean of the population is 29.5 (specifically, 29.49894), you can see that the sample means start to cluster around the true population mean—

Figure 7-4: Sampling Distribution of Offenders' Ages in Virginia

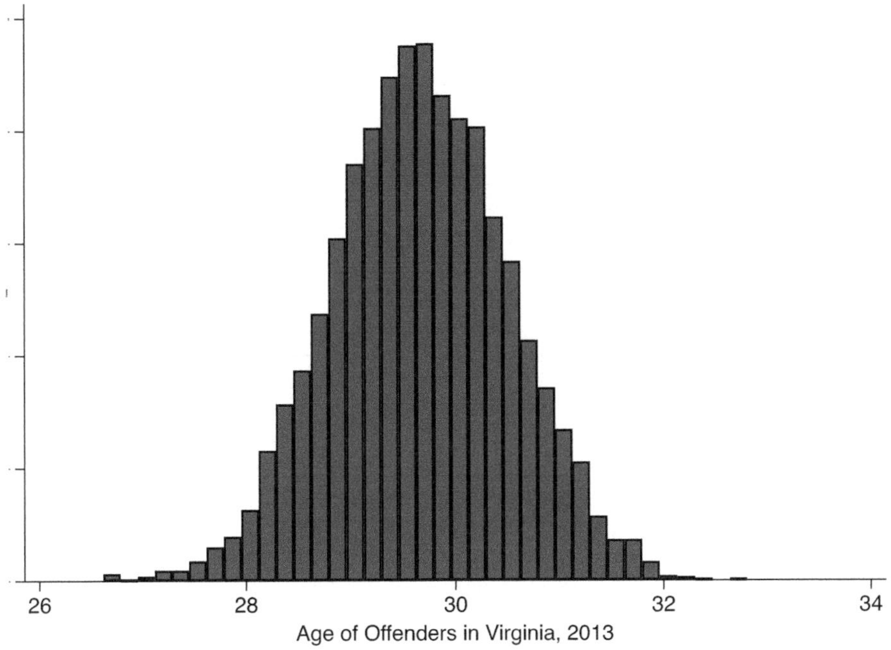

Age of Offenders in Virginia, 2013

there are more samples that are close to 29.5 than there are samples that are close to 32. This sampling distribution of thousands of samples starts to look like a *normal distribution*, which is also referred to as a bell-shaped curve. In fact, the mean of the means in this distribution is 29.49886—which is *incredibly close* to 29.49894. If you look back at Figure 7-4, you can see that there were some samples with very high mean ages—above 32! And some with very low mean ages—at around 27! Even though you took a random sample of 100 participants (which is a small, small sample considering the population size!), you could have taken a sample and had an average age of 33! And then, you would have inferred that the average age of offenders in 2013 offenses was 33 years old—yikes! There is always a chance that your sample is not representative. This is why we have *sampling error*, which is commonly known as a *margin of error*. We are not going to elaborate on how to calculate standard error, but do know that the standard error is for a sampling distribution what standard deviation is for a sample distribution. Specifically, the standard error attempts to account for how far, on average, each sample mean is from the true value of the population mean.

When you are able to calculate your margin of error, you can also construct *confidence intervals*, which provide a range of what the true population value is. So, if you had a sample with an average of 32 years old, but you had a sampling error of 4, then you could say that the average age of offenders in Virginia of offenses that occurred in 2013 is 32 +/– 4 years. To create a confidence interval out of this, you

Figure 7-5: Random Numbers Table for Simple Random Sampling Technique

133	140	429	448	249	281	228	406	365	55
327	73	75	150	113	17	178	411	400	329
12	142	3	279	153	442	461	395	427	374
458	434	351	156	402	404	479	443	347	6
356	59	176	24	155	16	292	166	87	474
160	51	199	287	263	180	486	231	233	308
247	206	397	1	204	322	37	301	162	438
253	242	171	490	381	28	115	92	8	182
236	269	215	260	352	410	14	217	335	183
285	188	349	81	71	0	319	210	358	445

would simply give that range (32 − 4 = 28 & 32 + 4 = 36), stating that the true value in the population is anywhere from 28–36. Now your statement is much more accurate, since that actual mean is 29.5!

It is important to remember that we can only make these estimates when we have used a *random/probability sampling technique.* As you can probably see, this is why they are considered so much better than *nonrandom or nonprobability sampling techniques*—you can do a whole lot more with determining the validity of them! However, even when we do use random sampling techniques, it is important that we replicate studies to gain sample statistics, which provide us a better understanding of the true values in the population!

Probability Sampling Techniques

Since we have discussed the importance of probability sampling, you should also know that there are different techniques you can use to obtain a random sample—it is not always possible to pull names out of a hat, especially when we are talking about larger target populations! There are four primary techniques of probability sampling: *simple random sampling, systematic random sampling, stratified random sampling,* and *multistage cluster random sampling.*

Simple Random Sampling Technique

Simple random sampling is just as we have described random sampling—pulling names out of a hat! However, you can actually use a random number table for purposes of this technique. If you have a target population of 500 people, you would take your *sampling frame* and assign each person a number (person #1, person #2, etc.). From here, you could use a random numbers table to select a sample of 100. The table might look something like Figure 7-5. If you used this, then those people assigned to each number would be selected for the study, and the others would be omitted. For instance, whoever is assigned as person #2 would not be selected for the study, but person #1 and person #3 would be selected for the study, since they are on the random numbers table.

In addition to using a random numbers table, we can also use a computer program. Microsoft Excel, for example, can provide you with a random sample of your sampling frame. Other programs that can do this include SPSS (Statistical Package for the Social Sciences) and Stata, both of which are statistics programs.

Systematic Random Sampling Technique

When our *sampling frame* is formatted into a list, a systematic random sampling technique can be ideal. Let's say that you have a target population of 500 and you want a sample of 100. You could take every n(th) one to obtain a sample of 100. Specifically, you can divide your target population number by your objective sample size: 500/100, which equals 5. So, if you took every 5th person or "thing" in your sampling frame list, then you would be using a systematic random sampling technique. What you want is a sampling frame list that is sorted in a truly random, non-meaningful order. If they are listed in any sort of nonrandom order, there is a potential for selection bias, due to periodicity, which is when the order of items in a list may fall into some sort of pattern, typically dealing with time.

Think about if you were trying to figure out what items were most often sold on Craigslist[2] in the Atlanta area. When you go to the ads on Craigslist, you can see that there are 1,072 ads over the last two months. You want to take a sample that makes up 25% of these ads. Therefore, you would want a sample of 268 ads, and you would select every 4th ad for inclusion in your study. If you look at Figure 7-6, you can see which ads you would specifically select. However, in this example, there is an issue of *periodicity*, because Craigslist ads are ordered by the time of posting. So, you may end up having an issue of sampling bias.

Stratified Random Sampling Technique

As we noted earlier, sometimes a random sample is not representative of the population. You may be particularly interested in making sure it *is* representative in some way. In this case, you would want to use a proportionate stratified sampling technique. Perhaps you are interested in looking at the rates of marijuana use by gender at your university, and you want to make sure that your sample is representative by gender. In this case, you could identify your target population's gender distribution (this in-

---

2. www.craigslist.com.

Figure 7-6: Systematic Random Sampling Technique

	1	Selling Furniture for Cheap! There is a collection …
	2	Need a Fridge? Here's one for almost free …
	3	We have trampolines!
Select →	4	Multiple laptops (gently used)
	5	Toner Cartridge refills
	6	Wooden Outdoor Patio Furniture
	7	Bed Frame and Headboard
Select →	8	Coffee and Side Tables
	9	Solitaire Diamond Ring
	10	Ford F 150 Pickup Truck, 2010
	11	Lockbox with Key
Select →	12	George Foreman Grill
	13	Firestone Tires
	14	Antique Desk for sale
	15	Vintage Side Table for Sale
Select →	16	Chickens
	17	Armoire TV Stand with Matching Coffee Table!
	18	Nativity Scene
	19	Gibson Guitar
Select →	20	Couch and Chair

formation is typically on the website of a university). Let's assume that your university is 40% male and 60% female. In this case, you would want to make sure that your sample is 40% male and 60% female. Therefore, you would split your sampling frame by the characteristic of interest (gender), which would create *sampling strata*, meaning layers of the target population. You would have two sampling frames: one comprised of males and one comprised of females. If you wanted to take a sample of 1,000, for instance, you would randomly select 400 individuals off of the male sampling frame and 600 individuals off of the female sampling frame.

At times, you may have multiple variables that you are looking at for representation. In this case, you will have multiple strata and multiple sampling frames. Let's say that you wanted to look at age groups, class, and sex. You would have to make sampling frames that account for all of these. For instance, one would be 18–20-year-old freshman females. As you can imagine, this can get complicated rather quickly, so make sure you identify your strata prior to attempting to sample!

There may be a time where you do not want a representative sample, but perhaps an equal sample across groups. Perhaps you want a sample that is equal in gender, meaning it is comprised of half males and half females. In this case, you would want to use a *disproportionate stratified random sampling technique*. You would follow the same protocol for proportionate; however, you would simply make sure that 500 individuals from the male sampling frame are selected, as well as 500 individuals from the female sampling frame.

Multistage Cluster Sampling Technique

Just as it sounds, a *multistage cluster sampling technique* requires multiple stages! This is often helpful when we do not have a list of all the elements (individuals/things) within our population to make a *sampling frame*. Elements of a sample often group together naturally, allowing us to sample from these groups or clusters. For instance, if I wanted to sample police officers in the United States, it may be hard for me to find a list of all police officers. However, I could randomly select states, randomly select police agencies within each state, and then randomly select police officers from each agency.

Different techniques could be used at each stage. In the first stage, I could use a stratified random sample to select one state from each region (see Figure 7-7). I could then use a simple random sample to select 10% of each state's police agencies. Lastly, I could use a systematic random sampling technique to select police officers within each agency.

Nonprobability Sampling Techniques

As we already discussed, probability sampling techniques are best when possible. That being said, I believe that lobster and champagne are best when possible, but I do not really have the money for that. Similarly, because we are typically sampling people, we run into a number of challenges in collecting random samples. Therefore, there are a number of nonrandom sampling techniques that we can use in hopes of providing some insight to a population. However, with nonrandom sampling techniques, we cannot provide specific estimates about the true values in the target population. There are four nonprobability sampling techniques: *purposive/judgment sampling*, *quota sampling*, *reliance on available participants/convenience sampling*, and *snowball sampling*.

Figure 7-7: Example of a Multistage Cluster Sampling Technique

Stage One: Select states using a stratified random sampling technique (stratified by region)	

Stage Two: Select police agencies within a state using a simple random sampling technique	

Stage Two grid:

1	2	3	4	5	6
7	8	9	10	11	12
13	14	15	16	17	18

Stage Three:
Select officers within each selected agency using a systematic random sampling technique.

Agency #2
Officers
Officer #1
Officer #2
Officer #3
Selected → Officer #4
Officer #5
Officer #6
Officer #7
Selected → Officer #8
Officer #9
Officer #10
Officer #11
Selected → Officer #12
Officer #13
Officer #14
Officer #15
Selected → Officer #16
Officer #17
Officer #18
Officer #19
Selected → Officer #20

Purposive Sampling

Often used for research that is qualitative (think interviews or field observations), a researcher may purposefully seek out participants who have various characteristics. For instance, if I were to conduct a study on methamphetamine users, I would have a hard time coming up with a sampling frame. Instead, I would want to find individuals who are serious users to really understand the effects. This would require me to purposefully seek out serious methamphetamine users. To do this, I would probably want to start in a state that is "meth heavy," like Tennessee, which had one of the highest number of meth laboratory incidents in 2013 and 2014 (Drug Enforcement Administration, 2014). I would then be likely to find counties or cities with that were known for having issues with meth, and then seek out individuals who were serious meth users. All stages of this selection were purposeful; thus, the sampling technique is purposive.

Reliance on Available Participants/ Convenience Sampling

While this technique has two names, I prefer convenience sampling, because it really tells someone what it is: I selected those people who were convenient to me! If I am trying to distribute a survey to university students and I use a convenience sample, I imagine it would be very heavy in criminal justice/criminology majors, as it is more *convenient* to me to distribute it to my own students and my department colleagues' students than other students at the university. Another example of using a convenience sampling technique is if you were to sit in front of Wal-Mart and ask people to fill out your survey instrument. This is only representative of those people who walked by that day (assuming everyone decided to participate), but there is no way to tell if it is representative of your actual population, which is likely those individuals residing in the local area.

Quota Sampling Technique

A quota sampling technique is very similar to a stratified random sampling technique; however, it does not use probability sampling techniques to obtain its sample. For instance, I may want a sample that is similar to my population of male and female college students (60% female and 40% male). Instead of randomly sampling from my male and female sampling frame, I may use convenience sampling to recruit individuals to be a part of my study. While my study would still have 60% female and 40% male participants, there is no way of determining whether that sample is representative of the population, since it was not chosen at random.

Figure 7-8: Recruiting Drug Dealers?

ATTENTION DRUG DEALERS!

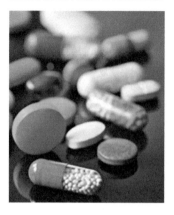

Have you been dealing drugs for over a year?
Do you have ten or more clients?

Participate in my Study!

Contact Researcher JANE at 555-555-2100

Snowball Sampling Technique

Like purposive sampling, snowball sampling is common in qualitative research, and is particularly applicable to hard-to-access populations. It uses chain recruitment and a referral system to find individuals who are applicable for your study. For example, if Researcher JANE wanted to study drug dealers, she cannot exactly post a flyer to recruit drug dealers. As you can see in Figure 7-8, this would be ridiculous! Most drug dealers do not like to openly announce that they are conducting illegal acts, so they likely will not respond to such an announcement!

Researcher JANE, however, may have a friend who knows someone who *is* a drug dealer and can get you in contact with them. This friend can serve as a *gatekeeper* to your possible participants. The thing about drug users and drug dealers is they often have a network. If Researcher JANE is able to gain the trust of one drug dealer, she may ask if they can get her in contact with one or two *more* drug dealers. Then she may ask those two drug dealers if they can get her in contact with one or two *additional* drug dealers, and so on.

Summing It Up

Prior to conducting a study, social scientists must determine the best technique to use to obtain an adequate sample. To determine if a probability sampling technique is possible, a researcher must be able to identify their target population and obtain a sampling frame.

Probability sampling techniques are best because they allow us to obtain samples that are *probably* representative of the population and allow us to estimate the true value of the population by using standard error and constructing confidence intervals. That being said, there is still a lot of utility in studies that use nonprobability sampling techniques! They are often used in an effort to understand a topic in more depth and can provide a better grasp of the relationship between variables of interest. However, when using nonprobability sampling techniques, the researcher cannot infer to the population and cannot make estimates of the true value in the population. While probability sampling techniques are great, it is important that studies are replicated using multiple samples. One small but random sample does not provide a full picture of the population!

Discussion Questions

1. How does the type of sampling technique affect the generalizability of a study? Provide an example.

2. Is study replication important in studies that use probability and/or nonprobability sampling techniques? Why or why not?

3. What are sampling frames?

4. What is the mean of a sampling distribution? Is it the same thing as the mean (average) of a sample? Explain.

5. Provide an example of a study that would use a quota sampling technique.

6. Provide an example of a study that would use a stratified random sampling technique.

7. What is periodicity? In what kind of sampling technique can periodicity occur?

8. Propose a study and identify the unit of analysis, the population, sampling frame, and the possible sampling technique(s) you could use within the study. Explain why one (or more) sampling techniques would not be feasible for your study.

Trying It Out

Your professor may ask you to complete the following companion assignment available from the publisher. Using the supplied worksheet form, you are going to identify the sampling technique used within each research scenario.

References

Drug Enforcement Administration. (2014). *Methamphetamine lab incidents, 2004–2014*. Retrieved from https://www.dea.gov/resource-center/meth-lab-maps.shtml.

Economics and Statistics Administration. (2010). *The impact of 2010 census operations on jobs and economic growth*. Retrieved from: http://www.esa.doc.gov/sites/default/files/economicgrowth.pdf.

Gallup Poll (2019). Presidential Approval Ratings—Donald Trump. Retrieved from: https://news.gallup.com/poll/203198/presidential-approval-ratings-donald-trump.aspx.

Gottfredson, M. R., & Hirschi, T. (1990). *A general theory of crime*. Stanford, CA: Stanford University Press

Maxfield, M. G. (2015). *Basics of research methods for criminal justice and criminology*. Boston, MA: Cengage Learning.

Press, A. (2010). 2010 census launches in remote Alaskan village. *The Times-Picayune*.

Section III

Doing Research: Types, Applications, and Methods (Chapters 8–11)

If you can recall back in Chapter 4 ("The Nitty Gritty"), we talked some about different types of data and different types of research. In these next three chapters, we are going to dive back into some of that, but in a lot more detail.

Some things that are important in considering how you should conduct your research include money, time, feasibility, and purpose. For instance, say you want to know about what types of organizations people belong to. So, you decide you want a national sample of 20,000 people. In this case, you better have a lot of money, time, and a really good reason for doing so. Instead of thousands upon thousands of dollars (and I mean thousands), you could just change your data type and use a secondary dataset—something like the General Social Survey. You can get the answer to your research question by using data that was already collected. We will talk more about these types of datasets in Chapter 9. Or maybe you want to survey college students at your college—that *might* be feasible (depending on money and time), but you will need to consider how you design the survey. To give you more information on this, Chapter 8 focuses on survey design and research. Lastly, maybe you do not want to do any quantitative research—you might think it is really important to get more in-depth to answer your research question. For that, we have provided more information about the forms of qualitative research in Chapter 10.

For this part, you can really start thinking about what your research question is, and how you can go about answering it. Just remember, money, time, and feasibility!

Trying It Out

Your professor may ask you to complete the following companion assignment available from the publisher. Using the supplied worksheet form, you are going to cite sources using different citation styles.

Chapter 8

Survey Research

Learning Objectives

- Describe the difference between a survey and a questionnaire
- Explain the role of survey research in the social sciences
- Identify and describe national criminal justice surveys
- Define omnibus surveys
- Assess the impact of response rates on the validity of survey research
- Summarize methods of survey distribution
- Examine the limitations of survey research
- Identify the strengths and weaknesses of mailed questionnaires
- Review methods of increasing response rates in survey research
- Discuss the role of Internet survey software and online marketplaces in survey research
- Apply the rules of survey construction
- Describe the parts of a questionnaire
- Apply the guidelines of questionnaire organization
- Define contingency questions
- Define Likert-type scales
- Explain matrix-style formatting
- Define and explain the importance of reverse coding, forced-answer questions, validity checks, and social desirability checkers
- Explain mutual exclusion and exhaustion
- Evaluate questionnaires in context of the "Dos" and "Don'ts" of survey research
- Define and explain double-barreled questions, biased questions, leading questions, and loaded questions
- Apply the steps of the survey research process

In a survey of 1,000 American adults on topics dealing with dairy products, researchers found that 7% of Americans think that chocolate milk comes from brown cows. Just in case you are not aware, chocolate milk comes from mixing—wait for it—chocolate and milk (Hanson, 2017). I used this example for two reasons: one, because I think it is important that we get that percentage *way* down, and two, because it is an example of survey research.

Here's the kicker: you have probably heard someone say, "I completed a survey," "I was given a survey," or "I gave out a survey …" A survey is not a tangible *thing*. A survey is a process of collecting the data. Typically, when people say they completed a survey, they are referring to a survey *instrument*, which is a tool that is used to collect the data. Oftentimes, the survey instrument is a **questionnaire**, which *is* tangible, as it is a tool that uses questions or statements to gather the data from its participants. A questionnaire can be answered directly by a participant (like taking a test), or a questionnaire can be used by an interviewer to ask the questions to a respondent/participant.

Regardless of these actual definitions, you will still hear "survey" used when someone actually means survey instrument or questionnaire. The way to remember that survey is a process and questionnaire/instrument is a "thing" is to think of land surveys. I am pretty sure that areas of land are not answering questionnaires about their own characteristics! A land *surveyor* is using an **instrument** (an electronic distance meter—those camera-looking things you see random guys using on streets) to record points and distances between points, which are often then used for mapping, transportation, etc. The land surveyor could say "I surveyed land today," and this would *not* mean that s/he distributed a paper-and-pencil questionnaire to areas of land and asked them to complete it.

Social scientists tend to be pretty big fans of survey research. It allows researchers to (potentially) find out a lot about a population's characteristics, and they tend to be cheaper and more efficient than a lot of other types of research. Further, there are times where survey research is the only feasible way to gather data. It can be used for multiple purposes of research: survey research can be used for description purposes (to describe a population or a sample), to examine a relationship (explanatory), to understand a phenomenon (exploratory research), or to evaluate a program or a policy. These purposes should sound familiar—we discussed them in the first chapter of this book ("Why Do I Care about Research? A Guide to This Book") under the purposes of research. Survey research can be used for both cross-sectional and longitudinal studies. If you remember from Chapter 4 ("The Nitty Gritty"), we talked about cross-sectional and longitudinal data. To refresh your memory, cross-sectional studies are those that look at one moment in time, while longitudinal research looks at least three points in time (usually over a *long* period of time—hence the name). Professor JANE might want to conduct a study to "answer" the research question, "What is the relationship between political topics and legalization of marijuana?" Professor JANE may survey college students, ask them about their opinions of legalizing marijuana, and also ask questions about their views on other politically controversial topics, like the death penalty, abortion, and welfare. This is an example of cross-sectional research because respondents are only providing responses once. Think about meeting someone only once—you often do not get an accurate impression of them. It takes meeting them multiple times, over time, to really know a person. This is similar to research. If you ask me about my job satisfaction on a day that I am grumpy and unhappy with some isolated work situation, then my answers would probably reflect that. However, if you ask me on a day when I have found out about a raise, or some student wrote me a nice note, my answers would probably reflect my pleasure with the job. Since it only captures one point in time, when a researcher uses survey research to conduct a cross-sectional study, that researcher is conducting *correlational research*.

Survey research can also be used for *longitudinal research*—a researcher could just distribute a questionnaire (with some modifications) to the same group of individuals multiple times. Take the example about Professor JANE examining the relationship between certain political views and the legalization of marijuana. Perhaps she decided to look at these relationships over time in Denver, Colorado. She would likely see some changes from before and after the legalization of marijuana in the state! She may also see that changes in views after legalization may be short-term or long-term changes. Professor JANE would likely want to survey her target population a few months after, a year after, two years after, etc. The good thing about longitudinal research is that researchers can begin to go a bit beyond simple correlations and can often begin to examine effects, because they are able to account for temporal ordering (remember—knowing which came first—the independent or dependent variable).

As I said, the reason(s) why a researcher may want to conduct survey research varies. One reason that researchers are looking to conduct survey research is to collect data on events or phenomena, so that researchers can make estimates about the prevalence of that phenomena in the population. In criminological and criminal justice research, survey research is often used for counting crime; meaning, for determining how frequently certain crimes occur. For instance, the Uniform Crime Report (UCR) is a form of a survey: The Federal Bureau of Investigation surveys participating agencies and asks them to provide the number of occurrences they had of different crimes in a given year. For instance, New Orleans Police could report that in 2014, they had 1,906 aggravated assaults (Federal Bureau of Investigation, 2014). Notice that within the Uniform Crime Report, data are collected in the aggregate; meaning, they are grouped together. The UCR (with the exception of the Supplemental Homicide Report) does not collect data about each case of aggravated assault, but instead asks for the group numbers. While the UCR undoubtedly gives a much better understanding of the number of crimes that occur, there are still problems due to the *dark figure of crime*, meaning, those crimes that were not reported to the police. The National Crime Victimization Survey (NCVS) is a great tool for attempting to count unreported crimes, as it surveys household members about any victimization they have experienced. The dark figure of crime is probably best known to exist within cases of sexual assault. Social science researchers can start to examine (on an aggregate level) how the rates of sexual assault that are reported to the UCR may be much lower than the rates of sexual assault reported to the NCVS.

Another reason researchers are looking to conduct survey research is to collect information about individuals; specifically, to collect self-report data, which is when someone reports information about their own demographics, knowledge, experiences, behaviors, actions, and/or feelings—essentially, individuals' perceptions or opinions about a certain phenomenon. Researchers can collect this information using a number of methods, which have only expanded as technology has made people so much more accessible.

There are a number of surveys that are large-scale and focus on collecting data from a nationally representative sample of individuals. Often, these surveys seek to find opinions or perceptions of a certain topic—these are often called polls. For instance, you have probably heard of Gallup polls. Gallup polls individuals randomly to be representative of either the general national population, or some subgroup. For example, they polled a sample of millennials about important aspects of jobs, in which the majority of millennials reported that work-life balance and well-being were the most important (Rigoni & Nelson, 2016). Often, large-scale surveys seek to find out more than just a few opinions or perceptions, but instead, either have a main focus, like the NCVS, or have a very broad focus, or no focus at all. These are called *omnibus surveys* (Bachman & Schutt, 2014). Specifically, researchers conducting omnibus surveys will examine a number of characteristics about an individual, including their perceptions and opinions, as well as demographic information, experiences, and behaviors. One example of this is the *General Social Survey* (GSS), which asks individuals about their political views, their demographics, their experiences, their emotions, and much, much more. Another example of an omnibus survey is *The National Longitudinal Study of Adolescent to Adult Health* (Add Health), which uses a nationally representative sample of adolescents. The survey asks about criminal behavior, but it also asks about biological data, the neighborhood in which they live, their family, their friends, drug use, etc.; however, they may also be used to collect a number of different *types* of data on individuals, so that researchers can use the data to examine different topics, including people's experiences, opinions, behaviors, demographics, and knowledge (NORC, 2016).

Focusing on Self-Report Questionnaires

As we discuss survey research, I am generally going to focus on how social scientists use questionnaires to collect self-report data on individuals. This is because it is likely the most common method of data collection within criminology and criminal justice. We will, however, talk about the use of survey instruments in other forms of research, including in-depth interviews and field research (see Chapter 10), as well as analyzing various forms of content (both qualitative and quantitative, see Chapter 9).

Back in the day (you know, before telephones, computers, and the Internet), there were only three methods of distributing questionnaires: by mail, in person using interviews, or in-person using paper-and-pencil questionnaires. However, with the introduction of different technologies, there are many more options regarding how researchers can distribute a questionnaire, as well as technological tools that aid researchers in the actual distribution of the questionnaire. Currently, researchers have four means of delivering a questionnaire: the Internet, telephone, in-person, or by mail. Additionally, there are four main *types* of questionnaires, which include electronic questionnaires, online questionnaires, interview questionnaires, and paper-and-pencil questionnaires. These methods of distributing the questionnaire are then combined with various questionnaire formats and tools to create different types of surveying.

Important Consideration in Survey Research: Response Rate

Another main concern with questionnaires is the **response rate**. A response rate is the number of people to whom the questionnaire is sent and the number of people who actually return it. You have probably received some sort of questionnaire in the mail before, asking you to rate your experience at a hospital, rate a restaurant, rate a product you bought, or something similar. You may or may not have chosen to respond to the questionnaire. However, the reasons you did or did not return the questionnaire are likely similar to other people's reasons for returning or not returning the questionnaire. People may answer a questionnaire for a number of reasons; however, here are a few possible ones: because they find the topic interesting, because they are sympathetic to the researchers who need responses, because they are bored and have a bit of extra time on their hands, because they are simply the type who believe they should do what they are asked. Those who do not respond likely do so for numerous reasons as well, but here are a few possible rationales: the person meant to complete it, but forgot or accidentally threw it away, they may have dismissed the request from the start, they may be too busy to take the time to complete it, they may not care about the topic, and/or they may not consider that the researcher needs responses. These reasons may point to distinct differences in characteristics of those who *do* respond and those who *do not* respond, making the sample not generalizable (meaning not representative) to the target population of the study.

Generally, the higher the response rate, the better. Meaning, the more people who you ask to participate in your study who do participate, the better. Some research has shown that the type of survey matters, but more than anything, giving people options and reminding them about the study will increase response rates (Kaplowitz, Hadlock, & Levine, 2004). The reason being that it would seem that the more who do not respond, the more likely there is nonresponse bias, indicating that those participating are different from those refusing to participate. There have at times been set standards of response rates. Generally, most resources will tell you that at least 50% is a standard goal for a study and that 50% is around the average response rate for published studies (Baruch, 1999; Baruch & Holtom, 2008). Yet, there has been some contradictory research on whether response rates are *that* important, and that at times a higher response rate actually *increases* bias (Pickett, 2017). Therefore, my advice is this: do what you can from the beginning before you start collecting data and try to increase your response rate. However, do not fret if your response rate is under 50% — but do worry if it is less than 10%! Further, look into more research on response rates before determining a strict standard of an acceptable response rate.

Methods of Questionnaire Distribution

In-Person Questionnaire Distribution

The first method of delivery is in person, which requires that the researcher (or a member of the research team) is physically in the same space as the respondent. Questionnaires can be delivered in person to individual participants using two different methods: interviewing and group administering. Additionally, the format of the questionnaire can be either electronic or traditional paper-and-pencil questionnaires.

In-Person Interviews

Researchers (or members of the research team) can interview participants using a questionnaire. Meaning, an interviewer, who is part of the research team, would meet the participant in person and read aloud the question and statements to the participant. The participant would then answer the questions orally, and the interviewer would record their answers. In Figure 8-1, I provide an example where the interviewer would ask the respondent (participant) what their age is, and when the participant responds, the interviewer would record the answer.

Figure 8-1: Example of In-Person Interview Question and Questionnaire

Interviewer: What is your age, in years?				
Participant: I am 27-years old.				
Participant's Age in Years				
20 or younger	21	22	23	24
25	26	27	28	29
30	31	32	33	34 or older

Questionnaire Types for In-Person Interviews

The *type* of questionnaire in in-person interviews can vary. For instance, the interviewer may use a traditional paper-and-pencil questionnaire to record the respondent's answers. The interviewer, however, could also use an electronic questionnaire, which is known as a ***computer-assisted interview (CAI)*** (Maxfield & Babbie, 2014). Specifically, computer-assisted, in-person interview questionnaires can be particularly useful when there are a lot of questions with some not being applicable to every person (more about that later)!

In-person interviews (with or without the use of self-interviewing) are an excellent method of surveying individuals, because there are fewer risks of respondents misunderstanding questions and not seeking clarification or answering a question in the wrong way. One example of this is in Figure 8-2. In this example, if the respondent were simply completing a questionnaire without a personal interviewer, s/he may

Figure 8-2: Clarifying a Question on a Survey Instrument

Interviewer:	On average, how many drinks do you have a week? One drink is equal to 8 oz. of beer, 6 oz. of wine, or one shot of liquor.
Respondent:	I do not know … it really depends.
Interviewer:	Well, if you had to guess the number of drinks for any given week, what do you think it would be?
Respondent:	Hmm. Well, I usually go out and drink about three times a week … I guess in each sitting I have about seven or eight beers.
Interviewer:	So, do you think about 24 drinks in an average week?
Respondent:	Yeah, that is about right.

have simply written in "it depends." This does not give much insight to the researcher! However, because an interviewer was asking each question, s/he was able to clarify the question and nail down a specific answer by *probing*, meaning getting more information from the respondent. A value of "24" means a whole lot more than an answer of "it depends."

One limitation of in-person interviews is that they require a respondent to feel comfortable enough to answer questions honestly to a stranger and do so face-to-face. A respondent may feel uncomfortable talking about private or sensitive topics (drug use, sexual behavior, criminal activity, etc.) and may answer in a way that s/he thinks the interviewer *wants* them to answer. This limitation is called *social desirability*—basically, people are people pleasers. For instance, if **Bob** the interviewer is surveying **Jane** the respondent about her drug use, and **Jane** (who is a frequent user of methamphetamine) senses that **Bob** is very "anti-drug," she may tell **Bob** that she only uses methamphetamine sporadically, or, even worse, she may tell him that she has never *tried* methamphetamine—this is because she senses **Bob** wants to hear that she has not used drugs. In these circumstances, a combination of surveying techniques can be used; specifically, in-person interviewing and self-interviewing. In these cases, the interviewer will directly ask the respondent the majority of the questions on the questionnaire; however, the sensitive questions will then be answered by the respondent without help from the interviewer (self-interviewing). The use of computers can be especially helpful in these situations. Specifically, a computer can be used for part of the questionnaire, and the respondent can actually take over the computer to answer sensitive questions. For instance, in a study on sexual behavior and sexually transmitted diseases, researchers examined whether answers on these sensitive questions would differ using traditional in-person interviewing versus computer-assisted self-interviewing (meaning the respondent answers the questions on the computer him or herself), and found that almost one-third of participants gave a different response when they had to answer these questions face-to-face with an interviewer versus when they were able to answer them on a computer (Kissinger et al., 1999).

Group-Administered Questionnaire

Questionnaires can also be administered in-person to groups of respondents. In these cases, the researchers do not act as interviewers, but instead, they provide the questionnaire in a paper-and-pencil format or electronic format. When using a *group-administered questionnaire*, respondents are able to answer the questions privately using a computer or a writing utensil; however, the researcher is able to deliver the survey to multiple participants simultaneously. A common example of this is when a researcher distributes a paper-and-pencil survey to a classroom full of students (perhaps at a high school or college).

This is obviously more economical and efficient than individual interviewing; however, there is a greater chance that respondents will not seek clarification as easily for any questions that might be confusing. This could lead to invalid responses on certain questions, that, had the researcher provided an in-person interview, could (or would) have been resolved. This goes back to the example in Figure 8-2 on average number of drinks. However, on the other side of the issue, omitting the role of the interviewer can be beneficial, because there is no chance of interviewer bias. Even in the example about average number of drinks, the interviewer showed some bias: the respondent said seven to eight beers in one sitting, and the interviewer interpreted that to be the higher number (eight beers three times a week is twenty-four beers).

Telephone Questionnaire Distribution

In their heyday, telephone-administered questionnaires were considered pretty awesome. Just like in-person interviews, telephone-administered questionnaires allowed researchers to make contact with respondents, clarify any confusing questions or ask for further clarification on any vague responses. Unlike in-person interviews, however, all of this could be completed at a fraction of the cost and a fraction of the time, yet still yield similar results as in-person interviews (Rogers, 1976; Tremblay, 1977).

Questionnaires for telephone interviews can take two formats: traditional paper-and-pencil questionnaires or electronic questionnaires. Similar to in-person interviews, there is *computer-assisted telephone-interviewing (CATI)*. Computers can also offer a number of tools to interviewers. Not only can questions be asked using an electronic form of the survey, but the computer can also assist in dialing the numbers of the respondents.

Random Digit Dialing

If you remember from Chapter 7 on sampling techniques, we discussed methods of collecting a representative sample using a probability sampling technique. When using telephone interviews, researchers can use a technique called *random digit dialing* (Glasser & Metzger, 1972). A telephone number consists of three parts: the area code, which provides information about the specific region or city of the number, the prefix, which provides a more specific location, and the last four digits which are the line number. For instance, Jackson, Mississippi, and its surrounding areas have three area codes: 601, 662, and 769. A researcher could then look up the various prefixes (such as 662-207-_ _ _ _, or 601-397-_ _ _ _) and then use a computer to select numbers randomly. While this method makes using a random sampling technique easier than most other methods, it also requires that those whom the researcher calls will actually want to participate. Also, if the researcher were looking for people in a certain area, this has become much harder than before, since people now, most often, have cell phones instead of landlines, and many individuals have a telephone number that does not represent their current address! There are methods that can be used to increase the likelihood of reaching a landline (Tourangeau, 2004); however, reaching individuals who have landlines will not yield a representative sample. This is because, one, it is—in the best-case scenario—representative only of those people living in households (so not of people who are homeless); and two, considering that as of 2016, less than half of the United States' population has a landline (Blumberg & Luke, 2017), it is only generalizable to less than 50% of individuals living in households.

Self-Administration Method of Delivery

A questionnaire is self-administered when respondents review and answer questions on a questionnaire with no direct contact or help from the researcher or research team. The two most common formats of self-administered self-report survey instruments are electronic (either online or emailed) and mailed questionnaires.

Mailed Questionnaires

There are certainly benefits to *mailed questionnaires* that researchers may be unable to obtain with other methods. Specifically, researchers are able to reach a wide (think distant) population with no travel, while also causing minimal interruption to the potential respondent (unlike a telephone call on a landline). Further, there are fewer time restrictions with mailed surveys; participants often have weeks to choose whether to complete it and return it.

Advantages and Disadvantages of Mail Questionnaires

Mailed surveys are much cheaper than in-person interviews, because there is no travel, and it eliminates the need to hire most individuals for a research team. Remember that the U.S. Census Bureau hired over 600,000 people to follow up with those who did *not* respond to the initial mail out—imagine if everyone filled it out from the beginning—that is a lot of money saved! It is also a lot of *time* saved, between travel, recruitment, and in-person interviews. Additionally, there has been some evidence that those who participate in a mail questionnaire provide more reliable or consistent answers as compared to those who respond to an electronic questionnaire (Savage & Waldman, 2008). Lastly, respondents are able to respond anonymously, and although the researcher knows to whom the questionnaire was distributed, the researcher is not aware who actually *responded*.

There are certainly disadvantages to mail surveys, too. Like group-administered surveys, an interviewer is not present to clarify any questions or confusing answers. However, unlike group-administered surveys, where someone is at least present *administering* the survey and thus providing the opportunity for a respondent to clarify or ask questions to a member of the research team. Mailed questionnaires are self-administered, meaning there is no research team member present; however, respondents are provided with contact information for the researcher(s) and the research team, so that they may call, write, or email to ask any questions or seek clarification.

Another concern with mailed questionnaires (that holds true for online surveys, too) is almost so obvious that it is easy to forget—sending out a mailed survey makes an assumption that *someone can read*. Considering that about 18% of the population cannot read at the most basic level, this is certainly a problem with mailed surveys that researchers do not face with in-person or telephone surveys. This can also create a significant distinction in your respondents versus your non-respondents.

Increasing Responses in Mailed Questionnaires

Another concern with mailed surveys is response rates and whether there is non-response bias. Do those people who complete mailed surveys vastly differ from those people who do not? It may depend on the survey instrument topic, its design, and/or the lifestyle of the potential respondents. This is certainly something to consider when giving mailed questionnaires. It may be best to follow methods to increase response rate and provide multiple options. There are four main methods that researchers can use in an effort to increase their response rate with mailed questionnaires. The first is making sure the instrument has a **professional appearance** and catches the eye. If the questionnaire is just a folded piece of paper in a traditional envelope, this certainly will not increase its perceived legitimacy! If possible, make it colorful, a bit of a different shape, use your institution's letterhead, and make sure it looks professionally done — the more impressed with the appearance, the more likely someone will respond.

The second technique to increase response rate is to first mail an **advance notice of the questionnaire**—meaning, provide a heads up that they will be asked to participate in a study and announce when the questionnaire should arrive (see Figure 8-3). At this time, you could also provide an addressed and stamped postcard that the respondent could mail back to you, that allows them to notify you of whether they will participate in the study. If you are trying to stick to a representative sample, then this is an excellent opportunity to replace participants, because you can keep record of which participants do *not* want to participate, as you do not have to promise anonymity (typically) for simply determining whether they will participate. So, if you have a 40-year-old white male from Kansas City, Kansas, you can attempt to replace him with another 40-year-old white male from Kansas City, Kansas. If you do not provide this option, then it becomes much more challenging to replace those respondents.

The third technique is to **provide incentives.** This may be anything from a little souvenir (like a pen or notepad) to a chance to win a cash gift card. Incentives for participation can be tricky, as some states do not allow it, so be sure to address this with your institutional review board first!

Figure 8-3: Advance Notice Mail-Back Card

Thank you for your consideration in participating in our research! Your participation is incredibly important to our study.

<u>Please select one of the following so that we can know whether to provide you with a questionnaire in the upcoming weeks:</u>

☐ **Yes**, I am interested in participating in the study.

My address is _____.

☐ **No**, I am not interested in participating in the study.

<u>**Thank you for your response!**</u>

The fourth technique is to *follow up* with participants. Send out a letter reminding participants of the study and its importance and request that they participate, if they have not done so already.

While mailed questionnaires are a much cheaper alternative to in-person interviews, they can still be costly. For instance, if you sent out advance notice, the questionnaire (with an addressed and stamped envelope for the respondent to return the questionnaire), and a follow up, the cost per participant is still significant for any individual. Considering that a postage stamp is 49 cents, you would need four per participant (the advance notice, the survey, the return envelope, and the follow up), along with the cost of paper, envelopes, and printing, you are looking at no less than two dollars, but probably more like three to four per person. If you send the survey to 500 people, then you would need anywhere from $1,000 to $4,000! It adds up rather quickly!

Online Questionnaire Delivery

One of the newest, yet most popular forms of delivering questionnaires is through the Internet. The Internet provides a number of options: researchers can distribute questionnaires through a website, provide them directly in an email, or can even use an online survey marketplace to find participants and distribute their questionnaire. Overall, there are many appeals to online delivery and formatting of questionnaires.

Their advantages are pretty obvious: they are incredibly inexpensive when compared to other methods of questionnaire distribution—in many cases they are free! Additionally, they take much less time than any other distribution method—for both participants and researchers. Lastly, it is easier to access populations that are incredibly far away, with no concern about the expense or added time (such as time for a mailed questionnaire to be delivered) (Wright, 2005). Particularly on its face, online questionnaire distribution seems like the dream, and in many ways, it is.

There is, however, the issue of whom you are surveying; meaning, who is the target population? If you are looking to survey prison inmates, they are not going to have access (in all likelihood) to the Internet. Conversely, if you are looking to survey CEOs of Fortune 500 companies, then it is probably a safe bet that they will have Internet access.

One of the strongest arguments against online questionnaires in the past has been that they simply are not representative. As of the year 2000, only 50% of American adults even *used* the Internet—meaning that if you were looking for a general target population of American adults, you already lost half your potential participants! However, this number has been creeping up annually, and as of 2016, only 23% of American households did not have a broadband Internet connection, and 13% of Americans do not use the Internet (U.S. Census Bureau, 2015; Anderson & Perrin, 2016). However, these 13% are likely distinctive from the 87% who *do* use the Internet: they make up over 40% of individuals who are over 65 years of age, 23% of individuals who make less than $30,000/year, 22% of rural residents, and 34% of individuals with less than a high school degree. So, if a researcher is looking for a general sample of the U.S., they must realize they will miss contact with 13% of their target population, while a researcher looking for a sample of individuals who are of retirement age would miss contact with over 40% of their target population.

Additionally, like mailed surveys, there are likely differences in those people who respond and those who do not, and the issue of potential respondents' reading ability also remains. It is important to keep these limitations in mind when conducting a survey using an online platform. First, determine whether most of the target population has access to the Internet. It is not a good idea for inmates, or rural-residing, poverty-stricken, or retirement-age individuals, but there will be little doubt that you'll be able to capture some of your population if they are college students, computer scientists, or Facebook subscribers.

One way that researchers can increase their response rate on either an online or web-based survey is to provide the *option* of completing the survey through the mail or an online format (Fricker & Schonlau, 2002).

Internet Survey Software and Online Marketplaces

Online Platforms for Online Questionnaires

There are a number of questionnaire distribution methods for online questionnaires. First, the questionnaire can be delivered directly through email; however, this is typically only applicable when there are no concerns about anonymity. Email can also be used to provide an anonymous link to the survey instrument, where participants will be able to respond to the questionnaire without any link back to them personally.

The questions are, to where does this link lead, and where can someone actually construct their online survey? There are actually numerous options—some of them free, and some of them not. If a questionnaire is short and simple and is being distributed to a small number of people, there are multiple free options. One popular online software program is Survey Monkey,[1] which has both free and paid options for users. Another popular online platform is Qualtrics.[2] While Qualtrics is not free, many universities have subscriptions to Qualtrics, which can provide free access to faculty and staff. Qualtrics has a number of types of products available to its customers and can get very fancy in terms of questionnaire construction. Both Survey Monkey and Qualtrics allow researchers to actually create their questionnaire on the Qualtrics platform, and then can provide the researcher(s) with links to provide to their targeted participants. Within both Qualtrics and Survey Monkey, when data collection is complete, the researcher(s) can simply download the data into a number of formats, including Microsoft Office Excel and SPSS (Statistical Package for the Social Sciences).

Online Marketplaces

One of the newest trends in research is online marketplaces, which are also known as crowdsourcing websites. While these have been around for quite some time, they've become more popular in recent years. Likely the most popular site for social science researchers is Amazon's Mechanical Turk. Researchers can post questionnaires as a "HIT" (Human Intelligence Task) and pay "workers" small sums to complete their studies. Researchers can also specify certain attributes they want in respondents. While this sounds like a dream, there are certainly concerns about individuals "working" to respond to questionnaires, and there has also been concern about how representative participants are (Casler, Bickel, & Hackett, 2013; Fort, Adda, & Cohen, 2011; Huff & Tingley, 2015; Ross, Zaldivar, Irani, & Tomlinson, 2010).

Constructing a Questionnaire: Guidelines and Rules to Follow

It may seem like writing questions for a questionnaire is easy, but unfortunately, it is kind of a pain. There are many ways that things can be interpreted, and naturally, we (meaning anyone) are kind of *bad* at writing these questions. It is important to really think through, plan, and design your questionnaire and then have a bunch of people tell you everything that is wrong with it. If no one finds anything, you need to find new people to look it over because I can promise you — something is wrong with it! First thing, as just a point of clarification: when I write "question" I may mean a question or a statement. When I write "construct" I mean a social construct that is measured by multiple questions (or statements), using an **index** or a **scale** (see Chapter 7). Also, I am writing this under the assumption that we are referring to a paper survey (just to keep things simple); however, the same rules apply to an online or telephone survey.

---

1. Access at http://www. surveymonkey.com.
2. Access at http://www.qualtrics.com.

There are three parts that we need to cover on questionnaire construction: The overall organization of the instrument, types of questions, and the guidelines of constructing questions. It may seem tedious (and that is because it is), but questionnaire construction is really important—you do not get what you need if you do not do it right, and then you have wasted a lot of time, money, and energy. It is like going shopping for twelve hours blindfolded, and ending up with a bunch of clothes that do not fit and a used computer from 1994—a bunch of time and money wasted!

Organizing Your Questionnaire

Even if you are a very creative, disorganized type person, you'll want to pretend otherwise with a survey. It should be clean, organized, and divided into sections. Before the questionnaire, there should be a **cover letter**. The cover letter often serves as the informed consent (or implied consent) from the participant. If you remember from Chapter 3 on ethics and research, it is important that a researcher informs the participants about what is going on in the research and what will be expected of them, as well as promises and resources available to the participant. For instance, a researcher may want to include resources like counseling services or crisis hotlines if there are any questions that might be upsetting. A researcher should also include contact information (professional, not personal) so that if there are any questions or a need to clarify, the participant has a way to get in contact with the researcher. If the intention is for the survey to be anonymous, state that. If there is a need for confidentiality, state that, too. Often, anonymity and confidentiality are both stated, which seems silly: if it is anonymous, why is there a need for confidentiality? However, it is a way to say that if somehow anonymity gets broken (like a participant provides a return address or writes their name on the survey instrument), that the researcher will keep that quiet and no one but the researcher and his or her team will be aware of that, and they will try to "get rid" of that identifying information quickly. Figure 8-4 has an example of a cover letter where Professor **Bob** was attempting to survey sex offenders to learn about their experiences being on the registry.

Variables of Interest

Participants tend to be paying the most attention at the beginning of a survey, so make sure the most important questions that measure your variables of interest go first. Group questions together that make sense together and are also measured the same way. For instance, if you have ten questions that are answered by checking "yes" or "no" put all of these together—even if they actually measure different things. If you have two variables, drug use and crime, and are asking about ever completing actions or using these drugs, you can put the questions together and group them separately. Figure 8-5 shows an example of this. Even though the questions are to measure two different constructs, drug use and criminal activity, since they both use the same answer type (yes/no) it makes it easy and clean to group them together.

Figure 8-4: Cover Letter for a Study on Sex Offender Experiences

---

The University of Nada

AUTHORIZATION TO PARTICIPATE IN RESEARCH

Project Title: Examining the Effects of Registration on Sex Offenders

Hello,

My name is Professor **Bob**, and I am currently an assistant professor at The University of Nada. I am researching the **effects of sex offender registration and community notification in the state. I am interested in how registration and notification affects sex offenders**. I am requesting your participation in this survey because according to the State, you are a registered sex offender who is subject to community notification. Many of the questions will be an attempt to understand how much the practices of sex offender registration and community notification have personally affected you.

This packet contains the survey booklet and a pre-stamped method for you to return the survey. The survey should take about **20 minutes of your time**. The survey contains questions about the crime(s) of which you were convicted, as well as questions pertaining to your negative and positive experiences with the sex offender registration.

Please be aware that your participation in this survey and research is **completely voluntary** and your **identity will always remain anonymous**. All answers will remain anonymous and will not be accessible to your probation officer or any other person besides the approved research staff and myself. At no point will anyone be able to connect your anonymous answers back to you personally. You may skip any question if you do not feel comfortable answering. Your choice to participate or not participate will remain anonymous and will not be shared or known by the researcher(s) or anyone else. It should be noted that you will not benefit in any way by participating in this survey nor will you suffer any consequences for not participating.

My hope is that by using this information, **researchers and lawmakers can better understand how these policies have affected you (both positively and negatively) and your life**. Should you choose to participate, I will be incredibly appreciative of your help, and your participation will aid in educating the public about sex offender laws.

I have supplied you with a stamped addressed envelope that you can use to return your completed survey. In the event you become distressed due to the content of this survey, you can contact the Crisis Line at 555-555-555 or 505-555-5555. If you have any further questions regarding this study, you may contact me at The University of Nada at 505-555-5592. Please make certain that you do not include any type of identifying information (e.g., your name) on the survey, as we want to make sure your responses are anonymous. This project and related consent form have been reviewed by the Institutional Review Board, which ensures that research projects involving human subjects follow federal regulations. Any questions or concerns about rights as a research participant should be directed to the chair of the Institutional Review Board, The University of Nada, 125 Nada Road, Nada, TN, 505-555-9215. I hope you strongly consider being a part of this important research. Thank you very much for your time.

Sincerely,

Professor **Bob**, PhD

Figure 8-5: Example of Question Grouping

Please indicate if you have used the following substances in the past year:		
Marijuana	☐ Yes	☐ No
Alcohol	☐ Yes	☐ No
Cocaine	☐ Yes	☐ No
Heroin	☐ Yes	☐ No
Ecstasy	☐ Yes	☐ No
Please indicate if you have done any of the following in the past year:		
Stolen something worth less than $50	☐ Yes	☐ No
Stolen something worth more than $50	☐ Yes	☐ No
Deliberately damaged someone's property	☐ Yes	☐ No
Gotten into a serious physical fight	☐ Yes	☐ No
Driven someone's car without their permission	☐ Yes	☐ No

That being said, you should be careful about response sets, which we will go over in the "Dos and Don'ts" section.

Besides making sure your variables of interest are included in the first part of the survey, you also want to make sure that your more sensitive questions are up front, so that they do not come as a surprise to the participant. If your focus is how often the participant has been a victim of various violent crimes, then you will want to include these questions at the beginning. Otherwise, due to the cover letter, the participant just knows they are coming, which can make them distracted while answering other questions. Any questions that are sensitive in nature should typically be in the beginning of the survey and then get less and less "stressful" for the participant.

Demographics Go Last

One of the first sets of questions researchers think about is demographics, meaning things like age, race, sex, socioeconomic status, etc. Even though these seem like a good place to start, demographic questions should go at the *end* of the survey. The reason is, participants will be paying less attention as they continue on with the survey, or, at the least, they will probably not be thinking as hard about each question. They certainly should not need to take the time to think about their age or their race. Demographics are the easiest questions to answer, so when the brain power is a little bit less (understandably so!), give them the easiest questions!

Figure 8-6: Information Gathered from Closed-Ended Questions about an Arrest

Have you ever been arrested?

✓ Yes

__ No

What was the crime for which you were arrested?

✓ Assault

__ Homicide

__ Sexual Assault

__ Other

Types of Questions in a Questionnaire

When designing a questionnaire and determining what type of questions to ask, one of the first questions to consider is what questions will be closed-ended and what questions will be open-ended. If you are creating a questionnaire for purposes of either in-depth interviews or in-person interviews, open-ended questions can be a fantastic tool. They provide a lot more information and context than closed-ended questions. However, too many open-ended questions will make for a tired, annoyed participant. There is, of course, a balance!

Imagine if someone had been arrested for getting into a physical altercation at a bar. If you asked closed-ended questions, you will not be able to get a lot of detail. Figure 8-6 provides an example of this.

Asking an open-ended question like "describe the circumstances of your arrest" can provide a lot more information — perhaps they punched someone because their friend was sexually harassed, or because they were defending themselves. Perhaps they punched someone because they felt like it. The motive and circumstances make those two scenarios sound like very different crimes. By only asking the closed-ended questions, this context would be missed. However, there is always the chance that the respondent will not provide the specific information that is sought. They may tell you the officer's name and badge number, but not provide information about the reason for the arrest. This is fine when the survey is being distributed by an interviewer, since s/he can follow up and make sure they have that information. When this is not the case (as it often is not), then it is important to weight the benefits and costs of open-ended questions. If the real interest is in the arrest, then it may be a good idea to include the closed ended *and* open-ended questions on the arrest. That way, the researcher has all the information s/he needs and hopefully, a bit more about the context.

Figure 8-7: Example of Contingency Question and Branching

1. In your lifetime, have you ever used marijuana, either legally or illegally?

   ☐ Yes

   ☐ No

   If no, please skip questions 2–4.

2. At what age did you first try marijuana?

   ___ years of age.

3. How many times have you used marijuana in the past year?

   ___ times.

4. Do you reside in a state where marijuana is legal?

   ☐ Yes

   ☐ No

Filter and Contingency Questions

The goal of any questionnaire should be to make things short, clear, and organized for the participant. Therefore, if a survey instrument asks a respondent "do you smoke marijuana" and they answer "no," then they should not have to answer any more questions about their marijuana use. This is where **contingency questions** and **branching** become handy (Nardi, 2015). If we were using a paper survey instrument (see Figure 8-7), the question on marijuana use would be a contingency question, and those respondents who answered yes would continue to answer questions about marijuana (branching) and those respondents who answered "no" to marijuana use would be asked to skip questions about marijuana use.

If using a self-administered paper survey, it is important not to have *too* many contingency questions, because this can be really confusing for the respondent! Imagine if every three or four questions you had to skip or continue on based on your answer for the last question. I know I would get lost very easily! However, if the survey is administered by an interviewer, s/he will be trained in determining what questions to skip and what questions to ask, which allows for more of these types of questions, as they will not confuse the respondent.

One of the amazing aspects of technology is that when using online survey software, like Qualtrics or Survey Monkey, you can build in contingency questions and "skip patterns." Meaning, you can tell the software that if someone answers yes to using marijuana, then present them questions two through four (from Figure 8-7), but if someone answers "no" then skip questions two through four, so that the respondent does not even see these questions. This allows a researcher to ask more of those contingency type questions without worry that the respondent will get tripped up with which questions they are and are not supposed to answer.

Likert-Type Scales

Questionnaires contain a lot of questions typically focusing on opinions or perceptions and/or frequencies of behavior. Something like "I believe that Research Methods is an awesome class" is an example of an opinion question, while "I have skipped my Research Methods class" could be an example of a frequency-type question. In the former (Research Methods is awesome), this could be a yes/no answer (which is dichotomous, meaning only two categories). However, that does not allow for much of an opinion to be expressed by the respondent. Instead, the questionnaire could be designed to allow the respondent to identify the intensity of their agreement or disagreement: they could answer strongly agree, agree, neutral, disagree, or strongly disagree. In the latter example (I have skipped my Research Methods class), could have similar levels of frequency, like never, once, two or three times, four or five times, and more than five times, or provide similar categories: never, rarely, occasionally, and often. These types of scales are referred to as Likert Scales, as they were designed by a man named Rensis Likert, who thought there was probably a better way to start measuring attitudes and opinions (Likert, 1932).

Matrix Formatting

In Figure 8-5, when we were discussing how to group questions, I provided an example about drug use and criminal activity. The questions were grouped together so that the same wording in a question did not have to be used over and over again. Here's what the questions would look like if we had not simplified the statements:

1. In the past year, have you used marijuana?
2. In the past year, have you used alcohol?
3. In the past year, have you used cocaine?
4. In the past year, have you used heroin?
5. In the past year, have you used ecstasy?

The questions in Figure 8-5 are an example of a *matrix format*. It allows a researcher to skip the same language on each question. Matrix formatting is especially great when there are Likert-type questions that are measured with the same categories. For instance, if there are multiple questions asking about the frequency of different actions then designing the questions using matrix formatting simplifies and shortens the instrument. An example of this is in Figure 8-8, from a survey instrument I distributed to a national sample of college students using the survey platform Qualtrics. In it, I have asked respondents to identify how often they had committed each act in the past year. By grouping them together, I only had to say, "In the past 12 months, how often have you ..." one time instead of sixteen times, which makes a big difference!

While grouping these types of questions together makes things more organized, it is important to avoid *response sets*, meaning that the respondent should not just get used to selecting one answer. For instance, if Researcher JANE was trying to measure political preferences, s/he may ask a few questions like:

Figure 8-8: Matrix Formatting for Frequency Questions on Deviance,
Created with Qualtrics Survey Software

	Never	Once or Twice	Three or Four Times	More than Five Times
Paint graffiti on someone else's property or in a public place?	O	O	O	O
Take something from a store without paying for it?	O	O	O	O
Deliberately damage someone else's property?	O	O	O	O
Get into a serious physical fight?	O	O	O	O
Injure someone badly enough that they needed to see a doctor?	O	O	O	O

I believe in a woman's right to choose.

I am against the death penalty.

I support gun control.

In all three of these, a traditional liberal would likely answer "agree" or "strongly agree" to each question. To make sure that the liberal respondent does not start guessing that s/he will select "agree" before really thinking about the question, it is a good idea to mix things up with **reverse coding**. An example of reverse coding would be to change "against death penalty" to "support death penalty." A traditional liberal would have to now select "strongly disagree" or "disagree," which avoids a response set.

Forced-Answer Questions

When asking respondent's opinions about questions, there are times when allowing a neutral answer is appropriate — they may *really* be neutral about certain topics and issues. However, it is important to ask whether neutrality is really an option in certain situations, particularly with one's own behavior. One thing you want to do is to avoid *fence sitters*, who are those who do not want to take a stance on anything (Bachman & Schutt, 2013). Another way to avoid fence sitting is to force a respondent to answer one of two or more choices. Basically, it is a formalized method of "would you rather ..." Something like "Would you rather read this Research Methods book or walk across nails?" Another example would be "Do you prefer going to concerts or movies?" Perhaps the respondent does not go to either, but in this choice, they have to choose one or the other.

The Dos and Don'ts

There are a bunch of rules and guidelines to follow to understand how to write questions, how to write questions for an index, and how to actually construct a questionnaire. First, we will review the dos and don'ts of writing an actual question. The dos: (1) make sure the question is mutually exclusive, (2) make sure the question is exhaustive, (3) make the question clear and simple, (4) consider your audience when writing the question, (5) have methods of measuring validity, (6) check the sensitivity of the question, and (7) be specific. The don'ts include avoiding the following: (1) biased questions, (2) double-barreled questions, (3) leading questions, and (4) loaded questions.

The Dos of Questionnaire Construction

(1) Mutually Exclusive

A closed-ended question has to provide options that are independent of one another. Meaning, the respondent cannot select more than one group. For instance, if a question asked to select a group for age range:

What is your age?
• 18–20
• 20–22
• 22–24
• 24–26
• 26–28
• 28 or older

In this example, someone who is 20-years-old could select the first or second option, someone who is 22 could select the second or third option, someone who is 24 could select the third and fourth option, etc. Each category should separate itself. This could easily be remedied by changing the groups to 18–20, 21–23, 24–26, 27–29, and 30 or older.

(2) Exhaustive

A closed-ended question also has to provide an option for each person to select. For instance, if we asked the age question:

What is your age?
• Under 18
• 18–20
• 21–23
• 24–26
• Over 30

There are two reasons this question is not exhaustive: what do you select if you are under 18? What do you select if you are 27, 28, or 29? Mutually exclusive and exhaustive are often directed together. The easiest way to remember these is "gotta fit in one group, cannot fit in more than one group."

(3) Clear and Simple

Make sure to break down a question to its simplest form. There is no reason to use flowery language and make things complicated. Do not ask "Do you think, in most cases, you probably eat ice cream?" Instead ask "How often do you eat ice cream?" We tend to **qualify** statements—to say something like "well, I could be wrong..." or "No offense, but..." Make sure to avoid this kind of qualifying in a survey instrument. Ask if any words can be omitted, and if they can—omit them.

(4) Consider Your Audience

Sometimes, college professors harp on you so much to make sure everything you write is formal, that you think that everything and anything you write for the rest of your life should be formal. Guess what? In most cases, it should! However, questionnaire construction may be an exception to this. Let's say that I asked, "How many hours do you use electronic devices (i.e., cell phone, television, computer, and/or gaming consoles) in an average week?" This may seem like a fine question—now imagine that I was asking this question to five-year-olds—it does not seem so fine now, huh? Your audience matters! If I were to ask five-year-olds about how much they use electronic devices, I would want to break it down and (assuming I am giving in-person interviews!) ask them if they use each one and how often they use it. Something like: "Do you watch TV at home?" "How many shows do you watch each day?" "Do you watch TV before dinner?" "What about after dinner?" "Do you have a TV in your bedroom?" We may not be able to get an accurate measure of hours from a five-year-old. This would also be a good time to consult with someone who does know about the cognition skills of a five-year old. Similarly, if we had questions about feelings or perceptions, we would probably provide smiley and "frowney" faces to describe their thoughts, not "agree" and "disagree." Similarly, I would not recommend asking inmates about their grocery shopping habits, or college students about their time in prison. Generally, it is important to ask questions applicable to your respondents and to do so in an appropriate way.

(5) Validity Checks

We already discussed one form of validity checks: reverse coding to avoid response sets. Another way to make sure that someone is paying attention is to ask them a very easy-to-answer question in the middle of the survey. Something like "I am paying attention to this survey" in the middle of a matrix formatted set of questions. They should, ideally check strongly agree! Something obvious like this can let a researcher know if a respondent has actually read every question carefully. A researcher can also ask some question about **always** or **never** in an effort to check for issues of social desirability. *Social desirability* is when a respondent answers a certain way because they think that is how the researcher or interviewer wants them to answer. A question like "I always tell the truth" could help determine if there is possibly an issue with social desirability. Always and never should be avoided in most cases, because it is rare that someone "always" does something. While often for good reasons, people lie—I have not met someone who has not told a lie—however, never say never! If someone selected "strongly agree" for the question "I always tell the truth," this could raise a red flag and the respondent's answers would have to be reviewed and interpreted with some caution.

(6) Check Sensitivity

As discussed earlier, when there are questions that are of more of a sensitive nature, they should probably be asked near the beginning of the survey. Additionally, the questionnaire should not include more specificity than needed. If studying sexual assault victimization, it is important to not get too specific in the details, as this may be upsetting, and may result in respondents skipping questions or terminating their participation. You do not want to ask, "Have you ever been physically injured by an intimate partner?" and then, "how many times this year?" followed by, "how many times this month?" and then, "were you physically injured by an intimate partner in the last week?" These questions should be combined to something like "In the past year, how many times have you been physically injured by an intimate partner?" This question could have an option of "0" for those who have never been physically injured by an intimate partner. Further, this question could serve as a contingency question and those who have been physically injured could be asked how recently they were last physically injured by an intimate partner. Similarly, when asking about sexual partners or some other issue that is considered private, do not get too specific with the categories. You may not want to give options of "0, 1, 2, 3..., 10, 11, 12..." but instead give "0, 1–3, 4–6, 7–10, 10 or more." It simply can feel less intrusive to a respondent to answer in a broader category.

(7) Be Specific

While it is important to avoid too much specificity with sensitive questions, it is also important to avoid vagueness or broad questions. There should be no doubt as to what the question is asking. Do not ask "Do you drink in an average week?" Instead ask, "How many alcoholic beverages do you drink in a week (1 drink = 8 oz. of beer, 6 oz. of wine, or 1 oz. shot of liquor)?" First, a lot more information is gathered from the second question, and two, the first question could be interpreted to mean "drink water" or "drink iced tea." It may seem like an obvious meaning, but it is important to not use the motto "you know what I mean …" in a questionnaire. No, they may *not* know what you mean.

The Don'ts of Questionnaire Construction

(1) Biased Questions

Have you ever been at a restaurant and been asked to fill out a questionnaire, where you rate your experience during that visit? I have seen a few that made me do a double-take:

1) Did you enjoy your experience at our fine establishment?

2) How did you enjoy the state-of-the-art facilities today?

3) Did you enjoy the food, cooked by our top-of-the-line chef today?

It is similar to if I asked you to rate this "awesome textbook." It is *biased*. It is fueled with language in hopes of making you lean in a certain direction to answer a question. No one should be able to determine what the researcher's beliefs and opinions are from the way the survey instrument is designed. It is actually pretty easy to avoid being biased—try to avoid any excessive adjectives or nouns. Not all adjectives, but if the word is not needed and describes something, it is probably excessive. If we did that with the three previous examples:

1) Did you enjoy your experience at our ~~fine~~ establishment?

2) How did you enjoy the ~~state-of-the-art~~ facilities today?

3) Did you enjoy the food, cooked by our ~~top-of-the-line~~ chef today?

(2) Double-Barreled Questions

In keeping a question short and simple, it is advised to not ask more than one thing in a question. If you were asked "Do you think this Research Methods book is thrilling and helpful?" You might think it is thrilling but unhelpful, you might think it is helpful but not thrilling, but you would be forced to answer "yes" or "no" even though you only agree with part of the question. It would be better to break this down into two single-barreled questions: do you think this Research Methods book is thrilling? Do you think this Research Methods book is helpful? Double-barreled questions are sometimes used to trip people for job interviews or background checks. "Do you get angry when people steal your cocaine?" For example, If you answer yes, then you are also implying that you possess cocaine. If in an interview and asked a double-barreled question, make sure to break it down to multiple single-barreled questions.

(3) Leading Questions

Just like attorneys in a courtroom, someone should object to a researcher asking leading questions on a survey instrument. An example would be "Do you agree that this chapter is long and tedious?" This implies that the writer of the question believes this chapter is long and tedious. Instead, the questions could just ask how much someone agrees or disagrees with the following statement: This chapter is long and tedious.

(4) Loaded Questions

Similar to leading questions, do not put the wrong type of descriptive words into a question. For example: "Should violent felons be sentenced to life without parole?" Yikes! The words "violent" and "felons" are loaded. The question should also be more specific: "Should individuals who have committed first-degree murder be sentenced to life without parole?"

Steps in the Survey Research Process

Conducting survey research starts the same way as any type of research: developing your idea and your primary research question! Typically, with survey research, you will also be developing hypotheses, particularly if you are conducting explanatory research to examine relationships, differences, or effects. From here, we can examine the specific steps of constructing a questionnaire.

- Following developing your research question and hypotheses, identify your variables of interest.
- Conduct your literature review.
  - While conducting your literature review, operationalize your variables of interest.
  - While conducting your literature review, identify your control variables. If you find a relationship between your independent and dependent variable(s), ask yourself what else would or could be affecting your dependent variable? Often, control variables include demographics, but there may be other variables that should be included. It is important to examine what past researchers have used for controls, and also what past researchers on your topic have included as their variables of interest.
- Identify your (probable) target population, sample, and sample size.
- Identify your method of delivery for the survey instrument (online, in-person interviews, group administered, etc.)
- Start to construct your survey instrument:
  - Begin to think about how you will measure social constructs and other variables in your questionnaire.
    - Determine if you will use a scale or index that is already established to measure your constructs (like political preferences), or if you need to construct your own. Hint: if there are reliable scales that measure what you seek to measure — use them!
  - If you need to construct your own scale, it is best to consult with other experts on the topic in which you are studying. You want to make sure that you have included items that, in their totality, encompass the construct. For instance, if you were looking to create items to measure a construct of job satisfaction,

it would be important to include one or more items (statements or questions) on pay!

- ○ Begin to determine how you will include your control variables.
  - ▪ Determine question format: matrix, open-ended, multiple choice, tick-marks?
- ○ Start to put the questionnaire together (not formatted at this point). Make sure that every question you are including is necessary and important to the study. Omit any questions that are not.
- ○ Examine the length of the survey — not just in the sense of number of questions, but how *long* it will take a respondent to answer (on average).
- ○ Start formatting the survey. Try to make sure it looks clean and organized and is easy to follow.
- ○ Make sure your questions are in a logical order: often, it is best to put the demographics last and the variables that are of most interest near the beginning.
- ○ Begin to develop your cover letter.
- ○ Edit, edit, and then edit again!
- ○ Examine the organization of the questionnaire. Consult peers, colleagues, and advisors to review the questionnaire to make sure it follows the guidelines of survey construction.
- ○ Apply for institutional review board approval.
- • Pilot the questionnaire.
  - ○ Make sure to complete the questionnaire yourself to see if there are any issues or confusing areas.
  - ○ Have friends and colleagues complete the questionnaire and identify any confusing items or questions — check answers to make sure that they understood the instructions and were able to answer correctly.
  - ○ Attempt to take a small sample from a population that is similar to your target population (if you are looking at college students, seek college students to pilot your study). Assess their responses in the same way to identify any possible issues or confusing areas. This pilot should be included in your application to your institutional review board.

Summing It Up

Survey research is incredibly valuable within social science research. Although there are concerns about issues with validity and responses, it still remains one of the most (if not the most) common method of research in criminology and criminal justice. It is important to consider the method of delivery of a survey instrument prior to designing it. Similar to all other research, a plan is key! Make sure to follow guidelines and rules of questionnaire construction and organization. Remember to have others edit it and pilot it!

Discussion Questions

1. Explain the differences between surveys and questionnaires.

2. Is it feasible to conduct a longitudinal study using survey research? If no, why not? If yes, how?

3. What is the dark figure of crime? How do the Uniform Crime Report and the National Crime Victimization Survey help reveal the existence of a dark figure of crime?

4. If you were to conduct research using a questionnaire, what method of delivery would you most likely use? Explain why.

5. What is social desirability and how could it affect a study's validity?

6. What is a validity checker? Provide an example of a validity checker that could be placed in a questionnaire.

7. Why should sensitivity be avoided?

8. Where should you place your variables of interest in a questionnaire? Why?

9. Where should you typically place your demographics in a questionnaire?

10. Why is specificity important in survey? Provide an example of how a participant might answer a question that was not specific.

11. A question on a survey instrument should be mutually exclusive and exhaustive. What does this mean? Provide an example of a question that is not mutually exclusive or exhaustive, and then explain how you could remedy it.

Trying It Out

Your professor may ask you to complete the following companion assignment available from the publisher. Using the supplied worksheet form, you are going to identify what is wrong with each survey question provided using the rules of questionnaire construction, and then rewrite each question to remedy the problems with the original question.

References

Anderson, M., & Perrin, A. (2016). 13% of Americans don't use the internet. Who are they? Pew Research Center. [Press release].

Bachman, R., & Schutt, R. K. (2013). *The practice of research in criminology and criminal justice.* Thousand Oaks, CA: Sage Publications.

Bachman, R., & Schutt, R. K. (2014). *Fundamentals of research in criminology and criminal justice* (3rd ed.). Thousand Oaks, CA: Sage.

Baruch, Y. (1999). Response rate in academic studies: A comparative analysis. *Human Relations, 52*(4), 421–438.

Baruch, Y., & Holtom, B. C. (2008). Survey response rate levels and trends in organizational research. *Human Relations, 61*(8), 1139–1160.

Blumberg, S. J., & Luke, J. V. (2017). *Wireless substitution: Early release of estimates from the national health interview survey, July–December 2016.* Centers for Disease Control and Prevention. Retrieved from https://www.cdc.gov/nchs/data/nhis/earlyrelease/wireless201705.pdf.

Casler, K., Bickel, L., & Hackett, E. (2013). Separate but equal? A comparison of participants and data gathered via Amazon's MTurk, social media, and face-to-face behavioral testing. *Computers in Human Behavior, 29*(6), 2156–2160.

Federal Bureau of Investigation. (2014). *Uniform crime reporting statistics.* Retrieved from www.ucrdatatool.gov.

Fort, K., Adda, G., & Cohen, K. B. (2011). Amazon mechanical turk: Gold mine or coal mine? *Computational Linguistics, 37*(2), 413–420.

Fricker, R. D., & Schonlau, M. (2002). Advantages and disadvantages of internet research surveys: Evidence from the literature. *Field Methods, 14*(4), 347–367.

Glasser, G. J., & Metzger, G. D. (1972). Random-digit dialing as a method of telephone sampling. *Journal of Marketing Research*, 59–64.

Hanson, H. (2017). Too many Americans apparently think chocolate milk comes from brown cows. *Huffington Post.*

Huff, C., & Tingley, D. (2015). "Who are these people?" Evaluating the demographic characteristics and political preferences of MTurk survey respondents. *Research & Politics, 2*(3). doi:2053168015604648.

Kaplowitz, M. D., Hadlock, T. D., & Levine, R. (2004). A comparison of web and mail survey response rates. *Public Opinion Quarterly, 68*(1), 94–101.

Kissinger, P., Rice, J., Farley, T., Trim, S., Jewitt, K., Margavio, V., & Martin, D. H. (1999). Application of computer-assisted interviews to sexual behavior research. *American Journal of Epidemiology, 149*(10), 950–954.

Likert, R. (1932). A technique for the measurement of attitudes. *Archives of Psychology.*

Maxfield, M., & Babbie, E. (2014). *Research methods for criminal justice and criminology.* Boston, MA: Cengage Learning.

Nardi, P. M. (2015). *Doing survey research.* Abingdon, UK: Routledge.

NORC. (2016). *The General Social Survey.* Retrieved from http://gss.norc.org/.

Pickett, J. T. (2017). Methodological myths and the role of appeals in criminal justice journals: The case of response rates. *ACJS Today, 41*(3), 61–69.

Rigoni, B., & Nelson, B. (2016). *Millennials want jobs that promote their well-being.* Gallup. Retrieved from http://www.gallup.com/businessjournal/191435/millennials-work-life.aspx?g_source=position1&g_medium=related&g_campaign=tiles.

Rogers, T. F. (1976). Interviews by telephone and in person: Quality of responses and field performance. *Public Opinion Quarterly, 40*(1), 51–65.

Ross, J., Zaldivar, A., Irani, L., & Tomlinson, B. (2010). *Who are the crowdworkers?: Shifting demographics in mechanical turk.* Paper presented at the CHI EA 2010: Proceedings of the 28th International Conference on Human Factors in Computing Systems, Extended Abstracts, New York, NY.

Savage, S. J., & Waldman, D. M. (2008). Learning and fatigue during choice experiments: A comparison of online and mail survey modes. *Journal of Applied Econometrics, 23*(3), 351–371.

Tourangeau, R. (2004). Survey research and societal change. *Annual Review of Sociology, 55*, 775–801.

Tremblay, K. R., Jr. (1977). Interviews by telephone and in person: Quality of responses and field performance. *Public Opinion Quarterly, 41*(1), 117–118.

U.S. Census Bureau. (2015). *Percent of households with a broadband interent subscription*. American Factfinder. Retrieved from https://factfinder.census.gov/faces/tableservices/jsf/pages/productview.xhtml?src=bkmk.

Wright, K. B. (2005). Researching internet-based populations: Advantages and disadvantages of online survey research, online questionnaire authoring software packages, and web survey services. *Journal of Computer-Mediated Communication, 10*(3), JCMC1034.

Chapter 9

Secondary Data, Available Records, and Crime Mapping

Learning Objectives

- Define available records
- Describe types of available records within criminal justice and criminology
- Describe some of the first uses of available methods in criminological research
- Describe data collected by the U.S. Census Bureau
- Define secondary analysis
- Distinguish between secondary analysis and secondary data
- Define quantitative content analysis
- Describe the procedure of conducting a quantitative content analysis
- List and define systems of quantification for quantitative data collection in content analyses
- Evaluate quantitative content analyses in context of their advantages and disadvantages
- Report the history of crime mapping
- Define crime mapping
- Define geographic information systems
- List and define types of features and data in geographic information systems
- Explain the process of geocoding
- List and define the four features that GIS software can generate
- Examine the use of GIS software in law enforcement

If you are like me, you probably use email a lot. My school is a Google campus, so I have a Gmail account—in fact, I have more than one Gmail account, because I really like the way Gmail is set up and generally think it operates on a pretty secure server (whatever that means—it sounds like I know about technology, right?). You probably think the primary reason that Google started Gmail was to provide its consumers with a platform for receiving email. Here's the kicker though—I am not a Google consumer.

I have not spent a single dime in helping Google (if either of your authors had invested with them, it is doubtful we would be writing this book right now). So, how does Google make its money? Advertisers—they are the real consumers. The primary reason Google created Gmail was so they could know more about you. I mean, within a recent update in the Gmail app, it now offers me automatic replies. So, when my friend sends me the fortieth YouTube cat video this month, Gmail might offer me three canned responses "Thanks so much" and "That's so funny" and "Why do you have no life?" (kidding—it is not *that* smart). While this is a cool and convenient feature, it is indicative that Google is reading my mail, and that means they know a lot about me—a *lot*. Email, Google search history, Google Chrome data, Google Earth, and Google Maps. It knows where I've been and what I've done and even knows that I am really the "friend" who is sending those cat videos (oh, the shame ... they are just so funny). So, Google's primary concern is collecting data, and their secondary concern is providing their users (not consumers) with email—but regardless of the intention and motivation, the data are collected. And these data are useful for a lot of reasons. While it would be unethical to collect an individual's search data (giving that it would be hard to make sure it is anonymous), there is a lot that researchers can learn from it. I wonder how much you would pay for someone's Google search data (whoever that person of interest might be). I also wonder how much you would pay *not* to have your Google search data revealed to everyone else!

This sounds all creepy, but it is not like Google employees are going around discussing your Google searches while they play volleyball, sit in their beanbag chairs, or whatever it is that they actually do at Google. These data are "big data," and there are too many of us Googling way too many things for any collection of individuals to maintain. Therefore, Google looks at aggregate (group) data and trends. Here's the cool thing— you, too, can look at Google search trends. For instance, the greatest number of searches for marijuana took place in November of 2016—you know, when a number of states voted to legalize marijuana for recreational and/or medical use. Unsurprisingly, a search that followed a similar trend was "Marijuana Dispensaries near me."[1]

Just like Google did not provide email service for me to have a better email experience, Google did not collect data on Google searches for me to have fun looking at trends. However, since these data were already collected, I can use them for my own amusement (or research)—it becomes a secondary purpose.

If you recall from Chapter 4 ("The Nitty Gritty"), we discussed how secondary data can take many forms. Sometimes data are secondary but were never put in existence for any sort of research purposes or even record keeping. For instance, 1990s Rom-Coms were not made for criminological or sociological researchers—however, they are a form of secondary data that can be analyzed. There are also data that were made for record keeping like birth and death records, or even incident reports of crimes. These can be used to create numerical (or other types) of datasets. Lastly, there are secondary datasets that were created for the purpose of research, but not

---

1. www.google.com/trends.

necessarily created for your topic or research question. Examples of this might be the *National Crime Victimization Survey* or the *National Longitudinal Study of Adolescent to Adult Health.*

We can use *traditional quantitative analyses* (like how many people used marijuana last year) for research-based secondary datasets, and sometimes record-keeping datasets. However, when we are looking at words, pictures, videos, locations, etc., then it becomes a bit harder to determine the right analysis. Generally, we want to use a form of content analysis (either qualitative or quantitative) and, if we want to look at geographic features of certain types of content, we would likely want to use some sort of crime mapping or geocoding. These types of secondary data and analyses are discussed in this chapter.

With the exception of the complete observer, the majority of the techniques we have described in the text thus far have required you as the researcher to be somewhat intrusive into the lives of your participants or respondents. Other methods of collecting data involve little or no intrusion on the part of the researcher. In this chapter, we will highlight some different approaches to using data that has already been collected by others, generally as part of their job or routine practice. Much of the data utilized in criminal justice research has been collected by state and local agencies such as police, courts, and corrections departments. Federal organizations such as the *Bureau of Justice Statistics (BJS), the Federal Bureau of Investigation (FBI)*, and *the Federal Bureau of Prisons* accumulate information about crime problems and criminal justice institutions.

We refer to such data as *available records.* These data are collected by agencies for the purpose of record keeping, but are then used by others (like criminal justice and criminology professors) for another purpose: research. Meaning, these data already exist, but not for purposes for why a researcher might be utilizing it. Recall from Chapter 4 that when using secondary data sources, the researchers do not actually make the data, but they still have to collect it and put it together in an original way that will work for their specific study. Researchers whose studies are funded by federal agencies, such as the *National Institute of Justice (NIJ)*, generally release their data for public use. For example, let's say you are interested in preventing gang violence in large urban cities, you might use data collected by Hennigan (2015) in her research examining gang prevention in Los Angeles, California. This chapter briefly describes some sources of secondary data as well as the strengths and weaknesses of using such data.

Finally, this chapter will conclude with a discussion of crime mapping. Utilizing software originally designed for use in the discipline of geography, *Geographic Information Systems (GIS)* allows researchers and police to utilize electronic maps to track and study crime. Similar to viewing a road map to get to where you need to go, crime maps offer graphic representations of crime-related issues. An understanding of where and why crimes occur can improve attempts to quell crime. Mapping crime can help police protect citizens more effectively. Simple maps that display the locations where crimes or concentrations of crimes have occurred can be used to help direct patrols to places they are most needed. Policymakers in police departments might use more complex maps to observe trends in criminal activity, and maps may prove invaluable in solving criminal cases (Johnson, 2000).

Secondary Data:
Available Records and Data Archives

As opposed to primary data that is collected by a researcher or team of researchers to answer a specific research question or line of inquiry, secondary data refers to the use of data that was collected by someone else for some other purpose (Crossman, 2017; Maxfield & Babbie, 2014). In this case, the researcher constructs questions examined through the analysis of a dataset that the researcher was not involved in collecting. The data were not collected to answer the researcher's specific primary or research questions and were instead collected for another purpose. So, the same dataset can be primary data to one researcher and secondary data to another. Since the researcher did not collect the data, it is important for the researcher to become familiar with the dataset, paying particular attention to how the data were collected, what the response categories are for each question, the population of study ... etc. Fortunately for criminal justice researchers, much of secondary data are available for criminological research, many of which are public and easily accessible, such as the *United States Census*, the *General Social Survey (GSS)*, and the *American Community Survey (ACS)* (Crossman, 2017).

Much of this written record is available to the public and can be referred to as available records. No, not the LP records that some of your parents used to jam to on the turntable when they were young. In this case, we are talking about written documents created to ensure the normal functioning of offices, organizations, and departments, to name a few, and are maintained at every level of government (not to mention by virtually every private business and organization) in every society throughout the world (Singleton, Straits, Straits, & Mcallister, 1988). These include *court records*, *state laws*, and *city ordinances*, to name a few. Many government agencies, most notably the aforementioned United States Census, also maintain numerous volumes of official statistics. Couple those with birth and death certificates, directories, almanacs, and publication indexes such as the *New York Times Index* and *Reader's Guide to Periodical Literature*, and one can imagine the massive amount of information available from public records (Singleton et al., 1988).

An especially rich data source is *vital statistics*, like those utilized by *Clifford Shaw* and *Henry McKay* in their groundbreaking research on *Social Disorganization* in Chicago in the early 1900s, which includes data on births, deaths, marriages, divorces, and the like. By law, all births must be recorded, and death records must be filed before burial permits can be obtained (Singleton et al., 1988). Birth records provide information not only on the child born but also on the parents, including father's full name, address, and age. These data make possible research ranging from a study of social class and infant mortality as in Shaw and McKay's research to a study of the criminality propensities in the birth of twins (Shaw & McKay, 1942). Similarly, death records contain data on the cause of death; length of illness; whether injuries were accidental, homicidal, or self-inflicted; and the location and time of death (Singleton et al., 1988). Much of what we know about death has come from the analysis of death records. Generally, these mortality records can be obtained from an agency such as the *Center for Disease Control*, which compiles data for the nation as a whole, or from international organizations such as the United Nations, which collect statistics for the world (Singleton et al., 1988).

One of the earliest studies to make use of official death records was *Emile Durkheim's* classic study *Le Suicide* (1897/1951). In the late eighteenth century, many European nations began to compile data from death certificates, including cause of death as well as personal characteristics of the deceased, such as sex, age, and marital status. Several scholars before Durkheim focused on suicide as a specific cause and further compiled and published data relating suicide rates to such variables as religion, season of the year, gender, and marital status (Singleton et al., 1988). Using these data, he took the official suicide statistics of different countries and analyzed them to see if he could identify variables that would mean that some people are more likely to commit suicide than others. He found, for example, that Catholics were less likely to commit suicide than Protestants. In this way, he took data that had been collected for quite a different purpose and used it in his own study—but he had to do a lot of comparisons and statistical correlations himself to analyze the data (Baltimore County Public Schools, 2017). After completing his secondary analysis, Durkheim rejected several hypotheses popular at the time, such as that suicide was exclusively the result of mental illness, and ultimately arrived at his influential theory that a lack of social integration contributes to suicides. Supporting his theory were data showing that suicide rates were lowest when social ties were strong (as among persons who are married and members of religions that emphasize social cohesion) and highest when social ties were weak (as among the divorced and members of religions that emphasize individualism) (Singleton et al., 1988).

Perhaps the most widely used public storehouse of data is that collected by the *U.S. Census Bureau*. According to the Constitution, every person in the nation must be counted at least once every 10 years. Data from these decennial censuses, which began in 1790, are made available in two different forms: aggregate and individual. Aggregate data describe various characteristics of the population of the states, counties, metropolitan areas, cities and towns, neighborhood tracts, and blocks. The censuses of population and housing gather detailed information on the composition of every household in the country, including data on the age, gender, race, and marital status of each person, and numerous household characteristics, such as value of home or monthly rent, and number of rooms. Researchers have utilized this data to study everything from the ecology of cities to residential mobility and racial segregation (Singleton et al., 1988). Therefore, publicly available data can examine questions about aggregated patterns or trends in drug use or crime in general, the covariation in two estimates of crime, or significant change in fatal violence. Publicly available data also have the advantage of being readily available; a web search or a trip to the library can quickly place several data series at your disposal (Maxfield & Babbie, 2014). You can obtain copies of most publications by the BJS and other Justice Department offices on the Internet; most documents published since about 1994 are available in digital and often times downloadable form. Some formerly printed data reports are now available only in digital format. Additionally, there are many advantages to utilizing digital electronic formats. Data fields may be read directly into statistical or graphics computer programs for analysis. Many basic crime data can be downloaded from the BJS website in spreadsheet formats or read directly into presentation software. More importantly, complete data series are available in digital formats (Maxfield & Babbie, 2014). Of particular interest to criminal justice and criminological inquiry are the original survey data. While the printed reports of the National Crime Victimization Survey (NCVS) limit you to summary tabulations, digital and optical media include the original survey data from 80,000 or more respondents (Maxfield & Babbie, 2014). As a word of caution, before using any secondary data sources, researchers must consider issues centering on reliability and validity, as well as how well the secondary data meet their specific primary and research inquiries (Maxfield & Babbie, 2014).

Secondary Analysis

As stated earlier, many government organizations routinely collect and publish compilations of data. Popular examples for criminological researchers include the FBI, BJS, and FBP, and over the last 40 years, the social sciences have seen a remarkable increase of data archives, which are repositories of data collected by various agencies and researchers that are accessible to the public. Many of these archives contain survey data as well as collections of ethnographies, as the use of data archives is an extension of both survey research and field research (Singleton et al., 1988). As such, each archival data source possesses both advantages and disadvantages associated with two different approaches to social research. One popular approach utilized by criminologists is the analysis of available survey data, called *secondary analysis.*

In most of the examples presented thus far, each survey had a central topic and the researchers were responsible for all phases of the study, from the formulation of the primary question and research design to the collection, analysis, and management of the data. This once was the most popular way to conduct a study; however, currently researchers are more inclined to analyze survey data collected by some other person or agency than to conduct an original survey themselves (Presser, 1985). The analysis of survey data by researchers other than the primary investigator who collected the data is called secondary analysis. The earliest application of secondary analysis was to census data and then, beginning in the 1950s, to opinion-poll data (Singleton et al., 1988). The major push for secondary analysis came in the 1970s with the advent of surveys designed specifically for the purpose of making data available to the social science research community A noteworthy example is the *General Social Survey (GSS)*, started in 1972, that was conducted annually (except for 1979, 1981, and

1992) until 1994. Each GSS involved personal interviews with about 1,500 respondents, drawn from a probability sample of the adult population of the United States (Maxfield & Babbie, 2014). In comparison to most surveys, which have a central topic, the GSS is diverse, with questions pertaining to a broad range of attitudes and behaviors. A portion of each GSS includes questions that are replicated across years to aid research on social trends. The remainder of each survey is devoted to topical and cross-national studies, which comprise blocks of questions relating to special topics. These enormous amounts of GSS data are deposited in two main archives: the ICPSR (Inter-university Consortium for Political and Social Research) and the Roper Center for Public Opinion Research (Maxfield & Babbie, 2014).

Quantitative Content Analysis

One of the problems with the analysis of written documents is the bias of who is doing the reading, which results in very different perspectives regarding the same information, leading to the lack of agreement or reliability. One way to overcome this problem is to be precise about how one should read the text. In fact, it is possible to develop systematic and objective criteria for transforming written text into useful quantitative or qualitative content analysis. That is the goal of content analysis. Researchers use content analysis to analyze the symbolic content of communication, especially verbal materials from the media (Maxfield & Babbie, 2014; Singleton et al., 1988). This involves selecting and defining a set of content categories, operationalizing and then sampling the elements of the text that are described by the categories, quantifying the categories (perhaps by counting their frequency of occurrence), and then relating category frequencies to one another or to other variables. More than just a single technique, content analysis is a set of methods for analyzing the symbolic content of any communication. The basic idea is to reduce the total content of a communication (e.g., all of the words or all of the visual imagery) to a set of categories that represent some characteristic of research interest. Thus, content analysis may involve the systematic description of either verbal or nonverbal materials (Maxfield & Babbie, 2014; Singleton et al., 1988).

Criminologists have utilized content analysis to examine interviews and have applied it to verbal responses that are designed to assess the psychological states of persons. So, its application is not limited to the examination of existing data. Still, its most common application is to the available printed or spoken word. Content analysis has been applied to written documents with varied and complex content, including newspaper editorials, recorded speeches, and television episodes, to name a few. One need only follow a few simple steps to ensure that the analysis is carried out correctly.

Operationalizing Content Categories

Selecting and defining the categories for content analysis is equivalent to deciding on a set of closed-ended questions in survey research. Instead of giving the questions to respondents who provide the answers, the researcher applies them to a document and codes the appropriate category. The "questions" applied to the document should be adequate for the primary and research questions, and the categories should be clearly operationalized, exhaustive, and mutually exclusive (Singleton et al., 1988). Regardless of whether a researcher codes firsthand or uses a computer to code, the reliability and overall value of the content analysis is dependent on the clear formulation of content categories and rules for assigning units to categories.

Operationalize the Type of Content and the Unit of Analysis

There are two primary types of content to analyze: manifest and latent. Manifest content includes that content which is objective, in your face—easy to read and not open to interpretation. Examples would be "How many people were quoted in the article?" or "Who were the people quoted in the article?" Latent content on the other hand is that content which is underlying—meaning it is more subjective and requires some interpretation from the analyst. To identify a tone of anger or sarcasm is latent content—this is not easy to read or objective. When conducting a quantitative content analysis, researchers will use manifest content only. Using a qualitative analysis (thematic analysis) typically requires examining latent content (in addition to manifest content). However, the two types of content are not mutually excluded to just qualitative or quantitative research (Neuendorf, 2002).

Researchers refer to the units of analysis as recording units (see Chapter 7 for more on units of analysis). The unit is that element of the text that is described by the content categories. It could be a single word or symbol, a sentence, paragraph, whole text, or some other aspect of the text such as a character (Singleton et al., 1988). Generally speaking, smaller units can be coded more reliably than larger units because they contain less information; however, smaller units such as words may not be sufficient to extract the meaning of the message, and there may be too many units for the researcher to manage. Because it may not be possible to place a recording unit in a particular category without considering the context in which it appears, researchers also employ the use of context units (Singleton et al., 1988). To fit properly into one of these categories, the coder would need to consider the larger context unit, meaning the sentence, paragraph, or possibly the whole work in which the words are embedded to ascertain the true meaning of the recorded word.

System of Enumeration for Quantitative Data Collection in Content Analyses

There are a number of ways to quantify data in a content analysis. Some of the most basic systems of quantification utilized are:

- *Time-space measures*: Early analysis of newspapers often measured the space devoted to certain topics. Whereas television content has been measured in time (e.g., number of hours of violent TV).

- *Appearance*: Simply recording whether a given category appears in a recording unit.

- *Frequency*: How many times a given category appears in a unit (the most common method of measuring content).

- *Intensity*: Used when attitudes and values are the subject of research. Asking "how important is money to you" rather than the standard "is money important to you" (Maxfield & Babbie, 2014).

How the researcher decides to enumerate the data is dependent upon the research question under investigation.

Conducting the Analysis

Coding Scheme

Determining how to code content often requires researchers to conduct a preliminary analysis—so they should look at the content or some sample of it to see what themes arise (Hsieh & Shannon, 2005; Neuendorf, 2002). This is particularly useful when enumerating data and using a deductive approach. However, if using an inductive approach (meaning no assumptions made about the content), researchers may use something called open coding (Strauss & Corbin, 1990). This is used so that the content determines the analysis (Braun & Clarke, 2006). In this case, the researchers would look at the data and start determining what content stuck out or seemed of interest—without trying to establish any themes. It would only be after full analysis that they would see what was coded as "of interest" to determine how that content is related and if that content can be collapsed into themes. This is not only of use with content using language—it can also be used for images.

As a very simple example, go to Google and search drug use. Then click on images and look at the first page or so of images that you see. Remember that we did not search "drug abuse" or "drug addiction" or "illegal drug use." Can you look at those first ten images and make some conclusions or connections about their themes? Considering that tobacco is the most used drug (to the best of our knowledge), it is interesting that none of these pictures have tobacco products in them. They represent illegal drug dealing, drug addiction, polydrug use, and seeking help for drug use. This could serve as a preliminary analysis; however, if we were using open coding, we would simply want to write down what is interesting about *each image*—what sticks out to us. Because a great deal of content analyses uses an inductive approach, there can be problems with biases—so it is often important to have more than one researcher conducting the analysis, as this can help to keep biases in check.

Advantages and Disadvantages of Secondary Data

The biggest advantage of using secondary data is economics, as it is cheaper and faster than collecting original data. Someone else has already collected the data, so the researcher does not have to devote money, time, energy, and resources to this phase of research. As Maxwell and Babbie (2014) contended, depending on who did the original study, you may benefit from the work of topflight professionals and esteemed academics (Maxfield & Babbie, 2014). Additionally, many times the data are already collected, cleaned, and stored in digital format, so the researcher can spend most of the time analyzing the data instead of getting the data ready for analysis (Crossman, 2017).

Another positive of using secondary data is the extent of data available. The federal government conducts various studies on a large, national scale. Many of these data sets are also longitudinal, meaning that the same data has been collected from the same population over several different time periods, allowing a researcher to look at trends, trajectories, and changes of phenomena over time.

A final advantage worth noting when utilizing secondary data is that the data collection process is conducted by those with a high level of expertise in data management that may be lacking in individual researchers or small research projects. For example, data collection for many federal datasets, such as NCVS (National Crime Victimization Survey), is often performed by employees who specialize in data management and have many years of experience in the subject area and with the instrument. A number of smaller research projects may lack that level of expertise, with a good bit of data being collected by graduate students (Crossman, 2017).

Some of the disadvantages worth noting when utilizing secondary data include that as-is, the data may not answer the researcher's specific primary and research questions. The data may also be from a different location or from different years than preferred, or from a different population that the researcher was not set to study. Since the researcher did not collect the data, they have no control over what is contained in the dataset. This can result in limiting the analysis or the researcher having to alter their original primary and research questions. A related problem is the variables within the data set may have been operationalized differently than the researcher would have preferred. For example, income may have been bucketed into categories for collection as opposed to collecting it as a continuous variable, or race may have been collected as "Black," "White," and "Other" instead of containing categories for the major races in the research location (Crossman, 2017).

A final disadvantage of note is that the researcher is not aware of how the data collection was done and how well it was carried out. The researcher is not usually privy to information about how the data is affected by problems such as low response rate or respondent misunderstanding of survey questions. Sometimes this information is available, as is the case with many federal datasets. However, a number of secondary data sets are not accompanied by this type of information and the researcher must learn to discover implied as opposed to explicit issues with the data and consider what problems might have tainted the data collection process (Crossman, 2017).

Crime Mapping

Crime mapping has been traced to the early 1800s when social scientists began creating maps to illustrate their crime theories and research. Social scientists Adolphe Quetelet and A. M. Guerry are credited as being two of the first researchers to utilize spatial analysis to examine crime. Using crime and other social data from France, they determined that crime was not evenly distributed across space, and it clustered geographically with other variables such as socioeconomic status and population density (Hill & Paynich, 2013). In the 1900s, New York City and other large metropolitan departments began utilizing the pin maps that you sometimes see in old movies or even utilized in *The Simpsons* by Chief Clancy Wiggum to catch the Springfield cat burglar.

It was not until 1960s and 1970s that crime maps were created using computers and not until the 1990s when these computers had the ability to be integrated with law enforcement record management systems and made mapping possible for many law enforcement agencies. In general, large departments with an extensive data collection personnel that serve a geographically dispersed population while providing adequate funding for training and equipment expenses have had the most success in adopting crime mapping as a strategy. Midsized and smaller agencies have been slower to adopt a crime mapping policy, largely due to a lack of data, resources, and personnel (Hill & Paynich, 2013). So how is all of this possible by simply having a digital map? It is possible because of the computer software known as *Geographic Information Systems (GIS)*.

GIS is a kind of computer software that allows users to process geographically related data. It uses geography and computer-generated maps to translate physical elements in the real world (roads, rivers, mountains, buildings) into forms that can be displayed, manipulated, and analyzed (Ferreira, João, & Martins, 2012). This information is stored in virtual layers (one layer for each variable) to be displayed on the computer in the form of a multilayer, virtual map (Hill & Paynich, 2013). These layers of data about the location of a crime, incident, suspect, or victim can be crucial in determining the method and intensity of police response as it enables the user to layer the data, via vector or raster, and view the data most critical to the particular problem facing law enforcement. Within a GIS environment, every element on the map corresponds to a row of data in an attribute table. *Raster data*, on the other hand, is an image, most commonly for criminal justice and criminology an aerial/satellite photo. The *raster image* is a grid formed by pixels and depending on its resolution can be larger (less resolution) or smaller (higher resolution) (Ferreira et al., 2012). GIS and crime mapping are used worldwide by law enforcement to provide mapping solutions for crime analysis, criminal tracking, traffic safety, community policing, and a number of other tasks.

So, where does all the information about different crimes come from and how does it get into the GIS software? Many times, this is accomplished by trained personnel within a police department or organization called a *crime analyst*. Their duties often include collecting, organizing, distilling, interpreting, and presenting data and information regarding all aspects of crimes law enforcement are called to investigate. They are typically tasked with a long list of duties, such as diagnosing emerging crime trends, creating administrative reports, and identifying likely suspects (White, 2008). The process of matching a call for service with a particular address where the incident took place is called *geocoding*. Before using GIS to analyze data, all the information must be geocoded. *Geocoding* is the process of linking an address with the map coordinates so that the address can be displayed on the map. Normally in crime mapping, the address of a record is geocoded to a line street segment which is dependent on the accuracy and the detail of the responding officer's report (Ferreira et al., 2012). A single layer may be displayed, or several layers can be combined to show relationships among the layers. In crime mapping, the layers sit atop one another, resulting in an overall picture of crime and its spatial distribution (Hill & Paynich, 2013). GIS allows the researcher to examine the layers individually or layer them over top of each other to gain a better visual representation of the entire crime problem of a given geography.

Many different types of maps can be generated; however, the real-world data in GIS are represented by four features within the software:

- *Point features*: A location depicted by a symbol or label. Different symbols represent the location of crimes, motor vehicle crashes, traffic signs, buildings, police stations, cell towers, etc.
- *Line features*: A geographic feature that can be represented by a line or set of lines, such as streets, rivers, and railways.
- *Polygon features*: A multisided figure represented by a closed set of lines, which represent the geographic location of neighborhood boundaries, census tracts, or city blocks.
- *Image features*: A photo (usually taken from an airplane or satellite) that is digitized and placed within the GIS coordinates that are associated with it (Hill & Paynich, 2013).

Each one of the four features contains data that describe it. Simply clicking on a point, line, polygon, or image can produce the data associated with that particular feature. For example, the researcher can identify a specific point on the map and be instantly given detailed information, such as victim and offender characteristics, motives for the crime, and temporal and spatial details about the incident in question (Hill & Paynich, 2013). The things that can be accomplished with crime mapping and GIS are numerous as they provide law enforcement the ability to:

1. Analyze crime data to identify crime patterns and series
2. Identify and highlight suspicious incidents and events that may require further investigation

3. Support pattern and trend analysis across multiple jurisdictions

4. Enhance the implementation of various policing methodologies to reduce over-all crime and disorder

5. Integrate traditional and nontraditional law enforcement data to improve overall analysis

6. Educate the public with visual information to clarify crime concerns and enlist community action

7. Understand events and dynamics in a neighborhood, including persons, events, and crime hazards.

8. Identify risk factors including businesses, buildings, or other locations that draw crime.

Risk Terrain Modeling (RTM)

Risk Terrain Modeling is an approach that utilizes separate map layers representing the spatial influence of features of a landscape created in GIS to assess relative risk of a given geographical area (Caplan & Kennedy, 2010). Combining risk map layers produces a composite risk terrain map with values that account for the spatial influences of all features at every place throughout the landscape. RTM represents a statistically valid way to articulate crime-prone areas according to the spatial influence of many features of a given landscape, such as parks, schools, bars, pawn shops, and entertainment districts providing users with a Relative Risk Value (RRV) for density or proximity of risk factors for a given spatial influence (often city blocks). These risk values do not suggest the inevitability of crime, rather they identify locations where, if the conditions are right, the risk of criminality will be high (Caplan, Kennedy, Barnum, & Piza, 2015, p. 8). As such, one or more features of the physical environment can elevate the risk of crime. As risk factors are identified, police and researchers can begin to implement strategies to mitigate the specific risks associated with the given geographic area. Additionally, police use RTM to be problem oriented and proactive in their effort to prevent new crimes (Caplan et al., 2015, p. 14). As all places may pose certain risks but, because of the spatial influence of certain features of the landscape, some places are no doubt riskier than others. RTM helps to explain why spatial patterns of crime exist in a jurisdiction and what can be done to mitigate risks, not just chase the hotspots. With such spatial intelligence (Kennedy & Caplan, 2012), key stakeholders can identify the most vulnerable areas in a jurisdiction, enabling them to predict, with a certain level of confidence, the most likely places where criminality will occur.

The reality of the situation is that law enforcement often suffers from limited resources. Crime mapping can help law enforcement efficiently and effectively match demands for service with service delivery. By knowing where the problems are, it also provides a visual means to proactively combat crime and communicate with citizens to build support (ESRI, 2008). Police working the street are aware of where the crime is flourishing. In addition to this knowledge, mapping over a period of months can help officers precisely view and understand underlying crime patterns and activities. For example, can certain types of crime be associated with a certain day of week or a particular time of day? Or, is a late-night alcohol establishment open till 5:00 a.m. a draw for criminals? Crime mapping can support law enforcement in developing more effective tactical approaches and deployment strategies for these specific days and locations, ultimately helping to inhibit crime by identifying trends and allocating resources to the problem locations (ESRI, 2008).

Summing It Up

The overwhelming majority of criminal justice and criminological research done today uses some version of secondary data in its analysis. Recall from an earlier chapter the expense that can occur from a simple mail-out questionnaire to 100 people. You must pay for the paper to create the questionnaire, the envelopes, the stamps, the follow up post-card, and the return postage. The cost of an easy survey can quickly spiral out of control, which led to our discussion of secondary data. Although it is often gathered by police departments, businesses, or government agencies for purposes completely different than the ones you might be interested in examining, these data are still a rich source of information for researchers. Whether one is utilizing secondary analysis of survey questions, using content analysis techniques on some old TV shows, or geo-coding 1,000 calls for service from the local police department into GIS software, they are all secondary data techniques and come with own set of pros and cons, as do techniques utilizing primary data collection. The researcher has to figure out which kind of data and analysis works best to answer their scientific query.

Discussion Questions

1. What are available records and how are they useful to social science research?

2. Describe how Emile Durkheim (in his book *Le Suicide*) and Clifford Shaw and Henry McKay (in their social disorganization research) used available records.

3. What is secondary analysis and how is it different form secondary data?

4. What is quantitative content analysis?

5. Imagine you were helping a fellow student understand the process of conducting a quantitative content analysis. Provide a plain-language example of conducting a quantitative content analysis using the steps from the chapter.

6. What are the systems of quantification? Name and explain each one.

7. Is crime mapping a new phenomenon? How and when was crime mapping developed?

8. What is Geographic Information Systems? What are the features of GIS?

9. What is geocoding? Explain the process of geocoding.

10. What are the four features that GIS software can generate? Explain each one.

11. GIS software is a valuable tool in law enforcement. Identify and describe two situations in which GIS software would be particularly useful.

Trying It Out

Your professor may ask you to complete the following companion assignment available from the publisher. Using the supplied worksheet form, you are going to explore what type of secondary datasets are available on crime and criminal justice.

References

Baltimore County Public Schools. (2017). Develop a research proposal. *Research Course*. Retrieved from https://www.bcps.org/offices/lis/researchcourse/develop_writing_data_secondary.html.

Braun, V., & Clarke, V. (2006). Using thematic analysis in psychology. *Qualitative Research in Psychology*, 3(2), 77–101.

Caplan, J.M., & Kennedy, L.W. (2010). Risk Terrain Modeling Manual: Theoretical Framework and Technical Steps of Spatial Risk Assessment. Newark, NJ: Rutgers Center on Public Security.

Caplan, J.M., Kennedy, L.W., Barnum, J.D., and Piza, E.L. (2015). Risk terrain modeling for spatial risk assesment. *Cityscape: A Journal of Policy Development and Research*, 17(1), 7–16.

Crossman, A. (2017). Pros and cons of secondary data analysis: A review of the advantages and disadvantages in social science research. *ThoughtCo*. Retrieved from https://www.thoughtco.com/secondary-data-analysis-3026536.

Durkheim, E. (1951[1897]). *The divison of labor in society*. S. Lukes (Ed.). New York: Free Press.

ESRI. (2008). *Crime analysis: GIS solutions for intelligence-led policing*. Retrieved from http://www.esri.com/library/brochures/pdfs/crime-analysis.pdf.

Ferreira, J., João, P., & Martins, J. (2012). GIS for crime analysis: Geography for predictive models. *The Electronic Journal Information Systems Evaluation*, 15(1).

Hennigan, K. M. (2015). Targeting youth at risk for gang involvement. Elsevier B.V. Vol. 56 (56), pp. 86–96.

Hill, B., & Paynich, R. (2013). *Fundamentals of crime mapping*. Jones & Bartlett Publishers.

Hsieh, H.-F., & Shannon, S. E. (2005). Three approaches to qualitative content analysis. *Qualitative Health Research*, 15(9), 1277–1288.

Johnson, C. P. (2000). *Crime mapping and analysis using GIS*. Paper presented at the Geomatics Group, Pune, India.

Kennedy, L.W., & Caplan, J.M. (2012). A Theory of Risky Places. http://www.rutgerscps.org/docs/RiskTheoryBrief_web.pdf.

Maxfield, M., & Babbie, E. (2014). *Research methods for criminal justice and criminology*. Boston, MA: Cengage Learning.

Neuendorf, K. A. (2002). *The content analysis guidebook*. Sage.

Presser, S. (1985). The use of survey data in basic research in the social sciences. In C. F. Turner & E. Martin (Eds.), *Surveying subjective phenomenon* (pp. 93–115). New York: Russell Sage Foundation.

Shaw, C. R., & McKay, H. D. (1942). *Juvenile delinquency and urban areas*. Chicago: University of Chicago Press.

Singleton, R., Jr., Straits, B. C., Straits, M. M., & McAllister, R. J. (1988). *Approaches to social research*. Oxford University Press.

Strauss, A., & Corbin, J. M. (1990). *Basics of qualitative research: Grounded theory procedures and techniques*. Thousand Oaks, CA: Sage Publications, Inc.

White, M. B. (2008). Enhancing the problem-solving capacity of crime analysis units. Center for Problem-Oriented Policing, Arizona State University. Retrieved from http://www.popcenter.org/tools/enhancing_capacity/.

Chapter 10

Ethnographies, Interviews, and Qualitative Content Analyses

Learning Objectives

- Evaluate the utility of quantitative versus qualitative research by examining research questions and purposes
- Compare and contrast qualitative and quantitative research
- Identify and define categories of qualitative methods
- Explain differences in qualitative data collection and qualitative analysis
- Compare and contrast inductive and deductive approaches
- Recognize types of qualitative research
- Describe research-participant contact in quantitative and qualitative research
- Evaluate the role of bias in quantitative and qualitative research
- Evaluate the role of language in quantitative and qualitative research
- Compare and contrast qualitative and quantitative interviews
- Describe the procedure for a study using qualitative interviews
- Discuss the strengths and weaknesses of focus groups
- Describe the importance of place in conducting interviews
- Identify the unit of analysis within qualitative research studies
- Recall issues that can arise when recruiting hard-to-access populations
- Describe the importance of reflexivity in qualitative research
- Determine how and when field notes should be recorded based off the situational context

While there are many interesting topics in criminology and criminal justice, one that seems to fascinate most students is the study of serial killers. While studying serial killers is challenging for a number of reasons, one reason is because it is hard to gain access to them. Keeping that in mind, what if you were a researcher and you had the opportunity to meet with some prolific serial killers? You have two choices:

you can interview them, or ask them to fill out a questionnaire about their crimes. Which would you pick?

I am assuming you picked interviews because there is so much information that you could gain from interviews. If you picked filling out a questionnaire—then I've completely failed in my example. Further, all you would have access to would be the responses from the survey instrument—there would be no follow-up questions. You would have to hope that you covered everything you want to know in that survey instrument. In a case like this, that is doubtful. While there are many reasons that interviews might be appealing, one reason is that there is no one strong theory to frame the motivations of serial killers, particularly because there are so few of them (in relation to, say, marijuana users) and one or two exceptions to a pattern has a much bigger impact on a small group rather than a large one.

When we lack a clear understanding of what it is we aim to study, we want to leave things open so that we can begin to develop a deeper understanding of the phenomenon. When we do not have a strong theoretical foundation, trying to conduct quantitative research is *hard*, especially if attempting to construct a survey instrument. It would become even more challenging to construct a survey instrument with closed-ended answer choices, because then you have to make sure that you know what to ask and how the research participant would answer. This would be similar to me attempting to write questions for an organic chemistry test. If I had a strong foundation, this would not be too challenging (especially if I also had access to textbook and class materials). However, without that foundation and class materials, I would only have one question for a test on organic chemistry: tell me everything you know about organic chemistry.

This is why qualitative research is valuable—it provides researchers with a place to start and to develop *deeper understanding* of some phenomenon. There are certain experiences in life that are not easily quantifiable. For instance, graduating from high school. If asked how excited you were on a scale of one to ten, you can report a ten—but that does not really get to the depth of your excitement. Or, perhaps, you reported a one, because you were not at all excited about graduating high school. Such an answer would warrant a need for follow-up and understanding about why you were *not* excited to graduate high school.

Qualitative research is just how it sounds—it deals with qualities of something. It is often focused on processes and how to contextualize those processes. Qualitative researchers seek to determine the meaning of these processes and social phenomena (Creswell, 2013). There are three main categories of qualitative methods: *fieldwork* (*participant observation*), *interviewing*, and *focus groups*. These methodologies, however, only focus on how the data are collected. If you remember, data collection and data analysis are two very different things! So, we will also talk about how qualitative data are analyzed through data reduction and content analysis.

Similar to most topics in this book, we will "hit the highlights" of each type of qualitative methodology, but please remember, this is only the tip of the iceberg. Just like quantitative research, qualitative research is hard and requires training, practice, and — to a certain extent — innate ability!

Quantitative vs. Qualitative Methodologies

Social science researchers tend to prefer either qualitative or quantitative methods. There are certainly strengths *and* weaknesses to both qualitative and quantitative methodologies, and in reality, there is a time and a place for each type of research.

Approach

From the example in the beginning of this chapter, researching serial killers, you have probably gathered that qualitative research, as compared to quantitative, has a different purpose from the start. This goes back to what we discussed in Chapter 1: there are two types of reasoning within research (and they are not always mutually exclusive): inductive and deductive. *Deductive research* is most often paired with quantitative research, and *inductive research* with qualitative. When there is already theory that is strongly developed, it is more likely that a researcher would use a deductive approach. However, when there is no theory, or theory that has not been strongly supported by literature, there may be a need to develop a new theory, or modify an old one.

In this case, qualitative methodology would likely be best. Qualitative research typically focuses on processes and not just results. A quantitative research question might ask "what" or "who," like "what is the relationship between marijuana use and brownie consumption" or "who are marijuana users?" A qualitative research question will most often start with why or how, such as "Why do people use marijuana?" or "How do marijuana users share their marijuana in social settings?"

Yet, let it be said that before developing any theory, there is a need to understand what actually exists. We cannot explain why chocolate chip cookies are so darn delicious if we cannot describe what a chocolate chip cookie *is*, how to make them, and what the ingredients are. Thus, before we just start trying to explain, we need to describe — and we do not need to describe just a little bit — we need to describe every single detail. This is often referred to as *ethnographic research. Ethnographic research* (or *ethnographies*) stems mostly from anthropologists, who would conduct ethnographies to study cultures and social dynamics. The outcome of ethnographies should be to answer the question — using a thick, rich, description — "what is going on here?" The report from an ethnographer on chocolate chip cookies would look similar to one of those food blogs — where all you want is the darn recipe but before then you have to scroll through how their kids wanted some chocolate chip cookies and they modified this old-time recipe to make something much more super-duper (and do not forget the endless Instagram-filtered pictures of the cookies, too).

Researcher-Participant Contact

Regarding *researcher-participant contact*, quantitative research generally requires little contact between the researcher and the research participants. For instance, if I were to give a survey to college students, the most in-person contact that might occur is when I (the researcher) handed out a paper survey instrument to the students. While other types of quantitative research might require more interaction (like in-person survey interviews or telephone surveys), there is still little *unstructured* interaction. Meaning, there is not much small or free talk.

Qualitative research (typically) requires a whole lot more interaction with participants, particularly when it involves interviews or fieldwork. Qualitative researchers rely on the openness of their participants to collect data. To gain openness from a participant requires **building a rapport**. Different qualitative researchers take different approaches on how to build that rapport, but small talk is almost always required! Research subjects have to feel some sort of trust with the researcher. This is more than just anonymity and confidentiality, particularly in criminological research. Participants want to know that you can understand their actions and motivations (in some way or another), and that you *will not judge them*. Who wants to open up to someone just to have them act judgmental? No one!

This contact between the researcher and participant is incredibly valuable to the study and to the development of theory and context. As a researcher, seeing the response "strongly agree" to a statement like "I feel guilty for the crimes I've committed" is different from a participant telling a researcher "I feel guilty for the crimes I've committed." One of the main reasons is because of body language, as it can transform the meaning of such a statement. If a research subject has their arms crossed and are smirking while saying this, the sincerity of that statement might be questionable. Conversely, someone who says they feel guilty while avoiding eye contact and looking down and also crying conveys an entirely different meaning, one that is completely lost within a quantitative survey instrument. While that contact is invaluable, it also has its downside. Contact and rapport leads to subjectivity and interpretations of body language and its meaning, which can threaten the validity of qualitative research.

Bias

One of the main concerns with qualitative research is the degree of *bias* that occurs within the study, and how that affects interpretation of the data. In qualitative research, the researcher is often the sole or primary research instrument, instead of a questionnaire. Even in interviews where there is a questionnaire of some sort present, the interviewer (typically the primary researcher or someone on the research team) has a big part in determining what from that questionnaire will be asked and can choose to ask additional questions. Also, how the actions and wording are interpreted are very much up to the researcher(s) and their perceptions.

We all perceive the world a bit differently. Imagine you and your friend **Bob** meet **Jane**. The two of you interact with **Jane** for a bit. When you and **Bob** leave, you turn to **Bob** and say "Wow, **Jane** was great, don't you think?" and **Bob** says "What are you talking about?! She was totally rude! I hope I never have to talk to her again!" You may have been in a situation similar to this (perhaps *as* **Bob**). This is because we interpret language, including words, gestures, and facial expressions, differently. Moreover, some people are just more attuned to people's behaviors than others. So, is bias possible with qualitative research? Certainly! It is rare that someone can have contact with research subjects and not have some sort of bias. However, to what degree that bias threatens the validity of the research is not within the bias itself— it is how the bias is recognized and how it is managed. The *denial* of bias is where the trouble can start!

Is there bias with my students? Sure! If I have had a student a few semesters and have developed a good rapport with them and seen them do well in my classes, I will initially have a different reaction to them doing poorly on an assignment compared to a student who has consistently done subpar work in my class. The initial reaction, however, does not affect the outcome—the grade is not different for either student. Another way (when feasible) that I attempt to *prevent* my biases from getting in the way is by not looking at who submitted the assignment. This is particularly useful when grading essays—I do not want to know whose is whose—that way, I do not even have to question if I allowed any biases to get in the way.

Therefore, just like we have sampling techniques and research designs to strengthen quantitative research, there are similar methods to strengthen qualitative research. However, in quantitative research, we typically try to control for validity before the study even starts. Qualitative research is a bit more challenging, as many of the threats to validity arise after a study has started. So, they must be worked into the study as it goes (the techniques for validity measures in qualitative research are audit trail; thick, rich description; and feedback/peer debriefing, which will be discussed later in this chapter).

Language

When it comes to *language*, qualitative research focuses on being thick and rich in its descriptions. Detail is key. In some ways, qualitative research is like creative writing: setting up the scene and providing context and understanding of the results to enhance their meaning. However, do not take this comparison to mean that the creative style of qualitative research diminishes its validity—it is simply another approach. Quantitative research, on the other hand, has dry and to-the-point writing, particularly when presenting the results.

To give you an example of qualitative research: in 2008, Heith Copes, Andy Hochstetler, and J. Patrick Williams published research that included interviews with male offenders (specifically, they were examining methods of avoiding being labeled crackheads). Within their results, they provided the following description of social connections:

> Another resource was the social connections that benefitted them in criminal pursuits. Most respondents liked to think of themselves in the center of a criminal network where there was some camaraderie or mutual respect based on one's character. Some interviewees reported social relationships that provided resources and respectful deference. Most had an abstract understanding that nothing was dependable in the hustling life. Nevertheless, a modicum of street success and display of success meant that other hustlers included them in crimes and shared with them. Also, drug customers, friends, family, or lovers would contribute to their needs and tastes, supporting their lifestyles and their leisure interests (p. 261).

Conversely, in 2002, using quantitative research methodology, Andy Hochstetler, Heith Copes, and Matt DeLisi examined the relationship between delinquent peer association and crime. The following is an excerpt from the results of their study:

> Turning to group crime, all independent variables were significant predictors of group offending. Predictably, significance levels dropped since there were fewer cases of group offending than total offending. Nevertheless, findings revealed that the effects on group crime held independent of the effects on attitude; the influence of friends' attitudes only fell to insignificant levels for assault. Friends' behaviors maintained its significance for all three crimes (p. 563).

Hopefully, you observed some differences in the writing styles. Also, I hope you noticed that two of the authors (Andy Hochstetler and Heith Copes) were *also* authors on the first article. However, their writing style was very different from one to the other—as it should be!

In addition to different writing styles, qualitative research projects typically result in longer manuscripts than quantitative research projects. A lot of this has to do with the writing style. Providing context and thick, rich description requires a few more words than reporting numbers! Additionally, when presenting the results, the researchers are often providing examples of their findings with lengthy quotations. If you have ever heard the saying that the "devil is in the detail," the same is true for qualitative research: the meaning is in the detail, too.

Interviews

The rules on survey research are pretty uniform. There are both ethical and methodological guidelines on survey construction and for survey distribution. Further, survey research can be learned. While there are guidelines for interviewing, many of them vary from person to person (and from discipline to discipline). There are three reasons that qualitative research (particularly good qualitative research) is so hard: one is that a lot of it can only be learned from doing it, there are unforeseen circumstances that arise in qualitative research, and to be a good qualitative researcher requires some innate talent. That being said, improvement does come with practice! Generally, a good interviewer must learn how to *establish rapport, communicate effectively*, and *think on their feet.*

When referring to interviews in qualitative research, I am generally referring to *in-depth interviews.* In quantitative research, interviews are used to deliver a survey instrument that often has closed-ended (or very short open-ended) questions. In-depth interviews are used by qualitative researchers to help develop theory and understanding of a particular issue. Remember that qualitative research is focused on processes, not just outcomes. Therefore, understanding the thinking process surrounding an issue is important within qualitative methodologies. In-depth interviews should result in data that contain detailed descriptions of certain phenomena and events within the participant's life. The researcher can then combine the data from multiple interviews to identify patterns and themes that emerge.

Interviews do not follow a strict set of rules because interviews are all so different, and there tends to be a degree of flexibility in the interview, often based on how the participant responds and perceives the questions. There are three degrees of structure within interviews that a researcher can execute: *highly structured interviews, semi-structured interviews,* and *low-structured interviews.* Those that are highly structured lack flexibility. The questions that are prepared are those which will be asked. There is little free thought or association from participants. While the interviewer will still record any additional information given by the participant, the interviewer does not usually encourage additional reflection/monologue from the participant. Highly structured interviews are typically reserved for quantitative research and not in-depth interviews. Semi-structured interviews are just how they sound: they are sort of structured. Interviewers still prepare questions and follow-up questions, but are not so structured that participants cannot take the conversation a bit off course. Semi-structured tends to build more rapport and make participants feel more at ease; and thus, they tend to give more open answers. In low-structured interviews, there are few (if any) questions, and none that the interviewer requires themselves to follow. The questions that are developed are broad and developed only to lead to understanding of the research question (Hesse-Biber & Leavy, 2010).

The degree of structure a researcher should implement in an interview is really dependent on how comfortable they are interviewing and what the goals are of the interview. If the researcher is trying to develop data that are thick and rich in description, then they likely want more long-winded, at times off-topic statements from participants. However, someone who is new to qualitative research should probably stick to semi-structured interviews. When possible, low structured should be left to the pros! Imagine the first time that you had to give a real presentation in front of a class. I am guessing that you had some sort of visual aids, note cards, a PowerPoint presentation — things like that. Now imagine all of that was taken away, and you were left with two questions on a sheet of paper. Some of you would probably respond splendidly, while others might freeze up! Until you know how comfortable you are and how you will react as the interviewer, give yourself more, not less, structure.

Interview Methodology and Questionnaire

Recruitment and Sampling

Qualitative research rarely uses random sampling techniques. One of the reasons is because, most often, qualitative researchers are not aiming to have their findings be generalizable. Instead, they are seeking to develop a deeper understanding of their research topic, develop theory, and understand processes. What they discover may or may not be true for most other people, but that tends to be immaterial to the qualitative researcher. Within interviews, what becomes of more importance is the quality and fit of the person who is being interviewed. If you have a dud fill out a survey instrument, this was not a great waste of time and energy. However, you probably do not want to spend two or three hours listening to a "dud" talk during an interview! For instance, if you were attempting to understand how burglars case houses, what characteristics they find appealing in homes, and what their steps of preparation are prior to burglarizing a home, you want to find a "real" burglar—not a teenager who broke into someone's home one time on a dare. Similarly, studying marijuana use should focus on participants who are habitual users, not those who used it once or twice in a social setting. Therefore, unlike in quantitative research, qualitative researchers might be a bit more selective in whom they interview (Marshall, 1996). Further, within criminological research, qualitative research is often reserved for those hard-to-access populations. This makes snowball sampling and convenience sampling prevalent within in-depth interviews.

Plan and Design

The flexibility that occurs within in-depth interviews should be saved solely for the actual interview. What makes qualitative researchers excellent researchers is the extensive planning that goes into the design of the study, prior to ever meeting with the participant. As the researcher, you should have a plan for the time questions should take, how you will record the data, who will be around, how you will provide informed consent, etc.

One of the best ways to plan is to practice and pilot the interviews. While it may seem best to just write what the participant says, this can create a formality within the interview that effects the candor of your participant, as they no longer feel that you are listening to them and reflecting on their thoughts and feelings. Also, you can miss a lot if you write things down! Tape recorders are often best for interviews, but these can affect how comfortable the participant feels, too. I would recommend not using some big clunky recording device, but something that the participant knows is there but can easily forget about (Davies, Francis, & Jupp, 2011).

When practicing for interviews, you will want to have someone around to critique your behavior and reactions. You want to remain objective to someone's statements so that you do not influence what they say next. If your participant informs you that they like to frequent a nudist colony, you have to be sure not to look shocked and be able to respond with something that is polite and respectful, all the while seeming natural and not-too-formal. It is important to picture yourself in the interview, and think about what might make the participant more comfortable. If you are going to interview men and women on Wall Street or if you are going to interview men and women who are currently homeless, dress accordingly! This does not mean that you perfectly mimic how they dress, but you want to fit in more than you want to stick out. The context and setup of the interview has an effect on the data you collect, which is why it is particularly important (Berg, 2004)!

Questionnaire Development

Within both semi-structured and low-structured interviews, there are usually topics that can be used as an interview guide for the interviewer. Even when there are few structured questions, the interviewer wants to make sure they have touched on each topic. If you have ever had a conversation with a friend and thought later "oh! I meant to ask them about …" then you are one who would benefit from an interview guide. It is like a checklist for conversation. You may not use the interview guide, but if you do, you'll be glad you had it.

There are likely questions that you will have that are closed-ended, such as demographic information. While this type of information is best at the end of a survey instrument, demographic questions (depending on the topic of the interview) can often be used in conjunction with small talk to create rapport and make the participant feel at ease.

One of my recommendations for early interviewers is to create the guide as an actual checklist. This way you can have what seem to be more open-ended, low-structured interviews that are actually a bit more semi-structured. For instance, say you want to know about marijuana use. You could simply ask "Tell me about your experience with marijuana." Then, your interview guide might include some specific topics that you hope they address within their statements and the conversation. Things like age at first use, use frequency, continued use over time, method of use, use in conjunction with other drugs, etc. are all possibilities. Each of these could be a subtopic, and if they do not address one of these areas, you can always follow up with an additional question. However, this will—ideally—keep you more focused on the answers they give rather than the questions you ask.

Interviewing Focus Groups

Another form of interviewing involves focus groups. As I discussed earlier, interviews are best when they seem like a natural conversation. This puts a lot of pressure on the interviewer! Sometimes, it is hard to play the role of the researcher, the interviewer, and the second person in the conversation. One method to increase the natural feeling of the conversation is to involve more people in it. Not only does this make things (hopefully) more natural, it also provides even richer data. While the researcher will still have questions (albeit, usually broader questions), the participants can often feed off of one another and might even ask their own questions. Further, they have no ethical quandaries about remaining objective. For instance, Interviewer Bob is interviewing Participant Jane about how she perceives the death penalty. Jane might tell Bob that she believes it is a just punishment for those who commit heinous crimes. While Bob can ask follow-up questions, he likely should avoid questions that may seem confrontational, as this may appear like he is challenging Jane. However, if Interviewer Bob were in a focus group, another participant, Shay, might ask seemingly confrontational questions to Jane, like "What about the cost of the death penalty?" or "What if someone was put to death who is innocent?" These types of interactions can make focus group data very rich in a way that one-on-one, in-depth interviews cannot achieve (Morgan, 1996).

The number of participants in a focus group can range from quite small to large; however, the ideal number is about four to eight people. Similar to a small discussion class, you want enough participants to create a group dynamic and conversation, but not so many that some are unable to speak and share their opinions (Kitzinger, 1995). Additionally, it is important to think about where the data will be collected (Kitzinger, 1995; Tong, Sainsbury, & Craig, 2007). If the conversation should seem natural, then it should occur somewhere that it is natural for people to have a conversation. That being said, there should also be consideration given to privacy and background noise (if planning to tape record the focus groups). Similar to other qualitative research, it is rare that a researcher will use a probability sampling technique for focus groups. One of the main reasons is because the individuals who are grouped together should most often be methodical. If Researcher Jane wants to examine individual's perceptions of police officers, she may want to consider whether she wants the group to be **homogenous**, meaning, all the same, or **heterogeneous**, meaning different. Perhaps Researcher Jane wants to have multiple groups that are comprised of participants who are demographically similar, but each group is distinct from every other, such as one group of upper-class white females, another group of upper-class Black females, another group of upper-class Hispanic females, another group of upper-class white males, etc.). Or, perhaps Jane wants the groups to be diverse. The methods used for grouping should be theoretically based and thought of in context of Jane's research goals. Sometimes groups may be naturally put together, such as people in the same classes, majors, workplace, etc. (Kitzinger, 1995; Morgan, 1996).

Field Research

My dog, Walter, goes to doggie daycare (yes, because I am that person). When he is at daycare, he acts totally different than when he is at home. He is much better behaved and less mouthy (though he still likes to bark quite a bit). Similarly, you probably act differently in the classroom than you do with your family, your friends, or when you are out on a weekend night. Those differences matter because they are layers of who you are and how your environment affects your behavior and your processes. Walter is no different—certain social cues affect his behaviors and thought processes, too.

When conducting interviews, researchers may often meet the participant on some sort of neutral ground. There are times when interviews are conducted at a place with which the participant is familiar (like their home or a local park), or at a place with which the researcher is familiar (such as the researcher's workplace). The place of data collection can be incredibly important in qualitative research, as it may affect how comfortable the participant is.

Another key part that is typically missing from interviews is the *effects of the place*. Unless the researcher has observed the participant's behavior in multiple environments, the researcher cannot be sure how their behavior changes due to the environment. For instance, I hate really, really fancy restaurants. One reason may be because I have not really frequented them! They tend to make me very uncomfortable. If a researcher were interviewing me at a fancy-schmancy restaurant, and has no interaction with me outside of the restaurant, they may not realize that I act differently when in another environment.

Interviews typically use individuals as the *unit of analysis*, but a lot of information can be lost this way. If Researcher JANE is wanting to research the process of drug dealing, interviews may not be the best methodological approach (particularly if it is the only methodology being used). JANE is not necessarily interested in *drug dealers*, but instead, she is interested in the *process* and *phenomenon* that is drug dealing. Her unit of analysis is more of a social artifact, but a "living" one, in that the processes are occurring in real time. The best way for her to understand drug dealing would be to observe drug deals and all the processes and preparation that go into each deal. This requires field work, which allows a researcher to collect data on a number of things: the environment, the individuals within that environment, and their inter-actions. Field research can involve frequent and short observations of participants, environments, or processes, or it can involve more in-depth involvement of the re-searcher—sometimes to the extent that the researcher actually lives in the environment they are researching. While this is quite a commitment, imagine that you want to understand homelessness. Which do you think would result in richer data and greater understanding of homelessness: observation and participation with homeless men and women or interviews with homeless men and women?

In the social sciences, a lot of our understanding of social dynamics and social phenomena have stemmed from field research. While this type of research is incredibly valuable, it is also incredibly costly, particularly in its time commitment. Additionally, while the data are incredibly valuable, there are a number of concerns with bias and subjectivity. Perhaps you are one who gets invested in characters when reading a book or watching a movie. I mean, people's feelings on *Star Wars*, Harry Potter, or *The Notebook* are not usually neutral and objective. That's because humans are emotional and caring, even with fictional characters! Now imagine how emotionally invested you can get with friends and family—even acquaintances. This does not get easier with field research, particularly when researching hard subjects like victimization, drug abuse, and criminality. Researchers often want to help, too. The question is, can a researcher be an advocate and not be biased? It is unlikely; however, bias is always within research—qualitative and quantitative. The validity of the study is not simply dependent on the bias of the researcher; it is the degree to which that bias is accounted for or controlled.

Gaining Access and Seeming Legit

The good news is that crime and those who commit crime are fascinating—and not just to criminologists! The general population happens to be very interested in crime (just look at the ratings for *Law and Order: SVU* or *CSI*). That being said, one of the things that makes these topics and people so interesting is that the more fascinating they seem, the harder it may be to gain access to them, particularly as a researcher. This is one reason qualitative research is so important—we cannot exactly put out a flyer recruiting all burglars to participate in our study (we touched on this in Chapter 7, "Units of Analysis, Samples, and Sampling"). Therefore, we need to access the population using creative methods. One method is snowball sampling, in which we might identify a gatekeeper. For instance, I may have a friend of a friend who has burglarized a few houses. Perhaps this friend of a friend knows other burglars, who—one by one—can introduce me to other burglars. Yet, there are many times when a researcher may not have such direct access to a burglar. This can become the biggest challenge of starting the research. Some other ways to find an initial gatekeeper is to think of some contact you have that is closest to being in contact with someone in your target population. Perhaps you do not know someone who burglarizes homes, but your shady friend **Bob** just finished community service (picking up trash on the highway). Perhaps Shady **Bob** met someone who has burglarized homes—Sketchy **Jane**—or perhaps they Sketchy **Jane** knows someone who knows someone. This is referred to as a ***chain of referrals*** (McCall, 1978; Wright, Decker, Redfern, & Smith, 1992).

There are times, however, when the *gatekeeper* is more than one person—it may be a group, an organization, or an entire culture. If you want to understand the world of strip clubs from the perspective of those who work in them, you are going to have to build some credibility and show that you are able to hang with them. They have to take you seriously in some context before they will probably trust you enough to share their thoughts and feelings. This can serve as an initiation of sorts—but it is important to remember that you are a researcher and any participation in activities should only be for purposes of research, while also not violating any ethical or legal boundaries. I (Vanessa Woodward Griffin) can probably not hang with an all-male motorcycle gang—I imagine I could not build the credibility necessary to establish rapport. However, Kyle Burgason might be able to, given his sex (male) and his stature (over six feet). However, credibility comes from more than just physical features—how one acts in situations will also affect whether rapport is built. You need them to be comfortable with you and your role as the observer/researcher (and rarely, participant, too)—so you need to be comfortable in your role as well. This does not mean to fake it—as the researcher, you should be honest about your intentions and who you are. That being said, the more you are like the population you aim to study, the easier it will probably be to establish rapport (Berk & Adams, 1970). This is one reason parents start having a hard time relating to their teenage kids. If parents start talking about "smoking the reefer" their kid will sense that there is a lot of social distance between them and their parents—meaning, to the kid, the social group to which the kid belongs seems nothing like the group to which his parents belong. While teens may find it laughable when their mom uses her own terminology, teens tend to be more accepting of this than when parents attempt to use their teens' terminology. For instance, if your mom said you were "on fleek" you would probably be horrified (let's be honest, I am too old to be saying it, too).

Additionally, within field research, you do not want to treat your participants as means to an end, but you also want to make it clear that you *really are just trying to collect data and conduct research—nothing more, nothing less.* **Richard Berk** and *Joseph Adams* outlined a number of rules for field researchers to build and maintain rapport, particularly with "deviant groups" (1970). They both state that rapport is more than just honesty—you have to follow through on any promises that you make, and you also have to explain your goals and your research in the right framework. For instance, if you wanted to interview sex offenders about their perceptions of the sex offender registry, you would not want to say to a potential participant "I want to understand how you're getting punished and how you perceive the government is keeping track of you to make sure you do not hurt women or children again." This probably will not gain you access to too many participants. Instead, you would want to say that you are attempting to understand their positive and negative experiences with being on the sex offender registry and what kind of impact it has had on their lives. You do not necessarily want to say they actually committed the crimes that they were convicted of, but instead, discuss the crimes as "what they were accused of" or "convicted of."

This line of thinking should extend into your research and data collection. You want to ensure that you are continually evaluating your own role within the research (by mentally taking a break and making sure you have not become too involved), and also to evaluate how you are reacting to those who are participating in your study. The attitude of a researcher is vital in field research (Berg, 2004). How the researcher approaches the subject with the participants will have an effect on how the participants respond. This is because in field research, the researcher essentially becomes the instrument. To validate "the instrument," biases have to be checked, and the researcher must also ensure that they are interpreting their observations correctly. For instance, if you judged certain actions on their face without context, you may interpret them incorrectly. In Venezuela, for instance, it is rude to show up on time.[1] If a field researcher did not know that, they might conclude that Venezuelans are not very con-

---

1. http://www.ediplomat.com/np/cultural_etiquette/ce_ve.htm.

siderate as they are always late! This is where *reflexivity* becomes a key aspect of qualitative research. Discuss how you have interpreted your observations with your participants to make sure you are correct. Further, when interviewing your participants, repeat back to them how you are interpreting their feelings and points (Berg, 2004).

It should come as no surprise that while interesting, there can be concerns about safety in criminological field research. *Jeff Ferrell*, a qualitative researcher who studied hip-hop graffiti, discussed the pros and cons of field research (Ferrell, 1997). He argued that some participation was necessary to gain access, and it provided a different perspective on the process of criminal experiences—but that becoming so immersed also led to walking fine ethical and legal lines. At what point does the researcher become that whom s/he is researching? If that line gets crossed, then the validity of the research (besides those legal and ethical issues) can come into question.

We generally suggest that any field work you do should be overt—meaning, all those involved should know who you are and what your purpose is. This is for the integrity of the research, the ethics of the procedures, and your safety—particularly when dealing with deviant groups of people. That being said, there are studies that have used covert methods of fieldwork, which can be very effective, particularly when there is concern about the *Hawthorne effect* (also called the *observer effect*). This is basically a concern within field research that people will act differently simply because you are there evaluating them. If you work any type of job, you might act differently when your boss is around versus when they are not (I know I have)! This is an example of the Hawthorne effect. Covert field research certainly has its place in research; however, these methods are controversial since they violate rules of informed consent with institutional review boards, as well as guidelines of honesty to establish rapport with your participants. Therefore, just like all other research, one should certainly weight the benefits versus the risks (for more reading on covert-type research methods, two suggested readings are Martin Bulmer's *When Is Disguise Justified? Alternatives to Covert Participation Observation* [1982] and Richard A. Hilbert's *Covert Participant Research: On Its Nature and Practice* [1980]).

Observations, Records, and Notes

Just as it is important to consider how the field researcher will interpret their surroundings and observations, it is also important to consider how those within the environment will interpret the researcher and their data collection. So, how data are collected in the field varies from situation to situation. For instance, JANE, the field researcher, is studying the culture of dog fighting. JANE may be able to actually video record a dog fight (assuming no onlookers are in the recording). However, if JANE goes to lunch with some folks who are involved in the dog-fighting business, she is probably going to be able to gain much more rapport if she just talks to them than if she takes out a tape recorder and a notepad. So, JANE will have to rely on her memory; and as soon as she is able, she will write down everything she can remember in as much detail as possible. There might be a few cheats for JANE. Perhaps she can

Figure 10-1: Example of Observation Instrument

Traffic Violations at the No Memory Bar

1. Time Entering Bar
   - ☐ 8:00pm
   - ☐ 9:00pm
   - ☐ 10:00pm
   - ☐ 11:00pm
   - ☐ 12:00am
   - ☐ 1:00am
   - ☐ 2:00am

2. Time Leaving Bar
   - ☐ 8:00pm
   - ☐ 9:00pm
   - ☐ 10:00pm
   - ☐ 11:00pm
   - ☐ 12:00am
   - ☐ 1:00am
   - ☐ 2:00am

3. Illegal Turn   ☐ Yes   ☐ No
4. Failed to Signal   ☐ Yes   ☐ No
5. Failed to Turn on Headlights   ☐ Yes   ☐ No

excuse herself to the bathroom and jot down some notes in the stall. What JANE should be primarily concerned with is making sure that her participants are comfortable with her being there — the more comfortable they are, the more they will act like they would in any other situation *without* a researcher observing them.

The notes that JANE takes are called *field notes* (see Figure 10-1). Sometimes a field researcher will need to jot down some notes at an unexpected point in time. This leads to some creative materials for record-keeping — perhaps pizza boxes, napkins, or paper towels become the available paper in those moments — perhaps an eyeliner pencil becomes the available writing tool. A field researcher should be able to think on their feet and be creative!

As discussed, field research is most often used for qualitative data collection (notes that consist of unstructured words, descriptions, pictures, etc.). However, field research can certainly be used to collect *quantitative* data using a structured, deductive approach (Bachman & Schutt, 2014). In this case, a researcher may be interested in how many drivers violate traffic laws when leaving a bar. BOB (the researcher — you remember BOB) may directly observe that when exiting the bar parking lot, a number of drivers took a left turn — even though it is supposed to be right turn only. He might also observe whether drivers signal to turn onto the main street, or if they remember to turn on their headlights.

The Good and the Bad of Qualitative Research

A lot of social scientists are either "Team Qual" or "Team Quant." In reality, both need each other! Qualitative research provides a strong foundation for quantitative research. Qualitative research can provide a more valid form of research if there is a need for context. For instance, in an online questionnaire, if JANE were to ask participants how many physical fights they had prior in high school, one guy might answer over 200. While it may sound as though that participant was incredibly violent, it may be that those physical fights were with siblings and were in jest. However, if the right questions are not asked, then JANE would probably conclude that this guy is super violent. As I discussed before, qualitative research provides context—especially field research.

However, the *reliability* (and at times, *validity*) of qualitative research can be called into question because of bias (as mentioned earlier). A researcher's interactions with participants combined with their own values can create a lot of subjective interactions. Remember in high school that student who was *always happy*? And I do not mean faking always happy—just sincerely happy … to be in high school (this example could be awkward if that happy person was you). Imagine you and that kid being asked to write a page describing high school. Do you think your observations and that kid's observations would be identical? Nope—perceptions matter, and they tend to pour into our research—and the more involved we are, the more we have to watch for that bias.

Lastly, another limitation of qualitative research is generalizability. BOB and JANE cannot go examine dog-fighting, drug-dealing gang members in one small town and expect that their observations would hold true for every other dog-fighting, drug-dealing gang member. However, qualitative research has never tried to be the type of research that generalizes—it wants to describe and explain that which it is observing.

Summing It Up

In this chapter, we discussed qualitative research, its components, the types of qualitative research, and its strengths and weaknesses. Qualitative research is focused on interactions, processes, and cultures. Its goals are to describe and explain through direct (and sometimes indirect) observation or interaction. A lot of qualitative researchers take on the role of observer-participant during field research, meaning that they might participate in some of the social interactions in order to better understand the dynamics and also establish rapport with their subjects. Qualitative research most often uses an inductive approach with a goal of eventually establishing theory.

Discussion Questions

1. Overall, do you believe qualitative or quantitative research methodology is more valuable? Defend your answer.

2. Provide an example of a study that would be better served with qualitative data collection and an example of a study that would be better served with quantitative data collection.

3. Provide an example of a study that would be best served using qualitative interviews, and then describe the procedure for conducting the study using the procedures for qualitative interviews outlined in the chapter.

4. What are the issues that can arise when recruiting hard-to-access populations?

5. Why is reflexivity in qualitative research important?

6. When and how should field notes be recorded? Does it vary?

7. What are the similarities and differences in qualitative and quantitative interviews?

8. How does qualitative and quantitative research differ regarding bias, language, and research-participant contact?

9. What is the effect of place in conducting interviews?

10. Do you believe the unit of analysis is typically clearer in qualitative or quantitative research? Why?

Trying It Out

Your professor may ask you to complete the following companion assignment available from the publisher. Using the supplied worksheet form, you are going to conduct your own qualitative content analysis.

References

Bachman, R., & Schutt, R. K. (2014). *Fundamentals of research in criminology and criminal justice* (3rd ed.). Thousand Oaks, CA: Sage.

Berg, B. L. (2004). *Methods for the social sciences.* New York, NY: Pearson Education.

Berk, R. A., & Adams, J. M. (1970). Establishing rapport with deviant groups. *Social Problems, 18*(1), 102–117.

Bulmer, M. (1982). When is disguise justified? Alternatives to covert participant observation. *Qualitative Sociology, 5*(4), 251–264.

Copes, H., Hochstetler, A., & Williams, J. P. (2008). "We weren't like no regular dope fiends": Negotiating hustler and crackhead identities. *Social Problems, 55*(2), 254–270.

Creswell, J. W. (2013). *Research design: Qualitative, quantitative, and mixed methods approaches.* Thousand Oaks, CA: Sage Publications.

Davies, P., Francis, P., & Jupp, V. (2011). *Doing criminological research*. Thousand Oaks, CA: Sage Publications.

Ferrell, J. (1997). Criminological *verstehen*: Inside the immediacy of crime. *Justice Quarterly, 14*(1), 3–23.

Hesse-Biber, S. N., & Leavy, P. (2010). *The practice of qualitative research*. Thousand Oaks, CA: Sage Publications.

Hilbert, R. A. (1980). Covert participant observation: On its nature and practice. *Urban Life, 9*(1), 51–78.

Hochstetler, A., Copes, H., & DeLisi, M. (2002). Differential association in group and solo offending. *Journal of Criminal Justice, 30*(6), 559–566.

Kitzinger, J. (1995). Qualitative research. Introducing focus groups. *BMJ: British Medical Journal, 311*(7000), 299.

Marshall, M. N. (1996). Sampling for qualitative research. *Family Practice, 13*(6), 522–526.

McCall, G. J. (1978). *Observing the law: Field methods in the study of crime and the criminal justice system*. New York, NY: Free Press.

Morgan, D. L. (1996). Focus groups. *Annual Review of Sociology, 22*(1), 129–152.

Tong, A., Sainsbury, P., & Craig, J. (2007). Consolidated criteria for reporting qualitative research (COREQ): A 32-item checklist for interviews and focus groups. *International Journal for Quality in Health Care, 19*(6), 349–357.

Wright, R., Decker, S. H., Redfern, A. K., & Smith, D. L. (1992). A snowball's chance in hell: Doing fieldwork with active residential burglars. *Journal of Research in Crime and Delinquency, 29*(2), 148–161.

Chapter 11

Program and Policy Evaluation

Learning Objectives

- Define evaluand
- Define defensible criteria
- Explain the difference between informal and formal evaluations
- Distinguish between merit and worth of evaluand
- Recall the two types of evaluand in the social sciences
- Identify stakeholders within an evaluation
- Recall the four standards of evaluation
- Distinguish between research and evaluation
- Describe the differences between formative and summative focuses of evaluation
- Recall and explain the five stages of evaluation
- Recall and explain the three types of assessment in evaluation
- Assess the importance of an expert or generalist evaluator in different evaluations
- Identify the advantages and disadvantages of internal and external evaluators
- List and define the four focuses of evaluation approaches
- Explain the differences between expertise-oriented and consumer-oriented approaches in judgments of evaluations
- Describe the development of consumers in evaluation over the last 100 years
- Assess the importance of validity and reliability in evaluation
- Define fidelity confirmation
- List and explain the steps of an evaluation
- Recall the five characteristics that goals should have
- Recognize the seven parts an evaluation plan should include

A friend of mine in graduate school, Sandra, had a goal while in school—to find the *best* of everything in town. It was a way for her and friends to make sure to try new places and get out of the house once in a while, since graduate school can keep you buried in work. She would be on a mission to find the *best* pecan pie, the *best* martini, the *best* pizza. If she were stuck between two places, she would go back and have both again. Determining what was the best started as a free exercise but started to get more technical with more people involved. People would debate, arguing in favor of the sweet potato fries at one restaurant over another. It became important to start identifying *why* Sandra or someone else thought that the sweet potato fries at the End Zone (a local bar) were the best. Sandra would identify characteristics or aspects of the food or drink: crispiness, flavor, sweetness, etc. Sandra, and all of us involved, were conducting evaluations.

I promise that you, too, have conducted evaluations before, albeit **informal evaluations**: looking at colleges, apartment hunting, determining your favorite restaurant, good and bad movies, etc. You identified the things you liked and those things you did not like—you established criteria and determined what fit those criteria and what did not. There is no strict definition for evaluation, but it basically is a technique aimed to provide a judgment about something using valid criteria. Specifically, an evaluation aims to determine what the **quality** is of the **evaluand**, which is the object of the evaluation. It probably sounds simple, but establishing criteria that everyone agrees upon, to where **BOB**, **JANE**, you, or I would all agree that *these criteria* are how we can determine if something is "good" or "bad." While it may be easy for one person to establish criteria, convincing everyone *else* that these are **defensible criteria** is where evaluation turns from an **informal evaluation** to a **formal evaluation**; specifically, creating objective, valid criteria that can be established as standards.

Evaluations can have numerous purposes: it may be to evaluate whether to implement cost-cutting methods in a business that needs to save some money, or it could be evaluating the short-term and predicted long-term success of a new television show. Evaluations can get complicated when determining specific types and approaches. First, there are types of evaluations, different evaluands, different approaches, and various sub-approaches to evaluation. We could write a whole book on all these approaches; however, the good news for you is that we will not dare do that. As social scientists, we are typically interested in two types of **evaluand**: **program evaluand** and **policy evaluand**. Particularly in criminal justice and criminology, it is important to be able to judge formally whether a program is meeting its intended goals (like a rehabilitation program for inmates) or if a policy is doing what the policymakers set out to do (like criminal justice reform policies). Program and policy evaluations have many aspects in common, but some important distinctions in approaches that can be used.

Quality

Quality is determined by assessing the **merit** or **worth** of the evaluand. They might sound like the same thing, but merit and worth are very different (Lincoln & Guba, 1980). Merit can be evaluated without context, while worth *requires* context. Imagine you are looking to buy a home. You could judge a home on **merit** for a number of aspects: its size, its foundation, how well-kempt it is, etc. However, the actual **worth** of the home depends on its context. The worth of the home would certainly differ in Missoula, Montana, compared to New York, New York—the context of location matters! An easy way to remember the distinction is a test grade. If your professor grades each of you independently, then you are being graded on your merit. If you are graded purely on a curve (meaning your grade depends on how everyone else does), you are being graded on your worth.

Parties Involved in Evaluation

There are typically a number of people involved in an evaluation, including evaluation subjects (those who are within the evaluation), the clients — those who fund the evaluation, those who are affected by the results of the evaluation, and anyone who is interested in the results of the evaluation. Evaluators are mainly concerned with **stakeholders**, who are primarily thought of as those who are funding an evaluation; but generally, they encompass other groups. For instance, if you were conducting a cost efficiency evaluation of a business, it would not simply be the business owners who had a stake in the results of the evaluation: employees' job roles could change, or the evaluation could result in them being laid off. In this case, they would certainly have a stake in the results of that evaluation!

Further, within criminal justice and criminology, there are other groups to consider. Typically, social scientists are not being paid to evaluate private businesses, but instead, are seeking to evaluate a not-for-profit program, a government-sponsored program, a state-level policy, or a federal policy. Therefore, there are typically no direct clients per se, and to receive funding, one would have to apply for a grant! Now, the grantor may be a government-funded program (like the National Science Foundation or the Bureau of Justice Statistics), or it may be a foundation. Regardless, it may be someone or some organization that may not be directly involved with the program or policy you aim to evaluate. Even so, they still have a definite stake in the evaluation process and the results of the evaluation (Yarbrough, Shulha, & Caruthers, 2004). There are multiple additional groups to consider depending the context. Therefore, if and/or when conducting an evaluation, think long and hard about who may have a stake, and then make sure to check with someone else to determine whom you are overlooking!

Role of the Evaluator

You know in books and television shows, how they often show a character pondering on what decision to make while listening to the guidance of a little devil on one shoulder and a little angel on the other? Now, imagine if there were a third party there, perhaps using the top of the character's head as their platform: The Evaluator. Generally, the role of the evaluator is to try and help gather and assess all the information necessary for the person(s) who is trying to decide. If a teenager is trying to decide whether to sneak out of the house, s/he'd be smart to listen to the evaluator, rather than the angel or the devil. The evaluator would attempt to show the cost and benefit of sneaking out (What if you get caught? How much fun will the party be? Is a two-hour party worth a possible two-week grounding?), and can provide the most objective approach. An evaluator should not be attached to the outcomes of the evaluation—the goal should always be to conduct a sound, comprehensive evaluation that provides the stakeholders with the information they sought.

That is not to say that an evaluator will not make recommendations—they will. An evaluation is, in itself, a judgment. In the case of the teen sneaking out, the evaluator would gather information and try to determine how likely it is that the teen would be caught and how fun the actual party would be—and would then recommend whether the teenager should sneak out of the house.

Standards of Evaluation

Not surprisingly, evaluation is very common practice in educational fields, particularly when you think about something like accreditation. For instance, if you attend a university or college in the Southern region, they are likely accredited by the Southern Association of Colleges and Schools Commission on Colleges (SACS-COC). There are similar associations for various regions. The point of these associations is to make sure a college is legit! You certainly do not want to pay for an education where you are not really learning anything. College is an investment, and one that should be made wisely, so these associations make sure that universities and colleges are not awarding degrees in underwater basket weaving. Additionally, accreditation and assessment of universities and colleges are to aim for some uniformity (while still maintaining some distinctions), meaning that a degree in psychology from one university would look similar to a degree in psychology from another university, with the idea being to aim for *some* standardization. Similarly, there are also accreditation associations for elementary, middle, and high schools.

So, it should come as no surprise that the model standards for program evaluation were developed in the context of educational evaluation. Specifically, in 1975, the Joint Committee on Standards for Educational Evaluation published standards for program evaluation (along with standards for other types of evaluations). There are four standards by which an evaluation is assessed: **accuracy**, **utility**, **feasibility**, and **propriety**. The **accuracy standard** is similar to validity in research: how valid the evaluation process, design, and results are. The **utility standard** can be judged by examining how the results of the evaluation were for stakeholders. Further, utility is judged by determining how those involved in the evaluation viewed the process: was the evaluation conducted in a clear and efficient manner? Did the process make sense and was the importance of each step clear? The **feasibility standard** is judged by the plan and execution of the evaluation: is it effective and efficient? Is it possible? Does the time and money it will entail correspond to the results gathered from the evaluation? Lastly, the **propriety standard** concerns how the evaluators and stakeholders treated the evaluation process in terms of rules, laws, standards, and ethics. Did the evaluators adhere to ethical practices? Did the clients adhere to ethical practices? How did the clients treat the evaluators? How did the clients treat the evaluation process? How did the evaluators treat the clients? How did the evaluators treat the process of the evaluation? How did the evaluators treat the evaluation subjects? (Yarbrough et al., 2004).

Research Methods and Evaluation Methods

I have often heard people refer to evaluation as the same thing as research—they are not the same. That is not to say there aren't a number of similarities. You can think of it as two peas on the same plant, but not two peas in the same pod. While one certainly needs research skills to conduct evaluations, they need to consider the differences in their purposes. Evaluations have stakeholders—those people who are invested in the results of the evaluation. Research should be used to enhance general knowledge, while evaluation is typically focused on enhancing stakeholder's insights of a program or a policy. While we assess research by looking at validity (internal, construct, external) and reliability, evaluations are judged on distinct criteria that were mentioned before: feasibility, propriety, utility, and accuracy. Meaning, an evaluation is judged on whether the evaluation process is practical, if the reports are useful, and if they portray the actual state of the program or policy (Fitzpatrick, Sanders, & Worthen, 2011). While criminological researchers stick with criminological research, evaluators are able to evaluate most anything, regardless of discipline or subject.

Evaluation Focuses, Approaches, Types, and Purposes

When we have talked about research, you have generally read that there is qualitative research and there is quantitative research. While we have other classifications (like survey research) it is pretty easy to classify the types and approaches to research. This is not to say that there are not many complicated approaches *to* research, but since research is discipline specific, it helps to simplify what we (as social science researchers) need to know. As I said before, evaluation is not discipline specific—it is interdisciplinary, which means that there are many types, approaches, and purposes to consider within evaluations. The good news is that this chapter will not address all of them, but I do want to make sure you know that there is a lot more to evaluation than what is covered in this chapter.

Determining Broad Evaluand: Program or Policy?

One of the first aspects to consider is whether the evaluation is a program or policy evaluation. While many of the same approaches can be used for both program and policy evaluations, the evaluand (what you are studying) can certainly affect other decisions. **Policy evaluations** typically have different stakeholders than program evaluations. Consider criminal justice policies: many of the policies in place lack any evidentiary support; however, policymakers are rarely held responsible for policies' successes or failures. Policies are often just symbolic and driven by fear and emotion, typically due to a recent event (Mears, 2010). Additionally, the stakeholders in policy evaluations are complex. If you were to evaluate sentencing policies for low-level drug offenders, there are many of them who would (or at least should) be interested in the results. Other stakeholders include not only those policymakers who made the original policies, but those in politics aiming to change or enforce those policies that are in place. Those working in the criminal justice system would be stakeholders, as well as any taxpayer or resident living in the United States! This makes the framework of the evaluation more complex in terms of the standard of feasibility. Further, evaluating policy depends on the current state of the policy: has it been implemented? Is it about to be implemented? Are stakeholders aiming to revise the policy?

When evaluating programs, it is often clear who the stakeholders are—this is particularly the case when evaluating a private program. If you were, for instance, going to evaluate an apartment company that owns one large complex, the direct stakeholders are much clearer than in policy evaluations: those who own, work, and live in the complex. However, there are still politics involved in these types of evaluations! Considering that those who own the complex are likely those who are funding the evaluation, this can certainly have a grave effect on the evaluation process, as they likely have a lot of control over how you evaluate the company. Similar to policy evaluations, it is important to examine the state of the program or company. For instance, is this a new apartment complex being built? Is it one that has been around for twenty years? Are they currently renovating? Are they attempting to change their marketing schemes or reinvent their image?

Determining the state of a policy or a program allows the evaluator to then decide what the **methodological focus** of the evaluation is. Generally, there are two main focuses: **formative** and **summative**, which can also be thought of as **during (formative)** and **after-the-fact (summative)**. Formative evaluations are focused on a part of the policy or a part of the program, and the evaluation is typically focused on the process; meaning, the purpose of the evaluation is to determine what about the delivery, the implementation, and the management of the program is effective and ineffective. A formative approach occurs "within" the program or policy. Conversely, a summative evaluation takes place *after* the implementation and/or the delivery of the program or policy. The difference between formative and summative evaluations can be confusing—the best example I've heard to distinguish between the two is that the evaluation is formative when the cook tastes the soup; the evaluation is summative when the guest tastes the soup (Fitzpatrick et al., 2011; Scriven, 1991). So, if you are asked to conduct an evaluation on a policy that is about to be implemented, you would likely conduct a formative evaluation. If you were asked to evaluate how effective a policy has been five years after its implementation, you would likely conduct a summative evaluation (Mears, 2010). The next question to ask is whether the goal of the evaluation is to describe a program or policy and its components, or to examine a relationship, difference, or effect. This is similar to focuses of research, for instance: is the goal to *describe* or is the goal to *explain*?

Table 11-1: Stages or Levels of Evaluation

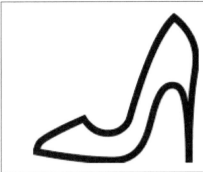

| 1. Do I need these shoes? |
| 2. Is the purchase and wearing of these shoes practical/logical? |
| 3. How and when will I wear these shoes? |
| 4. Will I reach my intended outcome (looking professional) when wearing these shoes? |
| 5. Is the benefit of these shoes worth the cost? |

Rossi et al. (2003).

The Evaluation Hierarchy

Prior to determining the focus of an evaluation, an evaluator should review the evaluation hierarchy to determine in what "stage" the program or policy currently is and what the goal of the evaluation *should* be. The **evaluation hierarchy** is applicable to both policy and program evaluations. **Rossi, Lipsey, and Freeman** (2003) developed these "building blocks" to examine program evaluations. Additionally, **Daniel Mears** (2010) applied the hierarchy to methods of evaluating criminal justice polices. There are **five stages or levels of evaluation**, including (1) **need**, (2) **design/theory**, (3) **process/delivery**, (4) **outcome/impact**, (5) **cost effectiveness/efficiency**.

Prior to embarking on an assessment of these five stages, it is important to conduct an **evaluability evaluation**. If you recall in the chapter on theory and research, we discussed that a characteristic of a good theory is testability—researchers can test the theory and determine if the research supports the theory or does not support the theory. Similarly, before spending a lot of time and money trying to evaluate a program or policy, it is important that an evaluator determines if it can feasibly be evaluated—this ties in with that feasibility standard mentioned earlier in this chapter. Typically, a program or policy *can* be evaluated, but the time, money, and effort it will take to conduct the evaluation should be assessed in context of the importance of the policy or program.

Getting back to the five stages: instead of first looking at a policy or program, let's imagine that we are talking about a pair of shoes (this example might resonate with some of you more than others—I realize that). Specifically, let's look at a pair of $600 Manolo Blahniks, which are something I have never been able to justify—no matter how hard I try (I've summarized the stages of evaluation in Table 11-1). The first stage of shoe shopping asks the questions: do I *need* this pair of shoes? Are they necessary? Will it affect my everyday life in a significant way? (2) Are the shoes a logical, sound purchase? Considering these are four-inch heels and I have the grace of a clumsy elephant, this purchase would likely not be based on practical or logical thinking. (3) How and when will I wear these shoes? When I teach? Probably not. When I go out? That would depend on how much and how far I would have to walk. (4) What is my goal in purchasing these shoes? Perhaps it is to look more professional. Is the purchase of these shoes going to result in that outcome? (Unlikely if/when I fall when wearing them). (5) Are the benefits of these shoes worth the cost? Do they contribute enough to the intended outcome to justify the $600 price? (I wish!)

Unfortunately, in this example, the evaluation of these shoes was pretty unfavorable. However, imagine that I was an Olympic athlete and was looking at spending a few hundred dollars on sneakers—these same questions might reveal a more favorable evaluation of the tennis shoes. The product, program, or policy is dependent on its context.

Using a more practical and applicable example, we may want to look at whether we need a policy, like harsher sentences for low-level drug offenders. Determining the (1) need of this would require looking at the context of such a policy. What are the issues with low-level drug offenders? Are they often committing other crimes? Are there successes in more punitive sentences for low-level drug offenders—what are the recidivism rates? When they do recidivate, what are the charges? Are there successes with other policies and programs that are less punitive, such as drug courts, rehabilitation, etc.? These questions also tie in to (2) design/theory—there should be a foundation in research, literature, and/or theory before implementing a policy. Is there literature, theory, research that has shown harsher sentences for low-level drug offenders decrease recidivism, crime rates, and victimization? (3) How will this policy be implemented? Will there be harsher sentences immediately? Where will the policy be implemented? At the federal level? Within one state? What sort of discretion will there be for those who are determining sentences? After the policy is implemented, (4) what are the results? Does it show trends/results that mirror its intentions? Is there a decrease in recidivism for those who received harsher sentences? If there is a decrease in recidivism, is it attributable to harsher sentences, or is there another explanation (think back to those pesky elements of causation)! (5) Lastly, does the cost of such a policy make sense in terms of how much change it is affecting? If we find that harsher drug sentences are costing the state of Missouri $500 million annually, and decreasing recidivism by 0.1%, then it probably is not very cost effective. However, if it is costing $500 million annually and decreasing recidivism by 48%, then we would probably conclude differently! Regardless, it is also important to ask if it is the most cost-effective policy to achieve these reductions in recidivism. There might just be a better way.

Now, in that example, we would need access to a lot of data that are not always accessible. Crime rates are "tossed around" as though they are fact, but a lot of times crimes are committed but go undetected. People who use drugs do not "get caught" every time; people steal and often are not arrested. It is important to understand the strengths and limitations of the data which you can gather or to which you have access, and do not take for granted that the data you have are wholly accurate and valid!

Types of Assessment in Evaluation

Within the evaluation hierarchy, we can pull three primary types of assessment: **need assessment**, **process assessment**, and **outcome(s) assessment** (Fitzpatrick et al., 2011; Mears, 2010). **Needs assessment** is focusing on whether there is a need for a program or policy, and how that need would best be served in the implementation and maintenance of the policy or program. **Process assessment** focuses on the implementation, administration, and delivery of the program or policy. Lastly, **outcome assessments** are focused more on the results.

In their book on program evaluation, **Jody Fitzpatrick, James Sanders,** and **Blaine Worthen** (2011) provide a detailed discussion of these three focuses and how each focus can be formative or summative in nature. Fitzpatrick and her colleagues recommend first determining the approach, and then determine the focus. If you remember, there are two main approaches: formative and summative.

It may seem that focusing an assessment on the process should only be formative, but this is not the case. For instance, an evaluator can assess the process and the implementation of a program or policy after the fact — they do not need to always assess it while it is still ongoing. A process assessment during the delivery or implementation phase would be a formative approach, while an after-the-fact process assessment would be a summative approach. Below is an example.

Example of Summative Process Assessment: Examining Delivery After the Fact

An example of this is the show *Firefly*, which was created by Joss Whedon (the creator of *Buffy the Vampire Slayer* and *Angel*), and starred Nathan Fillion (the main guy from the show *Castle*), and Gina Torres (who plays Jessica Pearson in the show *Suits*), as well as a number of other well-known actors.* Fourteen episodes were filmed, and yet, only eleven were aired when Fox cancelled the show due to low ratings. During and particularly since its cancellation, the show has developed an incredibly strong fan base. For instance, in 2009, Hulu named *Firefly* the top show in "Shows We'd Bring Back." Many fans have wondered what went wrong.

While there are likely many reasons the show did not see great success at the time, one reason is that Whedon and Fox had some artistic differences. The pilot was two hours (including commercials) and provided a lot of the backstory. Due to its length, Fox decided to air the second episode first, which omitted a lot of the characters' backstory. In fact, the pilot was not aired until December — three months after the show premiered on Fox. Some have criticized Fox for this decision and attributed it to the eventual cancellation of *Firefly*. While this certainly could not have *helped Firefly*, there were likely many other reasons that the show was cancelled so soon.

* https://web.archive.org/web/20100819073037/http://www.hulu.com/spotlight/huluawards.

Who Is the Evaluator?

Expert versus Generalist

Some evaluations require that the evaluators themselves are experts in the subject they aim to evaluate. This is similar to research—if you were a millionaire looking to fund medical research, you would probably pick a doctor over me, right? That would make sense. While in certain contexts expertise within the subject of the evaluation is necessary, there are many times that an evaluator is able to go across "disciplines" or subjects. The same general protocol and knowledge would be needed to evaluate a private physical rehabilitation business and to evaluate a drug treatment program in prison. While some knowledge of the area of focus within the evaluation can be ideal, there is often some bias on the evaluator's part that must be controlled. If I am assessing outcomes of a physical rehabilitation business, I probably do not have any overwhelming desire for the evaluation to reveal certain key findings. However, if I am conducting an evaluation of a prison drug treatment program, I likely have some desire for key findings to reveal themselves. That does not mean that the bias necessarily weakens the evaluation, it just is something that one should anticipate and control.

Expertise is common when discussing accreditation, which was mentioned earlier in this chapter. It is hard to evaluate certain parts of programs without some foundation or understanding of their focus. While accreditation is most often associated with academic programs (I used the Southern Association for Colleges and Schools earlier), there are many other accreditation-type bodies: for instance, the Food and Drug Administration. One of their roles is to evaluate how safe medications are (as well as a host of other things). This generally requires expertise that a **generalist**-type evaluator would not have. And I do not know about you, but I happen to like the idea of someone with a bit of science know-how is checking to make sure that the food and drugs I consume are safe. Now, this does not mean that there is no role for generalist-evaluators in organizations like the Food and Drug Administration—they just want to make sure that there are biologists and chemists involved, too.

Insiders and Outsiders

Being in-the-know has both its advantages and disadvantages, which is why evaluations can be conducted both internally and externally. **Internal evaluators** have some key advantages over **external evaluators**: they have context, history, and understanding that the external evaluator can never come close to gaining in the time of an evaluation. However, this also leads to bias, and a whole lot of it, which can be hard to control. For instance, I work at the University of West Georgia in the criminology department. What if I were asked by the state to conduct an evaluation to determine whether it would be beneficial to raise salaries of criminology professors in the Department of Criminology at the University of West Georgia, as some literature has shown that higher pay raises morale, and thus, would make us better teachers, which would allow us to increase our rate of retention? I promise you, should this ever happen, I have already decided what the outcome of my evaluation will be: yes, absolutely, raise salaries, and raise them by a good $100,000; it will certainly pay for itself in the long run. Now, I do not know if this is true—but as an insider, I am certainly attached to the outcome!

This is an extreme example but makes a point. Often internal evaluators should be used when there is less focus on outcomes and objectives and more focus on what is actually happening. Meaning, internal evaluations are great for purposes of descriptive-type evaluations. They are not ideal, however, for summative evaluations or those that are goal-oriented. An evaluator should probably not be evaluating something that could drastically affect the evaluator's life (raise, loss of job, change in job duties, etc.)

Approaches and Theories of Evaluation

As I previously stated, there are numerous approaches (or orientations) to an evaluation. These tend to focus on one party or one part/goal of the evaluation. Here's what is really confusing: an evaluation can take on multiple approaches. Evaluation approaches can be classified into four focuses: **judgment**, **features**, **changes**, and **stakeholders**.[1]

When formal evaluation techniques first really emerged, there were two main orientations: **expertise-oriented** and **consumer-oriented**, where the focus of the evaluation is to make a **judgment** about something in particular. I discussed expertise in the last section ("Who Is the Evaluator?"), but consumer approaches are also particularly important in understanding evaluation—because all of us, either formally or informally, have conducted our own consumer evaluation. If you have written a review on Yelp, Amazon, or something similar, then you provided others with the results of your evaluation. Consumer approaches to evaluation, combined with communication technology, have had a dramatic effect on the retail market. One of the first to pave the way for this was **Consumer Reports.** Just in case I am *really* old and you do not know what **Consumer Reports** is, it is a magazine started in 1936 that provided objective reports and reviews of products. Before the Internet, this was the best resource (in my opinion, at least) to determine whether something was worth its cost and lived up to its claims. This has become much easier: I can look at reports of a product on Amazon, and many other review sites; I can look at Yelp and Google Reviews to determine whether I should eat at a certain restaurant, I can go to Apartmentratings.com to find reviews of an apartment I am thinking about renting. While these reviews, at times, should be taken with a grain of salt

---

1. These classifications are modified from Fitzpatrick et al.'s (2011) classification schema on program evaluations.

(many are often emotionally fueled), they provide a great foundational knowledge to a product or service prior to us ever having to purchase or use it. If you try to sell an unworkable product and claim it works, you'll likely be called out sooner rather than later! While we typically do not focus much on consumer approaches to evaluation in criminal justice and criminology, they provide an understanding of the importance and effect evaluations (formal and informal) can have on the evaluand and its market.

The primary focus of the evaluation is often program or policy specific, like looking at some **feature** of the program/policy, determining whether the policy or program is designed most effectively for achieving its goals, whether the outcomes of the policy or program have supported the theory used to develop it, etc. For example, a police department may want to develop a model of community policing, based on theory and literature demonstrating its benefits (Stame, 2004). Their overall goal, however, is not to develop a model of community policing—it is to decrease the crime rate in their area. While there might be many ways to approach this evaluation, the focus could be the **objectives** of the organization to meet its goal, with community policing (and its specific requirements) being the objectives, and the eventual **goal** being to decrease crime. In reality, however, it may be necessary to conduct a formative evaluation on the community police model that is focused on its implementation—is the practice of community policing connected to the original intentions of implementing the model?

When the primary focus of the evaluation is to use the results to modify or maintain the current state of a program or policy, then an evaluation is really catered to answering particular questions to serve in those decisions. If the main goal of the evaluation is on maintaining, changing, omitting, or revising, then it is likely that the focus is on **change**. If Professor **Bob** allows students to use laptops and tablets in the classroom, he may want to conduct an evaluation on whether he should make changes to this policy: is it helping or hurting students? Should I not allow laptops and tablets? Should I only allow them during particular times of the class period? He hopes to shed light on what change (if any) he should make. Similarly, referring back to the police department who wanted to implement a community policing program, perhaps after they have implemented the program, they want to evaluate whether they should change it—is it increasing trust in police? Are citizens responding positively to it? Are there things that should be added or omitted? A change-focus evaluation does not need to be *summative*—it can occur before the program or policy has been developed—it can be a great tool for stakeholders to determine whether they should change the plan or implementation of the program or policy (Stufflebeam, 1983).

Lastly, the **focus of the evaluation** might be the stakeholders and their involvement in the evaluation. If a neighborhood association wanted an evaluation conducted to determine how they could lower crime in their neighborhood, one of the primary concerns of the evaluation would be how the residents of that neighborhood should be involved in that evaluation. They could help lead discussions on the problems in the neighborhood with other neighbors, they could encourage participation from other neighbors, they could provide context to judgments being made by the evaluator. The degree of involvement from the stakeholders is a primary focus because it has a significant effect on the value, feasibility, and outcome of the evaluation. If those affected do not participate, then the evaluation is neither feasible nor is the outcome valuable.

Values of Research Standards in Evaluation

Many of the rules of research apply to evaluation. One of the most important is that **validity** and **reliability** still matter just as much in evaluation as they do in any research. The focus, however, is typically on internal validity more than external validity. Evaluations are most often designed with a primary goal to make judgments/assessments about one program or policy. The secondary goal (if a goal at all) is to be able to apply the findings of the evaluation to other similar programs or policies. External validity becomes a challenge in evaluations, as one often cannot determine who is or who is not a stakeholder in a program or policy.

For instance, those who would be affected by a community policing program are not randomly selected. However, before the program was implemented, the police department and evaluator could **randomly assign** areas where the community policing program would be implemented and where it would not be. If they determined decreases in crime rates in all areas, (assuming that there are no other issues in the research design), then this reduction in crime rate is likely not attributable to the community policing program. Conversely, if they observed significant reductions in crime in those areas where the community policing program *was* implemented, then this begins to support the success of the program in meeting its goal (lower crime). While this could not be generalized to other communities by itself, replication of the program implementation and evaluation could be conducted (meaning, do the same thing in a bunch of other communities that have both similar and distinct characteristics), and if the findings showed support over, and over, and over again, then there is a much greater likelihood that the findings can be generalized to other communities. This is important stuff—evaluations like this can change programs, policies, laws, and governmental funding.

With accurate portrayal being a key goal of evaluations, internal validity can play a big role. Therefore, when possible, experimental designs should be used when the evaluation is assessing outcomes, or doing more than simply describing the state of a program or policy. Going back to the example from earlier (when discussing evaluation hierarchy), determining whether harsher sentences for low-level drug offenders are cost-effective would likely best be answered by using an experimental design. If an **experimental design** is not feasible (random assignment could be tough here!) then a **quasi-experimental design** would be the next best thing—just like research (Langbein & Felbinger, 2012).

One unique aspect about evaluations is that the goal is focused on providing a detailed, accurate picture of what is "going on" to the stakeholders. Therefore, using mixed methods (meaning, using both qualitative and quantitative approaches) is often ideal—the qualitative research provides more context to the evaluation, giving a more complete picture.

Let's say you owned a McDonald's and you had observed huge drops in the amount of money that McDonald's was bringing in—you might want to bring in an evaluator to help determine what the attributes of this decrease were. The evaluator could use quantitative methods and data and report back to you that job satisfaction is lower than average and that on average, the number of customers visiting the McDonald's has decreased significantly. While this might identify the main attribute (fewer customers coming in), it still does not get at *why* fewer customers are coming in. It might take some in-depth observations and interviewing to get to the truth of the matter: a McDonald's owned by someone else opened up three miles away, and the employees of your McDonald's found out that employees of the other McDonald's were making $1.50 more an hour. As a result, your employees feel unfairly treated and have been taking their anger out on the customers. With the option of another McDonald's relatively close by, customers have begun frequenting the other one, noting that the staff is much more courteous. Here is the heart of the matter—without the qualitative aspects of this evaluation, the results would hold little value to you, the primary stakeholder.

While qualitative research is often used in evaluations for purposes of providing context, it is also important for **fidelity confirmation**. The qualitative research can be used to confirm the findings of an evaluation. For instance, if conducting an outcome assessment of a drug treatment program that is founded on the theory of restorative justice, the qualitative research is a tool for linking the theory to the program to the outcomes (Miller, 2014).

Steps of an Evaluation

Unfortunately, the steps of an evaluation are really dependent on the focus, type, and approach. The best advice is to identify these first: formative or summative? Based on process, needs, or output? Is it primarily a feature focused, change focused, stakeholder focused, or judgment focused?

The first part of any evaluation requires planning, planning, and more planning. It is important to assess the goal of the evaluation, as well as the goal of the program or policy. There are five characteristics that goals should have to be **S.M.A.R.T.: Specific, measurable, attainable, relevant, and time-bound** (with a starting place and ending place) (Locke & Latham, 2002; Vito & Higgins, 2014).

However, planning should not mean that the evaluator strictly adheres to the plan. Things *change* in evaluations, and things are unforeseen, so the plan must come with room for change! The plan should involve (1) determining the approach and focus; (2) collecting information needed to understand the focus and (3) assess the information in context of the focus and need; (4) working with the stakeholders to make sure that there is a clear understanding of the focus, goals, and expectations of the evaluation; (5) identifying the role, rights, and boundaries of the evaluator; (6) reporting the plan to the stakeholders; and (7) determining changes to the plan after reporting to stakeholders.

The evaluation plan should consist of specific questions that are measurable and that (collectively) when answered, will meet the goal(s) of the evaluation (Fitzpatrick et al., 2011). For each question, the evaluator should have a specific plan on how to answer that question:

- What is the design (experimental, quasi-experimental, longitudinal, cross-sectional) for the specific question?
- What are the methods of collecting the data?
- Will the evaluator need to observe meetings or counseling sessions?
- Will they need to interview program participants?
- How many (sample size!) participants are needed?
- How long will this take?
- When will this occur in the process of the evaluation?
- How will the results be analyzed and by whom?
- How will they be reported and to whom?

Only after this plan has been developed should the evaluation begin. It is important that the evaluator know his or her place and his or her limitations. If they want to observe counseling sessions, this could be problematic—they need to know what is feasible and to what degree they can insert themselves without disturbing those involved.

Evidence-Based Practices

There is a tale about scientists putting monkeys in a cage with bananas on top of the cage and a ladder to reach those bananas. The scientists would observe the monkeys carefully, so that each time a monkey attempted to go up the ladder, the scientists would soak all the other monkeys in water. The monkeys did not like being soaked in water. Eventually, as a result of this, the monkeys would preemptively beat on the monkey climbing the ladder, which prevented the monkeys from being soaked. In time, no monkey dared to go up the ladder. When the scientists replaced one of the monkeys with a new monkey who was naive to the whole water/beating up thing, the new monkey would try to climb the ladder and get beaten up. The same thing would happen with each monkey being replaced with a new monkey until eventually, there were no monkeys from the original experiment in the cage. Thus, you had a bunch of monkeys beating other monkeys with no real understanding as to why they were doing it. Therefore, if you were able to ask the monkeys why they were beating the other monkeys, they would probably just tell you that is the way it has always been.[2] Often, we (U.S. residents) have been satisfied with practices simply because they are traditional. Police arrest people, courts sentence people to prisons, and correction workers enforce the imprisonment of people. This all was part of tradition and normality, and there was not a great movement to determine why—it simply seemed that it was the way things had always been.

In more recent years, there has been an increase in the demand for accountability from policymakers and program managers. People want to know that what they are paying for (think tax dollars) is effective and worth it. There has been a shift from "feel good" legislation (things that may not be effective but make people feel safer) to an expectation of accountability. The support and demand for **evidence-based practices** relates heavily to consumer evaluations—the market for public policy and government programs has shifted based off the knowledge and demand of the stakeholders (every person living in the U.S.). In criminal justice, this call for accountability and evaluation really rose after Robert Martinson (1974) concluded that "nothing works" in regard to treatment and rehabilitation. While the methods and findings of his evaluation have been largely refuted, there was some question as to why the government was funding these programs if they were not helping.

To gather evidence for evidence-based practices, evaluations are necessary. Not surprisingly, evaluation research has become a big part of the criminal justice literature. Some examples of recent criminal justice evaluation research have included process and implementation evaluations of reentry programs (Miller & Khey, 2016, 2017), effects of statistically driven profiles on arrest rates of burglaries (Fox & Farrington, 2015), and a descriptive evaluation of current super-max policies within each state (Butler, Johnson, & Griffin, 2014).

Two of the driving forces of a movement towards accountability and evidence-based practices are money and information. Technology has given people access to an abundance of information. Prior to the Internet, I would have had to gone into my college library and searched through articles, encyclopedias, and paper reports to try to determine the use of DNA analysis in the United States—and that is *me*, a college professor who has access to those materials. That often is not the case. The Internet has provided a wealth of information that is accessible to most people. And this technology has made many people more aware of issues, resulting in many accurate and inaccurate understandings of issues! One example of this is the *CSI* effect—jury members expect more forensic evidence but are also flummoxed at the complicated, time-consuming processes to obtain certain forensic evidence. The expectation is good, but the understanding is a bit inaccurate—DNA is not always available, and when it is, it takes a lot of money and a lot of time to run the analysis.

---

2. http://innovationforsocialchange.org/five-monkeys-experiment/?lang=en.

One realization that has been influenced by this wealth of information is that we (as a country) spend a *lot* on criminal justice. For instance, the cost of running prisons and jails across the nation might collectively be upwards of one trillion dollars *a year*. That is a lot of money! Similar to consumer-driven evaluations, no one wants to spend their money on a service or product if the conclusion is *nothing works* or if there is no evidence as to whether it does or does not work.

Summing It Up

One thing is for certain—the popularity of evaluations is not going anywhere in criminal justice research! Evaluations serve a very different role than regular research in that their concern revolves around the accuracy of the evaluation and its effect on stakeholders. There are different types and focuses of evaluation, including methodological focuses that are formative or summative, and assessment types that are needs-based, outcome, or process assessments. While there are many approaches to evaluation, they fall under four main categories: judgment focused, feature focused, change focused, or stakeholder focused. The methodological focus, approach, and assessment type must be determined prior to creating the evaluation plan. Each evaluation plan is unique in that it is dependent on the goals and objectives of the study and the goals and objectives of the program or policy. Lastly, remember that much of evaluation was discussed very broadly here and that we could write a whole book on it—others have!

Discussion Questions

1. Are evaluations and research the same things? Why or why not?

2. What are defensible criteria? Why are they important in evaluations?

3. What are some of the differences in informal and formal evaluations?

4. What is merit and how does it differ from worth? What are the roles of both merit and worth in evaluations?

5. Who are the stakeholders in an evaluation? Create an evaluation scenario and describe whom you would believe to be the stakeholders. Defend your answer.

6. What is fidelity confirmation?

7. Have consumer evaluations changed in the last 100 years? If yes, how? If no, why do you think they have stayed the same?

8. Are reliability and validity important in evaluations? How would you attempt to ensure that an evaluation is reliable, and how would you design your evaluation to safeguard against threats to validity?

9. Create your own evaluation plan and proposal. Describe the steps, the objectives, and your S.M.A.R.T goals, along with the seven parts of the evaluation plan.

Trying It Out

Your professor may ask you to complete the following companion assignment available from the publisher. Using the supplied worksheet form, you are going to see how people evaluate products on Amazon.

References

Butler, H. D., Johnson, W. W., & Griffin, O. H., III. (2014). The treatment of the mentally ill in supermax facilities: An evaluation of state supermax policies. *Criminal Justice and Behavior, 41*(11), 1338–1353.

Fitzpatrick, J. L., Sanders, J. R., & Worthen, B. R. (2011). *Program evaluation: Alternative approaches and practical guidelines* (4th ed.). Pearson.

Fox, B. H., & Farrington, D. P. (2015). An experimental evaluation on the utility of burglary profiles applied in active police investigations. *Criminal Justice and Behavior, 42*(2), 156–175.

Langbein, L. I., & Felbinger, C. L. (2012). *Public program evaluation: A statistical guide.* Armonk, NY: M.E. Sharpe.

Lincoln, Y. S., & Guba, E. G. (1980). The distinction between merit and worth in evaluation. *Educational Evaluation and Policy Analysis, 2*(4), 61–71.

Locke, E. A., & Latham, G. P. (2002). Building a practically useful theory of goal setting and task motivation: A 35-year odyssey. *American Psychologist, 57*(9), 705.

Martinson, R. (1974). What works? Questions and answers about prison reform. *The Public Interest, 35,* 22.

Mears, D. P. (2010). *American criminal justice policy: An evaluation approach to increasing accountability and effectiveness.* Cambridge, UK: Cambridge University Press.

Miller, J. M. (2014). Identifying collateral effects of offender reentry programming through evaluative fieldwork. *American Journal of Criminal Justice, 39*(1), 41–58.

Miller, J. M., & Khey, D. N. (2016). An implementation and process evaluation of the Louisiana 22nd judicial district's behavioral health court. *American Journal of Criminal Justice, 41*(1), 124–135.

Miller, J. M., & Khey, D. N. (2017). Fighting America's highest incarceration rates with offender programming: Process evaluation implications from the Louisiana 22nd judicial district reentry court. *American Journal of Criminal Justice, 42*(3), 574–588.

Rossi, P. H., Lipsey, M. W., & Freeman, H. E. (2003). *Evaluation: A systematic approach.* Thousand Oaks, CA: Sage Publications.

Scriven, M. (1991). *Evaluation thesaurus.* Thousand Oaks, CA: Sage Publications.

Stame, N. (2004). Theory-based evaluation and types of complexity. *Evaluation, 10*(1), 58–76.

Stufflebeam, D. L. (1983). The CIPP model for program evaluation. In G. F. Madaus, M. S. Scriven, & D. L. Stufflebeam (Eds.), *Evaluation models: Viewpoints on educational and human services evaluation* (pp. 117–141). Dordrecht: Springer.

Vito, G. F., & Higgins, G. E. (2014). *Practical program evaluation for criminal justice.* Abingdon, UK: Routledge.

Yarbrough, D. B., Shulha, L. M., & Caruthers, F. (2004). Background and history of the joint committee's program evaluation standards. *New Directions for Evaluation, 2004*(104), 15–30.

Section IV

The "How Tos" of Research (Chapters 12–15)

Section IV is different from the rest of the book. These four chapters are your research methods "manual." Imagine that you are studying to become a surgeon. You have to learn science first, right? This requires a bunch of classroom learning. These next chapters are more like you being able to observe a surgery while the surgeon provides you with some explanation of what s/he is doing. There should be little new terminology, per se, but a guide to how you can apply what you've already learned to creating your own research. These chapters are kind of like your step-by-step guide to research. Chapter 12 provides you with ways to take your research idea and form it into a research question and a research project. From there, you will learn some tips and tricks about how to read past research (Chapter 13) and how to write about past research and your own research (Chapter 14). Like history, we have to know what other people did in the past to make sure that we build on what has already been done and also avoid their mistakes. The last chapter (Chapter 15) is all about putting everything together and creating your own research proposal.

Trying It Out

Your professor may ask you to complete the following companion assignment available from the publisher. Using the supplied worksheet form, you are going to match each part of a research proposal with the examples given.

Chapter 12

Getting Started with a Research Idea

Developing a research idea requires planning several stages, but the stages do not always occur in the same sequence. Recall from earlier in the book, we reviewed some of the options available to criminal justice and criminology researchers for formulating research ideas (inductive, deductive, and retroductive, see Chapter 1 for details), but what if you wanted to conduct your own research? Where would you start? From where would your ideas stem? Then where would you go? How would you begin planning your research?

This chapter is dedicated to helping you with that task. In subsequent chapters, we will demonstrate how to read scientific research articles (which is where a good portion of your ideas for research may stem from), the research process, and finally taking you through how to write a research proposal (beginning with research questions and going through developing a budget). Earlier in the book, we discussed how a research idea can come to you at any time and from anywhere. You may be pumping gas at a service station, sleeping, or reading research when the idea strikes you — write it down! No matter how far-fetched the idea may seem, write it down so that you do not forget it, and make sure to come back to it so you can determine if it is worth using to form a primary question worthy of investigation.

Primary Question

The primary question (PQ) is just what its name says it is: it is the primary question that you are trying to answer with your research. It is true, this question can and should be a broad statement, which should be able to be answered by forming multiple research questions (RQ). Begin the PQ with the questions such as, "What is the relationship between …" or "What are the psychological factors that influence …" or "What are the correlates of …" or "What are the factors impacting…." One of the best ways to develop a primary question is to start with a problem that you are looking to find the answer to, and then using the primary questions to overcome that problem. For example, much is known about male sex offenders — their age, motivations, types of offending, etc., yet considerably less is known about female sex offenders. This could serve as the problem that you are looking to overcome via your research, and thus you could form a primary question in an attempt to examine female sex offenders in more detail. A possible primary question may be: *What are the characteristics of juvenile female sex offenders?* This addresses the problem of not knowing much about whom female sex offenders are, and it also lends itself well to having multiple research questions that can be produced in an attempt to answer the primary question. To aid in development of both primary and research questions, we offer three notes to keep in mind:

(1) Keep your literature review broad based. Utilize books, articles, speeches, addresses or anything else that can help formalize your questions.

(2) Have an idea of what you are looking for. Dismiss the literature that does not fit your questions. In the articles that do make the cut, try to find their PQ and RQs.

(3) Make a special note of the articles' methods, tables, and statistical analysis.

Decide if you are going to use their RQs, concepts, operant variables, etc.

One of the last and most important things to remember about the primary question (other than it is the basis for your entire study!) is that how well you meet the goals of your primary question will be the criteria by which your study will be evaluated in the discipline.

Research Questions

The research questions play just as important a role as the primary question, as they are utilized to answer the primary question and thus contain within them the concepts to be operationalized into the variables of the study. Because the research questions allow the primary question to be tested, each question should be separate and completely researchable, including having an analysis set up for each question from univariate all the way to multivariate.

Building on the primary question already utilized, we will now provide research questions along with a complete work through of how to identify concepts within the questions and operationalize those concepts so they can be measured and the questions tested.

After the PQ and each RQ is where you should include support for your research question (a full example of this will be provided in Chapter 14). This support will be similar to a miniature literature review for each question. What have other studies found in regard to demographic characteristics of juvenile female sex offenders and how it influences offending?

The next step is to clarify the scope of the research with an examination of the concepts and variables related to these questions, but first we will provide a technique to identify the concepts within the questions.

Example 1: Primary and Subsequent Research Questions

PQ—The primary research question of this study is: What are the characteristics of juvenile female sex offenders? As previously noted, the research on juvenile female sex offenders is limited in scope and based on small sample sizes. As such, they may not be representative of the true characteristics of juvenile female sex offenders. Using a large sample size and analyzing the characteristics of juvenile female sex offenders and the characteristics of the victim, this research seeks to add to the body of knowledge regarding juvenile female sex offenders.

RQs—In addressing the primary question of this research, four research questions are examined. These questions will provide additional insight into the population of juvenile female sex offenders.

The first research question is: What are the demographic characteristics of juvenile female sex offenders?

This research question focuses on age, race, and ethnicity of juvenile female sex offenders.

The second research question is: What are the demographic characteristics of the victims of juvenile female sex offenders?

This research question examines the number of victims, their age, sex, and race. It also focuses on actual relationship between victim and juvenile female sex offender.

The third research question is: What sex offenses do juvenile female sex offenders commit?

This research question focuses on the number of different crimes that fall under the category sex offenses.

The fourth and final research question for this line of inquiry is: What is the influence of alcohol and/or drug use on sex offenses?

This question sheds light on the role substance abuse may play in sexual assaults.

Example 2: Identifying Your Concepts

PQ—What are the <u>characteristics</u> of <u>juvenile female sex offenders</u>?

RQ1—What are the <u>demographic characteristics</u> of juvenile female sex offenders?

RQ2—What are the demographic characteristics of <u>the victims of juvenile female sex offenders</u>?

RQ3—What <u>sex offenses</u> do juvenile female sex offenders commit?

RQ4—What is the influence of <u>alcohol and/or drug use</u> on sex offenses?

Concepts

After underlining each of the concepts, at first glance, this may appear to be quite simplistic, but a good portion of critical thinking and research occurs now, specifically as you find supportive literature for your questions, operationalize your concepts, and finally discuss the measurement of the variables that have materialized from your concepts. If this sounds overwhelming—relax! I will take you through the process while explaining each step (also recall that in the next chapter we will be going through the entire process with a different set of questions).

The primary question conceptualization is slightly different from that of the research question as the concepts in the PQ are actually operationalized in the research questions. The concepts in primary question include characteristics and juvenile female sex offenders. These concepts will be operationalized in the research questions that follow. The first concept, characteristics, has multiple variables that stem from it that are operationalized in research question one, while the concepts of the victims' characteristics, sex offenses committed, and alcohol and/or drug use will be operationalized in research questions two, three, and four. Lastly, the concept in the PQ, juvenile female sex offenders, will be operationalized in research question one.

Concepts raised by research question one include demographic characteristics and juvenile female sex offenders. Again, demographic characteristics may seem like a simple concept, but in actuality, it can be one of the more tedious concepts to operationalize, as demographic characteristics can include a number of variables, such as the age and race of juvenile female sex offenders. As previously noted, the research exploring the characteristics of juvenile female sex offenders is relatively new compared to that of male sex offenders, and therefore, may be limited by relatively small samples. As such, there is a need for more information about the demographics of juvenile sex offenders as this information could be helpful in recognition and treatment of this group of offenders as well as aid in the development of a juvenile female sex offender typology.

Review of Levels of Measurement

Before we review how to operationalize a variable, it is important to remember those levels of measurement that were discussed in Chapter 4, "The Nitty Gritty." Just to review, there are four levels of measurement: nominal, ordinal, interval, and ratio. It is best to memorize them in this order, since there is a lot more numeric meaning in each level "up." Meaning, data measured on a ratio level has more numeric meaning than interval; interval has more numeric meaning than ordinal, and ordinal has more numeric meaning than nominal.

Data measured on a nominal level are categories that have no order. For instance, if you look at sex as male and female, you cannot rank order these! Female is not "higher" or "better" than male, nor is male "higher" or "better" than female.

Another example would be colors: red is not "higher" or "better" than blue, and blue is not "higher" or "better" than orange. These cannot be rank ordered. However, for statistical purposes, numbers *are* assigned to each category—but these numbers have no real meaning.

Data measured on an ordinal level includes categories that have an order, but the distance between each category is not equal. For instance, if you answered a question on a survey questionnaire that asked your current classification (freshman, sophomore, junior, or senior), the difference in these is not equal. For instance, there are some seniors who have been in college for many years (think Van Wilder, for instance), and a brand-new freshman who has not yet attended a college course is very different from a freshman who has almost completed 30 hours of coursework. One of the most common types of ordinal data we use in the social sciences are derived from questions measured on a Likert scale: like strongly agree, agree, neutral, disagree, strongly disagree or always, often, sometimes, rarely, never. While the distance between each category may seem equal, they are not. Take, for example, the statement "I am a big fan of Alabama football" with the choices "Strongly agree, agree, disagree, strongly disagree." Let's say you have three male participants (just to keep it consistent): Participant #1 (P1), Participant #2 (P2), and Participant #3 (P3). P1 responds with Strongly Agree, P2 responds with Strongly Agree, P3 responds with Agree. Let's say that we wanted to see what a "big fan" of Alabama football really is. We go to P1's house and it is painted in Alabama colors, as is his truck. Everything down to his dog has some sort of Alabama "symbol" on it. He goes to every single game—has not missed one in 20 years. We go to visit P2. There is no sign of him being an Alabama fan, except for a magnet on the fridge. He tries to watch most games and goes to a couple a season. Both responded "strongly agree," *yet there is no* real *"value" or definition for what strongly agree is—it is based on the participants' perceptions.* Next, we go and see P3, and his house looks just like P1's house. He watches every game and goes to as many as he can. He will record the games to make sure he can watch them later if he cannot watch them live. Now, based on our observations it *seems* like P3 is a bigger fan than P2—but P3 responded "agree"—not "strongly agree." The distance between each value (agree and strongly agree versus disagree to agree) are not equal, nor are the values themselves (strongly agree to strongly agree) necessarily equal. However, within the social sciences, they are often as close as we can get. So, while we identify them as ordinal (because they are), we will often treat them as interval.

Data measured on an interval level includes categories that have an order to them, *and* there is equal distance between each. The one thing it is missing, however, is a true zero, where zero represents that "absence of" something. One of the most common explanations for this is temperature Celsius. Even though there is zero in Celsius, this does not indicate the *absence* of heat—just that it is freezing outside. Further, sometimes there simply is not a zero on record. For instance, if we asked DUI offenders how many drinks they had when they were arrested, all of them would have to answer *at least* one. No one could answer zero. Similarly, if we asked prison inmates how many times they had been arrested, they would have to answer at least one—there would be no zero!

Lastly, data measured on a ratio level has all the components of interval, *plus* a true zero. What makes ratio more powerful is that you can actually make a *meaningful* ratio out of it. If I asked a bunch of college students how many alcoholic beverages they had in the last week, someone could respond zero, which would mean an absence of alcoholic beverages. If someone had two beers, they had half as many as someone who had four. Someone who had nine beers had twice as much as someone who had four-and-a-half beers. While you can often make a meaningful ratio with data measured on an interval level, it is not a definite!

You will need to discuss the **operationalizing** of each variable; for instance, the age of the juvenile female sex offender refers to the age in years of the juvenile female arrestee at the time of her arrest. That might seem like an obvious measurement, but what if I were looking at the age of puppies? I probably would not use years, or even months—I would be more likely to use weeks. The concept age of the juvenile female sex offender was operationalized into the variable *Age of Offender*. Let's say the categories range from 7 to 17 years of age, which can be ordered. For example, 15 is higher than 10 and lower than 17. Numerical values here are not just labels, they have real value, and the order cannot be arbitrarily changed. The equal interval is also the characteristic of this variable. The interval between the age categories is one year. For example, the interval between categories 7 and 8 is equal as the interval between categories 9 and 10, one year. The variable Age of Offender, however, does not have a true zero, which would indicate a lack or absence of age. Because there is an established order and equal intervals between categories but not a true zero, the variable *Age of Offender* is a variable measured on an interval level.

Race refers to the race of arrestee indicated at the time of arrest. Let's say there are four racial designations included in our study: White, Black, American Indian/ Alaskan Native, and Asian/Pacific Islander. The concept race of the juvenile female sex offender was operationalized into the variable *Race of Offender*. The first category, White, was coded with a one (1). The second category, Black, was coded with a two (2). The third category, American Indian/ Alaskan Native, was coded with a three (3). The fourth category was Asian/Pacific Islander and was coded with a four (4). When the race of the offender was unknown, it was coded as System Missing and excluded from the analysis. The four categories of the variable *Race of Offender* cannot be ordered. The values 1, 2, 3, and 4 are just labels that assist in the research. It does not matter if 1 is attached to White, 2 to Black, 3 to American Indian/Alaskan Native, and 4 to Asian/Pacific Islander, or if 1 is attached to American Indian/Alaskan Native, 2 to White, 3 to Asian/Pacific Islander, and 4 to Black. This variable is a word-oriented variable, and then numbers are used just for purposes of categories for statistical purposes. Because of lack of ordering, this is a nominal level variable.

Concepts in research question two would be demographic characteristics of victims of juvenile female sex offenders and includes: number of victims, age, sex, race, and victim's relationship to the offender. The age and race concepts would be operationalized and measured much the same way as they were in research question one. Let's say the concept number of victims refers to the total number of victims associated with the criminal incident. Let's say the incident report collects information on up to three victims. Therefore, the characteristics of the victim are available for up to three victims. The concept number of victims was operationalized into the variable *Number of Victims*. The categories of this variable represent the actual number of victims associated with each incident. These categories can be ordered, such that one is greater than the other. Two victims are more than one victim, and less than three victims. The numerical values are not just labels, they are quantifiably representative, and changing order would change the results of the study. Also, there is an equal interval of one between the categories. The interval between one and two victims is the same as the interval between two and three victims. It is always one. Finally, the presence or absence of a true zero was explored. Suppose that according to the data source there must be at least one set of victim data for each crime incident. Therefore, there is no true zero since there is always at least one victim associated with an incident. Since the categories can be ordered and there is an equal interval between them, but no true zero, the variable *Number of Victims* is measured on an interval level.

Victim's sex refers to the sex of the victim as indicated in the incident. Sex of the victim was available for up to three of the victims. The concept sex of the victim was operationalized into three variables: *SEX OF VICTIM-1, SEX OF VICTIM-2,* and *SEX OF VICTIM-3*. Each of these three variables was operationalized as Male was coded with a one (1), and Female was coded with a zero (0). The category Unknown, which represents missing data (occurs when no data value is stored for the variable in an observation), was coded into the category System Missing. The categories Male and Female cannot be ordered. The values 0 and 1 are just labels that assist in the research. It does not matter if 1 is attached to male and 0 to female, or if 1 is attached to female, and 0 to male, at least not for purposes of order. This variable is a word-oriented variable, and numbers are used simply for statistical purposes. Because of lack of ordering, this variable is measured on a nominal level. This variable is divided into two categories, Male and Female.

The victim's relationship to the offender refers to the relationship between the victim and the offender. Considering the relationship between victim and the offender, let's assume the data distinguishes three groups of offenders. The first group represents offenders within the family. These offenders victimized relatives (e.g., sibling, stepsibling, other family member). In the second group, let's say the offenders are outside the family but were known to victim. These offenders victimized acquaintances, friends, neighbors, babysitters, etc. The third group then consists of offenders who were not known by victim. This would be the case if the victim was a stranger or the relationship was unknown. Let's assume the victim's relationship to the offender was available for up to three victims. The concept victim's relationship to the offender was operationalized into three variables:

Vic1_off_rel for Victim1-Offender Relationship

Vic2_off_rel for Victim2_Offender_Relationship

Vic3_off_rel, for Victim3_Offender_Relationship

You have no doubt noticed that variable names are separated with underscores; the reason for this is twofold. First, it is quicker when writing out a number of different variables as opposed to writing out "Victim 1 relationship to offender." Second, there is some statistical software that limits the number of character spaces that a variable can have for a name. In HLM 7 (one such software program available) each variable can only be seven characters long, so you need to find ways to abbreviate variable names while remembering what each one stands for.

Each variable has the same four categories: Victim was Parent, Victim was Sibling, Victim was Acquaintance, and Victim was Stranger. These four categories cannot be ordered. Although we could say that the relationship between siblings, for example, is stronger than the relationship between acquaintances, we cannot say if the relationship between siblings is stronger than the relationship between parent and child. While the values assigned can be ordered in a meaningful way, the use of the assigned values to distinguish each type of the victim's relationship to the offender cannot be ordered in any meaningful way. The values easily could be modified to represent different types of the relationship, or different values could be used to represent the type of relationship, without distorting the understanding of the variables. Because of lack of ordering, this is a variable that is measured on a nominal level.

The third research question is "What sex offenses do juvenile female sex offenders commit?" Two concepts raised by this research question are juvenile female sex offenders, which was previously included in research question one, and sex offenses. The concept *sex offenses* refers to any completed or attempted offense which the data defines as a forcible or nonforcible sex offense. Let's say, according to the data, a forcible sex offense is any sexual act directed against another person, forcibly and/or against that person's will; or not forcibly or against the person's will where the victim is incapable of giving consent. Forcible sex offenses include forcible rape, forcible sodomy, sexual assault with an object, and forcible fondling. Further, the dataset defines nonforcible sex offenses as unlawful, nonforcible sexual intercourse, including incest, statutory rape, and pornography/obscene material. It does not include prostitution nor assisting or promoting prostitution.

Now, let's assume for simplicity that only the first sex offense listed on the arrest will be used for this analysis. Sex offense definitions are based on the common-law definitions found in *Black's Law Dictionary*, as well as those used in the *Uniform Crime Reporting Handbook*. Forcible rape is defined as the carnal knowledge of a person, forcibly and/or against that person's will. Forcible rape is also defined as the carnal knowledge of a person not forcibly or against the person's will where the victim is incapable of giving consent because of his or her temporary or permanent mental or physical incapacity, or because of his or her youth. Forcible sodomy is oral or anal sexual intercourse with another person, forcibly and/or against that person's will; or not forcibly or against the person's will where the victim is incapable of giving consent because of his or her youth or because of his or her temporary or permanent mental or physical incapacity. Forcible fondling is defined as the touching of the private body parts of another person for the purpose of sexual gratification, forcibly and/or against that person's will; or, not forcibly or against the person's will where the victim is incapable of giving consent because of his or her youth or because of his or her temporary or permanent mental incapacity. Statutory rape is defined as nonforcible sexual intercourse with a person who is under the statutory age of consent. Pornography/obscene material is defined as a violation of laws or ordinances prohibiting the manufacture, publishing, sale, purchase, or possession of sexually explicit material, e.g., literature, photographs, etc.

The concept *sex offense* was operationalized into the variable *SEX_OF*. This variable has seven categories which are sex offenses. For the purpose of this study, Forcible Rape = 1; Forcible Sodomy = 2; Sexual Assault with an Object = 3; Forcible Fondling = 4; Incest = 5, Statutory Rape = 6; and Pornography/Obscene Material = 7. These seven categories cannot be ordered. While the values assigned can be ordered in a meaningful way, the use of the assigned values to distinguish each type of sex offense cannot be ordered in any meaningful way. The values easily could be modified to represent different types of sex offense, or different values could be used to represent the type of sex offense, without distorting the understanding of the variables. For example, if 1 is attached to Forcible Fondling, 2 to Statutory Rape, 3 to Forcible Rape, 4 to Forcible Sodomy, 5 to Sexual Assault with an Object, 6 to Pornography/Obscene Material, and 7 to Incest, it would not change the results of the research. Also, 22 could be attached to Forcible Rape, or 25 to Incest, and again, that would not influence the results of the research. The numbers here simply indicate how the categories differ, but do not have real numerical significance. The only reason to use numerical values is to make mathematical operations possible. Because of lack of ordering, this is a nominal level variable.

The fourth and final research question is "What is the influence of alcohol and/or drug use on sex offenses?" The only concept in research question 4 not included in previous research questions is concept alcohol and/or drug use. Alcohol and/or drug use refers to whether the offender who was involved in the incident was suspected of consuming alcohol or using drugs/narcotics during or shortly before the incident. The concept alcohol and/or drug use seeks to determine the frequency of alcohol and/or drug use related to the sex offenses. The concept alcohol and/or drug use was operationalized into the variable *OFF_USE* for offender suspected of using alcohol or drugs/narcotics (aggregate). This variable has four categories. The first category, Alcohol, was coded with a one (1). The second category, Drugs/Narcotics, was coded with a two (2). The third category, Drugs/Narcotics and Alcohol, was coded with a three (3). The category Not Applicable, which was used for cases where the reporting officer did not indicate that any of the offender(s) were suspected of using alcohol or drugs/narcotics, was coded as System Missing.

The categories of the variable *OFF_USE* cannot be ordered. The values 1, 2, 3, and 4 are just labels that assist in conducting statistical operations. It does not matter if 1 is attached to Alcohol, 2 to Drugs/Narcotics, 3 to Drugs/Narcotics and Alcohol, and 4 to None; or if 1 is attached to Drugs/Narcotics and Alcohol, 2 to Alcohol, 3 to None, and 4 to Drugs/Narcotics. The categories cannot be ordered in a way that one is better or worse than another. The variable *OFF_USE* is word-oriented variable, and assigning different numerical values to the categories would not change the characteristics of those categories. Since there is a lack of ordering, variable *OFF_USE* is a variable that is measured on a nominal level.

Summing It Up

The preceding chapter demonstrates how to get started with a research idea by forming your primary question and creating your research questions to answer that primary question. Recall that your PQ should be a broad investigative question, while your RQs should all be independent testable statements that contain the concepts to be operationalized and measured. The easiest way to identify the concepts in your research questions is to write them out and underline the major words in each question. Next, you address each of the concepts in your PQ and RQs question by question, not moving to the next question until all of the concepts in the current question have been identified, supported by literature and/or theory, and variables stemming from the concept operationalized. Remember that we will be going through this process from beginning to end again in Chapter 14 so that you see additional PQs and RQs and how to identify and operationalize those concepts into variables. The next chapter in this section will teach you the techniques to reading scientific research articles so that you may use this newfound ability to help you identify good research questions and find other researchers' PQs and RQs.

Chapter 13

How to Read Research

For you to form a truly educated opinion on a particular phenomenon in criminal justice, you need to become familiar with current research in the field. As stated in Chapter 4, it is extremely important that researchers understand and review what past researchers have done so they may be aware of what other researchers have done in relation to what one is currently examining and to be sure that one's current research will add to the existing literature on the phenomenon of study. As such, you need to be willing and able to read scientific research literature for yourself. Make no mistake about it, reading a scientific article is a complex task. When you read a research paper, your goal is to understand the scientific contributions the researchers are making. This is not an easy task for someone new to the process, as it may require going over the paper several times while taking up to several hours to read a paper properly. However, all hope should not be lost, as you too can learn how to read and extract information from a research article, and like with any skill, it takes patience, and the more you practice, the better at it you will become.

Learning the Parts of an Article and the Proper Reading Techniques

From a beginner's point of view, research articles almost certainly appear intimidating and confusing, as they can contain technical jargon, intimidating statistics, and multiple tables and graphs. Reading a research article can be a frustrating experience, especially for those who have had little to no experience in the process or techniques needed to master art of reading scientific literature and extracting the information needed. Just like there are methods and techniques for mixing a drink or rebuilding an engine, you can also learn to read research articles by following a few techniques (Durbin, 2009; *Science Buddies*, 2018). First, it is necessary that readers become familiar with the structure of a research article just as they would with the parts of an engine or the different flavors of liquors and mixers. Along with knowing the components of the article, you will also become familiar with the purpose of each section and what information is generally found in each section.

Many research articles in criminal justice and criminology are written in a standard format set forth by the American Psychological Association (more on this in Chapter 14). This is a great benefit to readers, as it allows for the presenting of ideas and findings in a clear, systematic manner. It allows researchers to present their ideas and findings in a clear and well-organized manner. As a reader, once you understand this format you can approach a new research article regardless of its specific content. You will know where in the article certain information is found, making it quicker and easier to read through a research article. No matter what your reasons for reading a research report, a firm understanding of the format in which they are written will ease your task (Jordan & Zanna, 1999).

Most research articles in criminal justice will consistently contain the following sections: The title, an abstract followed by an introduction, literature review, methods, results, and discussion/conclusion. There can be additional sections depending on the article, or the section names may change slightly (e.g., the methods section might be referred to as methodology, or data, measures, methods); however, if you do not see these sections in a research article, then you should seriously question the quality of the article.

Reading and Taking Notes on Research Papers

Believe it or not, you should not read a research paper from beginning to end. Some people consider this approach—reading a research paper like a magazine article or a novel—to be one of the worst, if not the worst way to read a research paper. Reading scientific research articles is an active task, and you are going to need to take notes, highlight, and/or underline text as you progress through the article. It may sound lame, but it is good to approach it like a conversation: you should have questions, thoughts, and statements to make in response to what you read. The best place to begin is by examining the journal the article came from and the authors of the article. Take note of the authors and their institutional affiliations; some institutions are well-respected (e.g., SUNY Albany) while others may first appear to be legitimate research institutions but are actually agenda-driven. Also take note of the journal in which it is published. Be leery of articles from questionable journals (Fred's Mechanics & Criminology), or sites like Natural News, that might resemble peer-reviewed scientific journals but are not in actuality (Raff, 2014). Once you have determined that that both the article and authors are reliable sources of information on the topic, you can begin to read the article. Regardless of where you are reading in the article, there are a couple of guidelines you should keep in mind.

The way that you take notes when reading articles will vastly differ, and I cannot tell you that one technique is better than another. We (the authors of your book) will provide a few tips and tricks that have worked for us.

Kyle's Tips

1. *Be Critical*: Reading a research article is a critical process, and you should not assume that the researchers are always correct and all-knowing. To be critical

in this sense means to be questioning or to ask questions. If the researchers attempt to solve a problem, are they solving the *right* problem? Were there simple solutions the authors did not seem to consider? What were the limitations of the study; were there some limitations the researchers may have omitted? Were the assumptions the authors made reasonable? Is the logic of the paper clear and justifiable, or is there a flaw in the reasoning? If the authors present data, were the data gathered in the correct manner? Were the data interpreted in a reasonable manner? Were the analysis techniques appropriate given the structure of the data? (Mitzenmacher, 2015). In asking these questions and being critical of a research article, you are essentially setting yourself up to form *your own* research questions. As discussed in Chapter 12, developing your PQs and RQs is the first step to developing a research idea. So be critical and ask questions!

2. *Be Creative*: To be critical of someone's work is relatively easy; the real challenge comes when you must put forth a better or more efficient way to solve the problem. So, incorporate the strengths of the article you are reading with the problems of the paper, and see how to develop your own idea. What are the good ideas in this paper? Do these ideas have other applications or extensions that the authors might not have thought of? Can they be generalized further? Are there possible improvements that might make important practical differences? The answers to these questions can help you develop your RQs and possible additional research ideas (Mitzenmacher, 2015).

3. *Take Notes*: Some people cover the margins of their copies of papers with notes, others prefer electronic copies to highlight and make sticky notes via Adobe or a similar software; either method is acceptable and will need to be utilized for success. If you develop questions or criticisms as your read, write them down so you do not forget them. Underline or highlight key points, terminology, or other research articles the authors emphasize. Make a note of the data that appear most important or that may seem to be questionable. These techniques are helpful the first time you read a research article, and they are invaluable if you have to re-read a paper after a significant amount time.

Additionally, before and during your reading you should be asking yourself these questions:

1. Have I taken the time to understand all the terminology?

2. Have I gone back to read an article that would help me understand this work better?

3. Am I spending too much time reading the less important parts of this article?

4. Is there someone I can talk to about confusing parts of this article? (Purugganan & Hewitt, 2004).

After reading, ask yourself:

5. What problem(s) does this research address? Why is it important?

6. Are the methods utilized appropriate?

7. What are the specific findings?

8. Are the findings supported by convincing evidence?

9. How are the findings unique, new, or supportive of other work in criminal justice/criminology?

10. How do these results relate to the work I am interested in?

11. What are some of the policy implications (so what) of the ideas presented here? (Purugganan & Hewitt, 2004).

Vanessa's Tips

In additional to Kyle's comprehensive list, I (Vanessa) just wanted to provide some of my own tips and tricks for reading and summarizing research studies.

1. Rate research papers: sometimes after reading multiple papers, you may forget which ones really lined up with your own research. As a shortcut, you may want to provide a rating for each research paper after you read it. I typically rate from 1–10, with a "1" indicating little to no use and a "10" indicating that the paper was almost perfectly in line with what I plan to study.

2. Write a summary of the paper in plain language: After reading the paper write 4–5 sentences that explain the purpose and findings of the paper. This can serve as your own abstract. This should not be fancy, and it may be something like: Researchers examined how grades are related to cheating. Looked at a small sample at one college. Used college GPA and cheating scale to look at the relationship. Found positive relationship (GPA increase, cheating increased). Lots of limitations—see notes.

3. Write down the sources that the authors of the paper cited that you think will be applicable to your own study.

4. Write down any key findings, important notes, or quirks of the study.

5. Answer the five w's and one h (who, what, where, when, why, and how; see "Reading the Methods" section for details on these).

6. Go ahead and complete the citation for the article—it is tedious, but better than doing it five minutes before the paper is due!

Where to Start?

Back to Kyle's Guidance

The approach I provide is for reading research papers for the purpose of writing your own paper and developing your own research idea. Therefore, some of these techniques may not be applicable if you are *assigned* certain articles to read.

I like to start by reading the Abstract for an overview. Some people disagree with this approach vehemently; however, when you are reading on a subject or phenomenon for first time this should be the place to start. I personally hate wasting time reading an article if it is of no use to what I am researching. Reading the abstract first allows the reader to determine if this article is worthy of further consideration for my research or if it is off topic from the problem I am investigating.

After reading the abstract, I read the first couple of paragraphs of the introduction to get a sense of the issue being addressed by the research. Next, I skip to the last paragraph of the introduction (although sometimes this can be found at the end of the literature review) and read about the "so what" of the article. Here, there will generally be a couple of sentences about the questions the research is attempting to answer as well as the hypotheses for the study (should they have hypotheses). Next, I like to skim through the discussion/conclusion section to see how the study turned out. Again, nothing angers me more than wasting time reading an article if it is going to be of little to no use to me. By reading the first few and last few paragraphs of the discussion/conclusion section, you will get a brief overview of the entire study, including the major question attempting to be answered and, most importantly for our purposes, some of the main findings and the study's implications. If you get to this point and the main findings are not those that are going to aid you in your research in any way, you can abandon reading the article without having spent a significant amount of time reading through it.

Now you should go to the middle part of the research article and read the methods section in its entirety, and plan to re-read it, even a couple of times, to make sure you have a good handle on what the article is examining and how they are going about doing it. Then, read the discussion section. You may want to flip to the discussion/conclusion section for clarification of what the reported statistics mean in straight English as most, but not all, results sections have some descriptive sentences following the statistics that put into words what was actually found. It is important not to get bogged down in the details, both in the methods and in the results section, as you do not have to eat the whole cow just to get a good steak. Instead, try to gain a good understanding of how the hypotheses (or research questions) were answered. Next, read the discussion section more closely and in its entirety. Here you (hopefully) get a plain English explanation to statistics that you encountered in the results section as well as the "so what" to the research article. Lastly, read the entire article from beginning to end using the notes that you had taken in your first reading as guides. Again, you may have to do this several times to obtain the greatest comprehension from the research article.

Now that we have identified the techniques to employ while reading and the correct order to read each section in, we will turn our attention to what information is contained in each section and how you should read each section. Some sections are fairly straight forward, such as the title and abstract, but other sections, such as the methods, have specific information that you should focus on more than others.

Title and Abstract

Like the title of a film that attracts a moviegoer, the title of the article can serve to attract a reader in the first place. A good title can inform the reader a great deal about the study to decide whether to continue reading the paper or bypass it. Generally, the title presents a short statement of the issues being investigated, the criminological theory being utilized, and/or some of the variables that were studied. For example, the following title was taken from Kyle's curriculum vitae (CV):[1] "Close Only Counts in Alcohol and Violence: Controlling Violence near Late-Night Alcohol Establishments using a Routine Activities Approach." Just by reading the title, it can be inferred that the study investigated how alcohol use influenced violence around bars and clubs that were open late into the night. It also suggests that Routine Activities Theory was utilized as the study's theoretical framework. The abstract is also an invaluable source of information. It is a brief synopsis of the study and is generally limited to 150 to 200 words in the discipline of criminal justice. The abstract helps you determine whether you should read the entire article or not. Additionally, most criminal justice journals provide abstracts free of cost online, allowing you to decide whether you need to purchase the entire article. Abstracts in the criminal justice discipline contain information about the problem that was examined, the methods of how it was examined, the major results of the study, and some theoretical and practical implications of the findings. As such, the abstract is a useful summary of the research that provides a brief overview of the study. Abstracts within criminal justice generally appear in one of two ways. First, they can appear as written paragraphs much the same as a normal paragraph in a book. Second, some journals now have a structured abstract where one or two sentences appear in separate subheadings, like purpose, methods, results and conclusions, making it easier for the reader to identify important parts of the study quickly (Jordan & Zanna, 1999; Purugganan & Hewitt, 2004). Either way the information is presented, the abstract can be read in an orderly way and provide the reader with some preliminary ideas of what the study examines.

Reading the Title and Abstract

Reading these is pretty straightforward. As stated above, the title and abstract of a research article are similar to a movie preview. Just as a movie preview highlights the important aspects of a movie's plot, and provides information for one to decide whether to watch the whole movie, titles and abstracts highlight the key features of a research article, allowing you to decide if topic fits with your line of inquiry. Also, just as movie previews do not give the whole story, reading only the title and abstract is never enough to fully understand a research article (Jordan & Zanna, 1999). When reading the title and abstract the things for the reader to take note of include the pur-

---

1. A curriculum vitae is a detailed resume for academics. It provides information on anything someone in academia has published, presented, taught, etc. Fun Fact: curriculum vitae is actually Latin for "course of life." (We figured this was great bar trivia.)

pose of the study, the methodology, the key findings, and any conclusions that may have been reached.

Introduction and Literature Review

Even though researchers will not come out and say it in writing, the introduction begins the main body of a research article. Here, the researchers set the stage for the study. They present the problem under investigation and state why it was important to study. The literature review section contains existing knowledge and previous research as well as theory that is relevant to the central issue being examined. Additionally, the researchers want to illustrate that the problem they are examining is a real problem that you should care about. If the researchers are studying racial profiling on the part of the police, they may cite statistics that suggest this form of discrimination is prevalent, or describe specific cases of racial profiling in the news. Such information helps illustrate why the research is both practically and theoretically meaningful, and why you should bother reading about it. The researchers will often place the study in a historical context by identifying gaps in the literature and how those gaps spurred the researchers to develop a new study and suggest how their study advances knowledge of the phenomenon. Typically, this section concludes with the researchers restating their aims and objectives, or the "so what" of their research, meaning why their particular study is important and what gaps in the extant literature the research will fill (Subramanyam, 2013).

Reading the Front End
(Introduction and Literature Review)

When reading the introduction and literature review, do so carefully, but choose carefully what to focus on; and remember, as some literature may be more in line with your own study than others. To comprehend an introduction and a literature review, you need to understand the researchers' hypotheses and results, and how they were derived and/or influenced by theory, informal observation, or intuition. Other information, particularly in the literature review section, may be intriguing but not necessarily critical to understanding what the researchers did and why they did it (Jordan & Zanna, 1999). While reading the introduction and literature review sections, take note of these questions: What problem was studied, and why? Did other researchers also study this problem? Or a similar version of this problem? What theories did the researchers utilize to guide their study? How did the researchers derive their hypotheses? What questions do the researchers hope to answer with this study?

If you are writing your own paper, the literature review can also serve as a key to what literature *you* should be examining. This is why it can be important to look at the year the research paper was published. For instance, if you are looking at a research paper from 1910, it may provide a good foundation; however, you should also make sure that your research sources and papers include more recent research. A paper from 2016 will probably serve as a better guide to what research studies you should be reading, especially when the research study is in line with your own study.

Methods

This section gives the technical details of how the study was carried out. Generally, researchers translate their research questions hypotheses into a set of specific, testable hypotheses. This is where the researchers outline the main characters of the study; often, in criminal justice, we are talking about subjects or respondents or events. They can be participants in a survey, inmates in a prison, or a number of arrests. Participants in criminal justice and criminological studies can be students, police officers, and even inmates; as such they are not always initially told the true purpose of a study. If they were told, they might not act naturally. Thus, researchers frequently need to be creative, presenting a credible rationale for complying with procedures, without revealing the study's purpose. The researchers will generally describe the characteristics of participants (gender, age, etc.) and how many of them were involved. Then, they describe the materials (or apparatus), such as any questionnaires or special equipment, used in the study. Finally, they describe chronologically the procedures of the study, such as how it was conducted. Often, an overview of the research design will begin the method section, providing a general outline of the research design; however, the data and methods can be presented in great detail so that other researchers can recreate the study to confirm its results (Jordan & Zanna, 1999).

For our purposes, this detailed information is not necessary to comprehend at this point, so do not get overwhelmed trying to memorize the particulars of the procedures. Focus on how the independent and dependent variables are measured. Within the criminal justice discipline, you often will find the analytical strategy within the methods section. This is fancy terminology for what kind of statistical analysis is going to be run on the data that has been collected. It can range from simple univariate statistics all the way through multivariate nested regression and anything in between. The last thing that can be included in the method section by some researchers is the descriptive statistics; however, it is also common for these to be found at the beginning of the results section as it is up to the individual researcher as to where s/he prefers to put those particular findings.

Reading the Methods

While reading the methods section, try putting yourself in the place of a participant in the study, and ask yourself if the instructions given to participants seem sensible, realistic, and engaging. Imagining what it was like to be in the study will also help you remember the study's procedure and aid you in interpreting the study's results (Jordan & Zanna, 1999). The reader should become familiar with the procedures and analysis used for data collection and manipulation and find out whether they are appropriate. As noted above, the methods section is often difficult to read, especially for students, because of technical language and a level of detail sufficient for another researcher to repeat the experiments. However, you can more fully understand the design of the experiments and evaluate their validity by reading the methods section carefully (Purugganan & Hewitt, 2004). Make note of these questions as you progress carefully through the methods section: How were the data gathered? How were the concepts operationalized from the research questions? How were the variables of interest measured? Did the measures used adequately reflect the variables of interest? For example, is annual income an adequate measure of social class? Was the analytical strategy appropriate given the nature of the data?

You can also think through the four w's and the one h: who, what, where, when, and how? (We save "why" for the discussion section.)

Who: Who are the participants? Of whom is the sample comprised? Of whom is the population comprised? Depending on your unit of analysis (see Chapter 7), the answer to "who" might really be a what. For instance, if your unit of analysis is social artifacts, you may be looking at newspaper articles.

What: What is the goal of the research? What are the research questions? What are the hypotheses? What type of research is being conducted (explanatory, exploratory, etc.). What are they trying to study? What are the variables of interest? What are the control variables? What are the data? What is the unit of analysis? What is the sample size? What is the sampling technique? What is the instrument used (such as interview, online questionnaire, in-person questionnaire, field observation)?

Where: Where were data collected? Is there a specified state, city, school, prison, etc.?

When: When were data collected? Over what period of time were data collected?

How: How were data collected? How were concepts operationalized? How were variables of interest measured?

Results

In this section, researchers provide details about the analysis run on the data collected; generally, this information is provided via figures, tables, and graphs while the data is described and statistical techniques are presented. Because of this, the results section can seem rather intimidating to readers who have little or no experience with statistics and interpreting data. Stumbling through complex and unfamiliar statistical analyses is no doubt confusing and frustrating and can often lead to individuals skipping over this section. We advise against such a strategy, as the statistical findings of research are the foundation to the science of criminal justice, and even the most prestigious criminologists were once in your shoes and shared the same apprehensions and concerns that you may be experiencing.

Often, in criminal justice and criminology, research articles' specific hypotheses are not explicitly stated; however, you can generally determine the hypothesis that was tested by reading the narrative description that accompanies the result, and referring back to the front end (introduction/literature review) of the article to locate a hypothesis or research question that corresponds to that result. Sometimes you may encounter an article where the analyses presented in a research article tests a specific hypothesis. Generally, in this case, each analysis presented is preceded by a reminder of the hypothesis it is meant to test. In both instances, after an analysis is presented, researchers generally provide a narrative description of the result in plain English (Jordan & Zanna, 1999). Even following the most complex statistical analysis, there will be a written description of what the result means conceptually, and this where you will want to focus your attention. Focus on the conceptual meaning of research findings, not on the procedures of how they were found (unless you feel comfortable interpreting statistics).

Reading the Results

The reader should thoroughly go through the results section of the manuscript and find out whether the results were reliable (same results over time) and valid (measure what they were supposed to measure). An important aspect is to check if all the topics present in the front end of the research article (i.e., research questions, hypotheses, theories) were accounted for at the end of the study. If the answer is no, the reader should check whether any explanation was provided (Subramanyam, 2013). While reading the results section, make note of the following questions: Did the researchers provide evidence that the independent variables had predictive value? For example, if testing for behavioral differences between violent criminals and nonviolent criminals, did the researchers demonstrate that one group was in fact more dangerous than the other? What were the major findings of the study? Were the researchers' original hypotheses supported by their observations? If not, look in the discussion section for how the researchers explain the findings that were obtained (Jordan & Zanna, 1999).

To provide another example: a researcher may hypothesize in their article that there is a relationship between boredom and learning techniques about how to read research. As a reader, you could go to the methods and see how these concepts, "learning techniques about reading research" and "boredom," were measured. You could then go to the results and find those variable names that were referenced in the methods. You should be able to (ideally) find them in tables if the study is quantitative, and the authors will probably mention it in the writing of the results. Looking for key words like "hypothesis supported" and/or "significant relationship" are also important—the authors are telling the reader that there is a relationship between particular variables—it is just important to make sure you know which variables they are referencing. If you are still confused, the discussion/conclusion section can also help clarify things.

Discussion/Conclusion

This can easily be considered the most important section of a research article because this is where the research questions are answered and the meaning of analysis and interpretation of the data are presented. In criminal justice and criminology, the discussion section generally begins with a quick overview (generally the first paragraph or two) of the purpose of the study. This can include restating the problem statement or primary question of the study; restating some of the gaps in the current literature with regard to the phenomena of interest, the theoretical framework, and hypotheses the study utilized; and restating some of the major findings. Next, the study results are discussed (in plain English) in regard to how well (or not) they answered the questions of the study and filled in the identified gaps in the literature. Additionally, the results are compared within the context of other studies, explaining in what aspects they were different or similar. Ideally, no new data should be presented under discussion, and no information from other sections should be repeated. Furthermore, this section also discusses the various strengths and limitations or shortcomings of the study, providing suggestions about future research or areas that need additional explanation. It is important to remember that the discussions are the researchers' interpretations and opinions and not necessarily facts (Subramanyam, 2013). It is also possible that these two sections can be split into a separate discussion section and conclusion section. When this is the case, generally the same information is presented, except separated into the different sections. The conclusion section will now contain the "so what" portion of the article along with the policy implications and the directions for future research.

Reading the Discussion/Conclusion Section

As I just discussed, the value in reading the discussion/conclusion can vary depending on when you are reading it — at the beginning of article reading or the end. Some readers find it useful to read the first few paragraphs of the discussion/conclusion section before reading any other part of the research article. Similar to the abstract, these few paragraphs usually contain all of the main ideas of a research article: What the research questions/hypotheses were, the major findings and whether they supported the original hypotheses, and how the findings relate to past research and theory. Having this information before reading a research article can guide your reading, allowing you to focus on the specific details you need to complete your understanding of the article. The description of the results, for example, will alert you to the major variables that were studied. If they are unfamiliar to you, you can pay special attention to how they were conceptualized in the introduction, and how they are operationalized in the method section (Jordan & Zanna, 1999). In reading the discussion/conclusion section from beginning to end, one should look to see if all the results are thoroughly explained and grounded in the literature and theoretical framework utilized the front end of the article. Consider the researchers' explanations carefully, and see if they seem plausible to you. Also, be sure to pay attention to the policy implications of the findings as well as the limitations and future research advocated by the researchers. While reading the discussion section, make note of these questions: What conclusions can be drawn from the study? Were the results adequately explained in plain English? What new information does the study provide about the problem under investigation? Does the study help resolve the problem? What are the policy and/or theoretical implications of the findings? Did the results contradict past research findings? Did the researchers note the limitations of the study? Is there anything I can examine to address these limitations (Jordan & Zanna, 1999)?

Summing It Up

Each of these sections normally contain easily recognized conventional features, and if you read with an anticipation of these features, you will read an article more quickly and comprehend more information. Remember, the more you practice these techniques the faster you can process a research article with accuracy and precision.

References

Durbin, C. G. (2009). How to read a scientific research paper. *Respiratory Care*, *54*(10), 1366–1371.

Jordan, C. H., & Zanna, M. P. (1999). How to read a journal article in social psychology. *The Self in Social Psychology*, 461–470.

Mitzenmacher, M. (2015). How to read a research paper. Retrieved from https://www.eecs.harvard.edu/~michaelm/postscripts/ReadPaper.pdf.

Purugganan, M., & Hewitt, J. (2004). How to read a scientific article. Cain Project for Engineering and Professional Communication, Rice University. Retrieved from http://www.owlnet.rice.edu/~cainproj/courses/HowToReadSciArticle.pdf.

Raff, J. (2014). How to read and understand a scientific paper: A step-by-step guide for non-scientists. *Huffington Post*. Retrieved from https://www.huffingtonpost.com/jennifer-raff/how-to-read-and-understand-a-scientific-paper_b_5501628.html.

Science Buddies. (2018). How to read a scientific paper. Retrieved from https://www.sciencebuddies.org/science-fair-projects/competitions/how-to-read-a-scientific-paper.

Subramanyam, R. (2013). Art of reading a journal article: Methodically and effectively. *Journal of Oral and Maxillofacial Pathology: JOMFP, 17*(1), 65.

Chapter 14

How to Design a Research Article

In the first two chapters of the "How To" section, you learned how to begin a research study by forming primary and research questions of interest as well as how to read scientific research articles, which is one of the main ways a researcher can find and identify gaps in research and thus fruitful research ideas. In this third chapter, we will combine the first two sections and take you through the process of designing a research article. Beginning with the role of the literature review and where to find the research articles you will need, through the operationalization of the concepts identified in your research questions, to the applications of the findings to policy—our goal with is to take you step by step through the process so that you may look back on this section as a sort of template to utilize as you design and write your own research articles.

The Role of the Literature Review

You have probably noted throughout the text we have referred to "the literature" a number of times, and by this point, you have undoubtedly figured out this is an invaluable part of any research article. You have read about how you need to read about previous research similar to your own ideas to gauge what has been done, the way it was done, and what the remaining gaps or questions that need to be addressed may be. What has been missing up until this point? How should I write a literature review? How do I find sources to include in my study? How do I identify to the reader which articles I have used? We will first turn our attention to how a literature review should be written and the role it serves for your readers.

Almost without exception, the majority of research articles begin with an introduction to the topic and statement of purpose, followed by a mandatory review of the literature, which is where the author typically attempts to place the current study in context of previous research in the area or on the given phenomenon, as the literature review is useful as a starting place when beginning a new line of research or an indicator of the major sources in a given area. The most useful literature reviews are those that serve as a launching pad for the current discussion (Walker, 1998). When writing a manuscript, a literature review should be framed in such a way that the purpose of the article is well established in the introduction and then the literature is reviewed in light of that purpose. In this manner, sources may be compared to show how the current work overcomes the limitations of some research, expands and refines other research, and complements still others. This keeps your reader attached to the main purpose of the article while providing the appropriate context (Walker, 1998).

As previously stated, literature reviews are an important method by which to introduce the reader to the topic of study; however, they also serve as a platform to introduce both new and complex terminology or concepts that will be a part of the current discussion. For example, researchers who are working in the area of risk-terrain modeling or environmental theory may have to introduce the reader to a completely new way of thinking and new terminology with which they may be unfamiliar. As such, this can more easily be accomplished with a review of previous works rather than having to break the flow of the writing with a lesson on new concepts. When a review of concepts and terminology is included with the literature review, it also allows the researcher to direct the reader to additional sources of information where they may find a more detailed discussion.

Common Problems with Literature Reviews

Introducing readers to new concepts and terminology and setting the context for the current study are two broad goals of a literature review that are often not met because a researcher may approach the literature review with the wrong objectives in mind. One of the most common problems of literature reviews that diminishes their usefulness is that they are typically poorly organized and thought out. Researchers will attempt to include as many references as possible, oftentimes in a list that runs on longer than the paragraph of text. What often ends up as the result of these kinds of citations strings and literature reviews is that all but the most dedicated readers quickly tire of the discussion and move on. Some researchers think this is acceptable; after all, there is incentive for the reader to care more about my work than someone else's. This makes for extremely tedious reading and does little to nothing to introduce the reader to the subject matter or provide a foundation for the current line of inquiry. This type of literature review often follows a chronological format (sources cited from earliest published to most current) rather than one of logical flow and often includes sources that are scarcely, if at all, related to the topic of study. Researchers with this type of review could lessen their work and anxiety, and create a literature review that is much more useful, by simply reducing the amount of material covered and making the review flow from the introduction to the primary topic of the article. A shorter and more relevant review would be much more interesting and prepare the reader for what lies ahead rather than having a reader that is weary from citation fatigue (Walker, 1998).

Researchers should also be aware of the format of the literature review. Although there is typically a heading between the introduction and the literature review, authors often begin the review with a continuation of the introduction. While this can serve as an important transition from the researcher's work to the literature review, it can result in a long and rambling segment of text where it is difficult to determine where the researcher is citing previous studies and where they are offering their new perspectives and assertions (the "so what" of their contribution).

As Walker noted, the exact opposite of this can also be problematic. This happens when researchers begin the article with positive, active writing and then change the tone completely in the literature review section to that of a lock-step of phrases; "Bill and Joe (2010) argued …." or "Lisa and Brittany (2005) proposed…." Nothing loses a reader's interest quicker than a monotonous and repetitive approach to presenting prior literature.

Final Thoughts on the Content of a Literature Review

As Walker contended, with the explosion of interest in criminal justice and criminology disciplines in the past twenty years, it is not possible to stay abreast of all relevant literature in the discipline. For this reason, when writing a literature review, you should attempt to inform the reader about the subject from a perspective that they might not possess, meaning that a researcher should strive to have a well-rounded, organized, and informative literature review to enhance the reader's understanding of the particular topic area of an article. Simply demonstrating that a researcher has access to one of the many bibliographic databases from which one can list dozens of sources rarely meets these requirements. While it may be true that citing every relevant article in the history of the topic does prove that the researcher has done their homework, this can be established in a much shorter and more relevant review and by demonstrating an understanding of the material regarding the researcher's own contribution.

To summarize and reiterate what is required of a good literature review, recall that first, you should make sure that each of the sources reviewed are relevant to the purpose of the article. The literature should not read as if you took it from another source. It should flow from the introduction and provide a firm foundation for the discussion to follow. The review should also establish as quickly and concisely as possible the researcher's credibility and understanding of the material. Convincing readers, your professors, and eventually editors and reviewers that you understand the material and topic is important, but it should not consume half of the article in a barrage of repetitive statements. Additionally, the review should be written for the reader, not for the researcher; this is an especially important distinction to make as a student when writing for your professor versus an editor or reviewer. The literature review should introduce the reader to the topic of the article, establish the parameters of the topic at hand, provide the reader with the necessary information to understand the topic, and clarify the conceptual framework of the study. Lastly, maintain contact between the literature review and the new material to be presented by discussing the literature in light of your own contributions and the discussion to come, but be diligent to separate the critical review of the literature from new arguments.

Finding Literature:
Where to Find Sources

So now that we have identified the role of the literature review and what content should be included in it, we move to actually finding the sources one would draw information from when writing the literature review. Because we are living in a digital age where technology is part of everyday life, a major foundation for identifying sources can be found online, via both traditional search engines such as Google and Bing as well as specialty sites like Google Scholar and ResearchGate.

Search Engines

Let's start with the websites that are generally the most familiar to all of us on a daily basis, popular search engines. Just as you might type in a search on Google for a recipe for oatmeal cookies, you can also look for sources to include in a research article. In fact, Google is often the preferred method of identifying certain types of sources, like expert interviews in the media, or if you are trying to find a government report that may have been put out by a local, state, or federal agency, such as Federal Bureau of Investigation or the Bureau of Justice Statistics. These sources will appear like any other Google search, with a list of links that will take the researcher to a link where they will often have the ability to open and download either an HTML or PDF version of the interview or report (it is always important to cite the web address of these links; more on this later).

University Library

Another popular place to find sources for your research article, in particular scholarly journals and books, is your university's library. I know it seems like the obvious place, but in today's age of technology, it is surprising the number of students (and some faculty) who do not know the value and the resources that are in their own university library. In addition to the books that you can find under the criminal justice/criminology section, libraries also have a large number of research articles available to researchers. Usually, your university library will have a section that is called "Periodicals"; this is fancy name for research articles. Often, they are bound by journal title and grouped by year or groups of years and can be requested to be brought directly to you by library staff. Additionally, as with the World Wide Web, a large number of the sources within a library's archives are accessible via the Internet. Generally, you can log into your university's library system with your student ID and password and instantly have access to a host of dissertation and thesis archives as well as access to any academic journals that your university subscribes to on a yearly basis. You should be able to either download these to a thumb drive or cloud software or print them out to read as a hard copy. What research article databases that are available in your library will vary, but some popular databases that you can often find access to include JSTOR, Academic Search Complete, and LexisNexis. These databases work similarly to how a search engine of a website functions. For a broad search, you can type in key words that may be part of your PQ and RQs, such as Juvenile Female Sex Offenders. A list of research articles will appear that contain the key words that you typed; if the library has access to those articles, you should be able to download and/ or print a copy of the article. Additionally, there are advanced search options that let you narrow down your search, including limiting your search criteria to a certain number of years, or only showing articles that contain the searched phrase in that exact order, as well as a host of other options.

Fear not if there is an article, book, or book chapter that you have found online but your library does not have because there is one last service that the majority of university libraries have, and it is a lifesaver for researcher—I am referring to the Inter-Library Loan (ILL) program. If you come across a source that you need but cannot obtain at your library or through an online database you can always get it through the ILL. The ILL is kind of like a movie rental store (Blockbuster) for academic sources. Generally, you have to use your student ID and a password to sign up for an account via your university library. Once the account is created, you are able to enter the information about the source that you need to borrow. You will be asked to identify the title of the journal or book, the author, and the year of publication. For articles, it will also ask you to include the volume and issue number of the journal the article was in, as well as the specific page numbers from that journal that you are requesting. Once you have entered the information and submit it to the library, they begin contacting other libraries that have the ILL program to see if they have the source, you have requested. When they find another university that has the source they will either attach an electronic copy of the article if they have one, make a photocopy of the journal article from their bounded versions, or in the case of a book chapter, make a photocopy of the chapter requested. In the case of requesting an entire book, they will mail the book from their university library to yours. The best part of this is the simplicity of what you have to do as the researcher. After you enter the information about the source, all you have to do is sit back and wait for it to arrive to your account. Generally, you will receive an email in your university email account that a source you requested has arrived. In the case of an article or photocopied chapter, you do not have to do anything except log onto your ILL account and download the source to a drive, or you can print it. In the case of an entire book, you will have to go to the library circulation desk and pick up the text; they will check it out to you much the same as a regular book you have borrowed from the library, complete with a return date and fines if you lose or fail to return the text on time. The best way to become familiar with any and all of these resources is to start using them.

We would be remiss at this point if we did not tell you about the employees that work at the library, especially if you are a student seeking information for research purposes. Many libraries have specific staff whose purpose of employment it is to aid students and faculty with research. Please, take advantage what these people have to offer and the knowledge and resources they can provide to you. Oftentimes, not only can they help you one-on-one but they offer to come to a class (such as a

Research Methods class) and provide a full overview of the variety of services that they can offer.

Research Search Engines

One of the most popular, if not the most popular, research websites today is Google Scholar. It works very much the same way as the regular Google search engine, except it is already limited to academic and research sources. It appears to be very similar to the regular Google search engine with the exception of the whether you are looking for articles or case law as will be designated by the circle checked below the search box. When looking for sources for a research article, you generally will want to go with the default and have "articles" checked, unless you are searching for specific cases. This search bar works the same as those discussed above in that you generally want to search for something that is specific to your research idea, perhaps a key word or phrase from your PQ or one of your RQs. A search on Google scholar for our example topic, Juvenile Female Sex Offenders, returned approximately 95,700 sources including books and articles. The list of sources appears the same way that hits do for the Google search engine, except that in the case of Google Scholar, each title in the list shown is linked to an academic article or book. Clicking on the title will generally take you to a page with more information about that source. With articles, you are usually taken to a page where you can find the journal title, author's names, and the volume and issue number to the journal the article was available in; sometimes an abstract, references, and related works can be present. You will also find that the full versions of these article are not generally available, but some may be. You will notice tabs that may say "login" or a button that will let you purchase and download the article for a price. Why this may be an option to some, prices can be steep, and there are better ways to obtain the article, mainly the ILL we previously discussed. If the full version is not available for the article you want, the page that you were brought to when clicking on the title provides all the information to fill in the form on your university's ILL website and will save you great time and effort. Returning to the list of sources from our initial search, if the full text to the article is available you will most likely see a link, light blue in color, to the right of the title that says something along the lines of "[PDF] tandfonline.com" or "[PDF] sagepub.com" or "[HTML] google.com" or some variation of this. This means that there exists a PDF or HTML copy of the article that you can access and download for free without having to go through ILL. Similar to searching the aforementioned databases mentioned above, you can do an advanced search to narrow down the criteria of the sources that you are looking for. If I limit that same search to sources published since 2010 it returns approximately 17,600 sources, and then I would be searching more contemporary perspectives regarding juvenile female sex offenders as opposed to the entire history of the topic. Google Scholar is also great place to visit when you need to cite a source in a particular format (more on this later).

Tips and Tricks for Google and Google Scholar (and Other Search Engines)

Boolean Operators

There are other tools that Google Scholar offers. (We should mention that many of these same types of tools are available in other search engines, too.) First, you can use Boolean search operators (instead of advanced search tools) to find what you are looking for. For instance, if you want to make sure that an article contains the phrase "punitive sentencing" you should search it just like that—quotation marks and all. If you do not use the quotation marks, it will result in every article that says "punitive" and "sentencing" and "punitive sentencing." If you have more than one phrase you want in an article, you can use AND to make sure that it includes both. For instance:

"restorative justice" AND "sex offenders"

Perhaps you want articles that include at least one of those phrases (restorative justice or sex offenders). For this, you can use OR instead of AND:

"restorative justice" OR "sex offenders"

What if you want a phrase, but are unsure of one of the words that you want in the phrase? Like "sentenced to a ____ security prison"? (High, low, or medium.) You could do three separate searches, or you can use an asterisk, which signifies that you are flexible on what word fills in the blank.

"Sentenced to a * security prison"

You can also use a hyphen (-) to signify that you do not want a certain word in there. Perhaps after reading our book, you want to make sure that you never see anything with the names "Vanessa Woodward Griffin" or "Kyle A. Burgason" again. If this is the case, you could say:

-"Vanessa Woodward Griffin" -"Kyle A. Burgason"

Specifying Citations

You can also use Google Scholar to narrow down your selections a bit more. For instance, if your topic was on juvenile female sex offenders and shame, then you might already know that disintegrative and reintegrative shaming was developed by John Braithwaite, in his book *Crime, Shame, and Reintegration* (Braithwaite, 1989).

When we discussed searching for juvenile female sex offenders, Google Scholar originally approximately 95,700 sources, including books and articles. If you know that you really want to first focus on how this topic has been studied in the context of shaming theory, you can search *only* those sources that have cited Braithwaite's book. Simply search Google Scholar for Braithwaite's book (*Crime, Shame, and Reintegration*). When it comes up (should be the first result), you should see a link under it that says, "Cited by 5,121" (or some number close to that). This is a link. You can select it, which will take you to a new results window that includes all the results/sources that have cited Braithwaite's book. Before the first result, you should see where the window says "Crime, shame and reintegration" and a check box that says, "Search within citing articles." Now, in the search bar, search female juvenile sex offenders, (no quotation marks) and select the checkbox: "search within citing articles." What this does is allows you to see only those articles that discuss juvenile female sex offenders (or a similar topic on sex offenders, like juvenile sex offenders or female sex offenders), and also talked about (and cited) Braithwaite's *Crime, Shame and Reintegration*. Now, you have gone from almost 100,000 sources to less than 1,200! This can help you start with more specific results and then broaden out, instead of trying to do it the other way around.

ResearchGate

The last website that I am going to mention is an interactive site that you can become a member of even as student, ResearchGate. I like to refer to ResearchGate as Facebook for researchers. You have the ability to join the group and create your own profile as you would with Facebook and add friends (researchers) and see their profiles. Instead of the last thing you ate or pictures from you last vacation, on ResearchGate you post the articles, books, and reports that you have published as well as the projects that you are currently working on. Other researchers can friend you and follow your work as you can to them as well. Comments and questions can be posted to profiles much the same way as they are on Facebook, and if you are seeking a particular work from an author, you can send them a direct message and request it or ask questions about it.

Citing Sources in a Research Article

In a literature review (and throughout a research article), it is not enough that you locate and read several sources just so you can set up your study with proper context and inform the reader of previous work, but you must give credit (or cite) to all the studies that you mention and all the information that you provide that is not common sense or is not your own. If you do not cite this information, you are guilty of what is known as plagiarism, and as some of you may know, this is strict liability offense. Meaning that you do not need intent to plagiarize—in other words, whether you meant to do it or if it was just an accident, the result is the same ... you are guilty of plagiarizing.

So how do you go about citing (giving credit to) the work of others throughout your research article? First, it depends on what style you are writing your research article in. That is right, you might not have thought (especially after reading this book) researchers had style, but indeed we do. Now, we are not talking about goth, preppy, or hipster style but rather ASA, APA, and Chicago, to name a few of the popular versions in the social sciences. In criminal justice and criminology, you will be dealing with either APA or Chicago. Some of you probably learned or at least heard of MLA style in high school or at the very least in your English 101 and 102 classes at your university. Our conversation shall stick to the APA style, as that is the style that most papers are written in for the discipline of criminal justice and criminology. As you have or will read through a research article, you will no doubt see some of the citation that I am referring to within the article. They often appear after the statement of fact or finding discussed by the author. For example,

> It was recently found that 95 percent of the students who read this research methods book thought it was the best book they had ever read (Woodward Griffin & Burgason, 2019).

The previous sentence is a factual statement that contains a percentage (in actuality, it is a pretend citation) and therefore needs to be cited correctly to give the researchers proper credit. This was done by giving the in-text citation at the end of the sentence. For APA style (which is shown) the in-text citation needs to contain the author's surname (last name) and the year the source was published; in this case, the authors were Vanessa Woodward Griffin and Kyle A. Burgason and the source was published in 2019. This information can also be presented as part of the sentence, and in that case, would usually come at the beginning of the sentence. For example, Woodward Griffin and Burgason (2019) recently found that 95 percent of the students who read this research methods book thought it was the best book they had ever read.

Both versions of this style are correct and can be used interchangeably throughout a research article. You probably noted the use of the ampersand (&) as opposed to the word "and" with the end of sentence citation. That is a unique feature to the APA style and is utilized to save time and space when writing in-text citations and listing references at the end of the research article. Sometimes, researchers need to paraphrase what another author stated, or better yet, use a direct quotation from another researcher's study. For both styles, this requires a little bit more information about the source. Let us use a quotation from the same pretend source we just used, a research article by Woodward Griffin and Burgason written in 2019 that deals with student enjoyment of reading their research methods book. This time, imagine that we want to cite the sentence in the study on page 150, where Professor Burgason claims that "the current edition of the research methods book is a fantastic example of scientific inquisition." The quotation should be cited as follows:

> The book was met with such excitement that "the current edition of the research methods book is a fantastic example of scientific inquisition" (Woodward Griffin & Burgason, 2019, p. 150).

Or

> Woodward Griffin and Burgason (2019) stated that "the current edition of the research methods book is a fantastic example of scientific inquisition" (p. 150).

Again, either version of this citation is acceptable. The small difference that you may have noticed is that with a paraphrase or a direct quote, APA style requires you to include the page number as part of the citation.

There are subtle differences between the different styles of citations, such as where you use an ampersand in APA style, Chicago style requires the word "and," but all the information provided by both is essentially the same and has the same end goals: to give credit to the proper researchers and to help those reading your research in the future find that particular source you utilized and read it for themselves.

Each of the writing styles has an accompanying manual that can be purchased that will take the researcher step by step though citing almost any kind of source possible, from research articles to movie clips; however, in the days of technology this valuable information can also be found on the Internet. One the most popular websites that offers this information for free is the Purdue Online Writing Lab or Purdue OWL, as it is known. A simple Google search for Purdue Owl will lead you to its homepage, where you can explore a vast array of different in-text citation styles, several reference styles, and a whole host of information that is specifically designed to help students in writing a paper.

References

You have probably noticed that at the end of many of the research articles you have read, there is a long list of studies, which are generally listed in alphabetical order. This is what is referred to as the reference section, and it is just what its name suggests. This section gives full credit to those studies that were "referenced" in your research article. Just like we discussed giving credit with in-text citations throughout the literature review, those in-text citations (researcher's surname and year of publication) are linked directly to a source in the references, except in the references, all the information about the source is provided, including researcher's name and year of publication, the title of the article or chapter, the title of the source (name of journal or name of book), the volume and issue number, inclusive page numbers, and publication information if it is book. This is done so that if anyone is curious about one of the sources that you cited in your literature review and wants to find and read that source for themselves, they can flip to the reference section and easily see where to find the particular source for which they are searching.

Like in-text citations, references also follow a certain style; for criminal justice and criminology, we are generally talking about APA or Chicago. Again, we will go with APA style for examples because it is the most popular style utilized by the journals in our discipline. Let us use our example from above with Woodward Griffin and Burgason (2019) as the in-text citation. Each in-text citation must correspond to a source in the references section, and these are linked via the first author's (Woodward Griffin) last name. In the reference section, you would see a whole host of sources listed before you got to the last name Woodward Griffin, as references are listed in alphabetical order. When you arrived at the correct source, it would look something like this (keep in mind this is a fictitious source):

Woodward Griffin, V., & Burgason, K. A. (2019). Research methods rocks. *American Annals of Criminology*, 25(4), 145–160.

Notice that we have both of the authors' names and their first initials. Remember, this is for APA style — other styles may have different requirements for references, such as in the Chicago style, where references are required to show the full first and last names of authors (there will be a full list of references accompanying the research article example at the end of this part). The Purdue OWL is a great online resource to help with this aspect of your research article as well. Another great website for references is a return to Google Scholar. Once you have located and read an article you are going to cite in your research article you can easily use the Google Scholars "cite" link to put that source if your references with ease. When looking at the article title on Google Scholar you should notice a list of blue symbols and words below the author's names and the abstract. Generally these symbols and words are: ☆, ", Cited by 10, Related Articles, All 5 Versions, and ››. If you click on the quotation mark symbol (") a box will pop up with the reference already cited in the proper format. Ideally, all you need to do is copy and paste the citation into your reference section, or you can import the citation to one of a couple of popular bibliography managers, such as EndNote or RefWorks. (Sometimes, however, these are not formatted correctly — you will have to use all your newfound knowledge on citation styles to discern whether it is correct!)

You should also be aware as there can be different styles within styles. For example, there are multiple versions of Chicago style, including "R" style and "B" style and while each one generally provides the same information, there are little nuances to each style that can make a big difference — particularly if you are writing for a professor who requests a certain version. Always be diligent and check to make sure that you are using the correct format for your references.

An Example Research Article

The following appendix will give you in detail an example of a research idea taken from conception of PQ and RQs through the literature review and methods section of an article, as these are the sections that are most often required when submitting a research proposal (more on this in Chapter 15). This example will include not only development of PQ and RQs as did the example in Chapter 13, but it will also include the literature that should accompany the conceptualization and operationalization of variables. This example will also include a theoretical framework so that you may see how to incorporate a theory into your research proposal and eventually a research article suitable for publication. It is the author's hope that this full example can be utilized as a guide or template for the student as they embark on their own research. The following example in the appendix is a theoretical research article centered on optimal foraging theory and how it can be used to help identify the search patterns of online sex offenders (Burgason & Walker, 2013). Additionally, this example will be provided in Chicago "R" style to expose the reader to the other major style in the criminal justice/criminology discipline.

In addition to conceptualizing and operationalizing variables, the researcher must decide who to study and where to obtain those observations. As stated in Chapter 7, researchers are rarely able to study all the members of the population that interests them; however, they can utilize a sample of subjects for study and draw inferences. In the current study about the online search behavior of sex offenders, the relevant population would either be the Internet logs of computers obtained from sex offenders via police or the online sex offenders themselves.

In interviews with the offenders themselves or via their Internet logs, you can ask or assess all the questions raised during your conceptualization. How much time did they spend searching for a website? What drew the offender to one website over another? How much time did the offender spend within particular website? And so on.

The researcher can finally analyze the collected data for the purpose of drawing conclusions that can answer the research questions, fall in line with the theory, and finally answer the primary question that initiated the inquiry. Lastly, the final part of the research article should help to inform policy or what is known as the application stage. The researcher will mostly likely want to disseminate (share) their findings so that others will know what they have discovered. This can be accomplished in several ways, depending on the situation of the researcher, the purpose of the research, and the robustness of the findings. The researcher may deem it appropriate to publish the article or make a presentation in class or at a local, regional, or national conference, as others will most likely be interested in what you have learned about the search behavior of online sexual predators. As such, the research might actually be used by parents, schools, or even computer forensic investigators to monitor and help protect certain segments of the population while they are online. Finally, you should consider what needs to be done to further research on the subject. What mistakes should be corrected in future research?

Perhaps you obtained all your information from Internet access logs, or perhaps you could suggest an actual interview with the offenders. What new lines of inquiry did your study open that might not have been there prior to it? If you can track and help predict search behaviors online, perhaps you can track and predict search behavior in real-time, and your study could be the first in a series of steps that leads to new monitoring and apprehension of sexual predators.

Summing It Up

It was the goal of this chapter of the "How To" section to consolidate what was described and learned in the first two chapters of this section of the text so that students could be exposed to the different elements that make up a research article and how those elements come together to form a research article. Hopefully the example in the index of what a research article should contain (introduction, literature review, theoretical framework, methods, results, and discussion/conclusions) will help you when developing your own research ideas and writing your own research proposals.

References

Braithwaite, J. (1989). *Crime, shame and reintegration.* Cambridge University Press.

Burgason, K., & Walker, J. (2013). Optimal foraging theory's application to internet sex offender search behavior: A theoretical model for computer forensic investigations. *Journal of Forensic Investigation, 1*(1), 6.

Walker, J. T. (1998). The role of a literature review in publication. *Journal of Criminal Justice Education, 9*(2), iii–vi. doi:10.1080/10511259800084271.

Chapter 15

How to Develop a
Research Proposal

Everything that you have learned in the first three chapters of this section will be put to use to help you draft your own research proposal. The good news is you already know most of the parts that are required in a general proposal and have been studying them in the past three chapters of the "how to" section. If you undertake a research project, be it in class or through a foundation or government-funded organization, you will most likely need to provide a research proposal describing what you intend to undertake, why you want to do it, and how you are going to accomplish your research objectives. We will conclude this text with a discussion of how you might prepare such a proposal. Lastly, in the appendix you will see an example research paper, so that you can see how we have applied the information we are providing to you.

Purpose and Parts of a Proposal

A research proposal is intended to convince others that you have a worthwhile research project and that you have the competence and the work-plan to complete it. Generally, a research proposal should contain all the key elements involved in the front end of a research article (which is why we provided multiple examples) and include sufficient information for the readers to evaluate the proposed study (Wong, 2002). Most often, like the research article, a proposal introduces a problem, purpose, and significance of a study as well as the researcher's primary and research questions and hypotheses. It also gives a brief explanation of the theory guiding the study, a review of relevant literature pertaining to the theory, and the procedure for the experiment (University Writing Center, 2011). Like a research article, the introduction explains in detail several components of the experiment that must be included in any proposal. The main purpose of the introduction is to provide the necessary background or context for your research problem. As such, after reading the introduction, the reader knows why the researcher is conducting the study and why it is important—specifically, how it will impact the discipline, the academic community, and/or society at large. For this paragraph, it is necessary to grab the reader's attention, introduce the topic at hand, and provide a brief overview of the theory from which the study is based (University Writing Center, 2011).

Problem Statement

The "Problem Statement" is a vital part of the proposal; considering that, for research to be conducted, one must notice a problem in the existing literature that has not been previously addressed. For this section, the following questions should be answered: What exactly do you want to study? Why is it worth studying? Does the proposed study contribute to our general understanding of crime or policy responses to crime? Does it have practical significance? Answering these questions will allow readers to understand why this study is important and how the study will attempt to answer new, never-before-asked questions.

Literature Review

The literature review provides the background for the research problem and illustrates to the reader that the researcher is knowledgeable about the scope of the theory. What have others said about this topic? What research has been done? Are the findings consistent, or do past studies disagree? Are there flaws in the body of existing research that you feel you can remedy? The literature review is your chance to act like a news reporter. You want to present what is "going on" within the literature without imputing your opinion. This should be a comprehensive unbiased report that still frames your eventual study, as it should serve as a foreshadowing tool for your study. Recall that literature reviews serve several important functions, including:

- Ensuring that you are not "reinventing the wheel."
- Giving credit to those who have laid the groundwork for your research.
- Demonstrating your knowledge of the research problem.
- Demonstrating your understanding of the theoretical and research issues related to your research question.
- Showing your ability to critically evaluate relevant literature information.
- Indicating your ability to integrate and synthesize the existing literature.
- Providing new theoretical insights or developing a new model as the conceptual framework for your research.
- Convincing your reader that your proposed research will make a significant and substantial contribution to the literature (i.e., resolving an important theoretical issue or filling a major gap in the literature) (Wong, 2002).

Research Questions

Mirroring a research article, it is important to provide the primary research question and other research questions that your study will try to answer. Given what others have found, what new information do you expect to find? It is useful to view research questions as a more specific version of the problem or objective described earlier (Maxfield & Babbie, 2014). In addition to identifying the research questions of the study, the researcher should also include the hypotheses for the study. Meaning, based on your research questions and review of literature, what do you think the relationship between your variables is going to be? What do you think you are going to find with this line of inquiry?

As did the research article, this section should detail the theory that is guiding the proposed study (as optimal foraging theory does in our appendix example). From this theory, the researcher can inform the statement of the problem, the purpose of the study, and the questions and hypotheses. In this section, explain the major tenants of the theory as well as how the theory relates to the proposed study. Remember that the eventual findings of the experiment will be discussed in terms of how they relate to the theory (University Writing Center, 2011).

Methods

Many subcategories can fall under the methods umbrella, as this is the most important section in the entire proposal. It explains each step the researcher will take to conduct his or her research, and it tells your reader how you plan to tackle your research problem. It will provide your work plan and describe the activities necessary for the completion of your project. The guiding principle for writing the method section is that it should contain sufficient information for the reader to determine whether the methodology is sound (Wong, 2002). Ideally, it should give enough detail that the reader could replicate your study using your methods section as a guide. A lot of times some of this information might get cut (for actual publication). Yet, it is better to start too detailed than too broad, particularly so you do not forget what it is that you did! This section generally includes research design, measures, sampling, and data collection methods and analysis.

Research Design and Sampling

Include the proposed research design of the study, whether it is a survey, experiment, observation, or using secondary data for analysis, and explain how this design will produce fruitful results. Briefly discuss how the data will be administered and collected, including how the subjects will participate in the study. This section should include an expanded discussion of the sample. First, discuss the population under consideration. From where will participants be selected? Second, give the sampling method to be used. Which specific sampling method will be used to select participants? Lastly, list the elements that will be characteristic of the sample, such as sex, age, etc. (University Writing Center, 2011). If there is any possibility that your research will have an impact on those you study, how will you ensure that they are not harmed by the research? Finally, if you will be interacting directly with human subjects, you will probably have to include a consent form that describes what efforts will be taken to protect human subjects (Maxfield & Babbie, 2014). Reiterate that the respondents' participation is voluntary and that they can choose to withdraw from the study at any time. Describe how the respondents' confidentiality will be protected and how they may receive a copy of the study when it is finished, (University Writing Center, 2011) as this will be required by your university institutional review board and all government and foundation research institutions.

Measurement

This is where you should describe the key variables in your study and how you arrived at those variables. This is good place to employ the conceptualization and operationalization techniques demonstrated in the previous examples. If you have already developed your instrument (a questionnaire, for example), you should include a copy in an appendix to your proposal, as your university's IRB will require you to include it (Maxfield & Babbie, 2014).

Analysis

Obviously, you do not have results to report at the proposal stage (though some preliminary results are acceptable); however, you need to have some idea about what kind of data you will be collecting and what statistical procedures will be used to answer your primary and research questions and/or test your hypotheses. The research should briefly describe the kind of analysis you plan to conduct from the univariate through multivariate. Spell out the purpose and logic of your analysis. Also, include what statistics or analytical tools will be used for analyzing the data. For instance, you may want to address what software you plan to use (some examples might by Microsoft Excel, SPSS [Statistical Package for the Social Sciences], Stata, or Mplus). Second, you should address what statistical techniques or other analytical techniques you plan to use to analyze the data (content analysis, ordinary least squares [OLS] regression, chi square, etc.). Some of these techniques and software may sound foreign to you, which is perfectly okay! Most of this will be addressed in statistics courses.

Discussion

It is important to convince your reader of the potential impact of your proposed research. You need to communicate a sense of enthusiasm and confidence without exaggerating the merits of your proposal. Always think about your reader like your funder—they are giving you a million dollars to conduct the study, and they want to know how their money is being used and that it is a good investment. The researcher should focus on the implications of the proposed study, such as how the study's results will affect future research, theory, policy, etc. Therefore, write this section with the focus on how the study's results will benefit others. Address how well the study will do in terms of internal and external validity, and discuss the implications of the study affecting practice, policy, and scholarly/future research (University Writing Center, 2011). Additionally, it is a good idea for the researcher to state the possible limitations and weaknesses of the proposed research, which may be justified by time and financial constraints (Wong, 2002).

Schedule and Budget

These are two new elements that we have yet to discuss in the "how to" section but are important parts of the research proposal. It is often appropriate to provide a schedule for the various stages of research. Many of the national foundations and research institutions in the country (NIJ, USDA, etc.) not only require a schedule, but also require reports to be filled out throughout the duration of the research as to the progress you are making toward your completion of the research. As Maxfield and Babbie (2014) noted, even if you do not do this for the proposal, do it for yourself. Unless you have a time line for accomplishing the several stages of research and keeping track of how you are doing, you may end up in trouble.

Regarding the budget, if you are asking someone to give you money to pay the costs of your research, you will need to provide a budget that specifies where the money will go. Such expenses can include personnel (graduate students), equipment (tape recorders and statistical software), supplies (paper for questionnaires, stamps for mailing recruitment letters), and expenses (travel, copying, and printing). As noted in Chapter 8, even for a simple survey of university students, the costs can quickly total a couple of thousand dollars, from office supplies, photocopying, computer disks, postage, and telephone calls. As such, it is a good idea to spend some time anticipating any expenses that may be involved over the course of the project. As noted by Maxfield and Babbie (2014), if you are interested in conducting a criminal justice research project, it is a good idea to prepare a research proposal for your own purposes, even if you are not required to do so by your instructor or a funding agency. If you are going to invest your time and energy in such a project, you should do what you can to ensure a return on that investment.

Summing It Up

The main purpose of a research proposal is to show that the problem you propose to investigate is significant enough to warrant the investigation, the method you plan to use is sound and reasonable, and the results are likely to prove fruitful and will make an original contribution to the discipline, the academic community, or society at large. Additionally, the researcher should never view writing a proposal as a worthless endeavor, but rather you can use it to your advantage. It always forces you to think about your topic, to see the scope of your research, and to review the appropriateness of your methodology. Having something in writing also provides an opportunity to your supervisor to judge the practicality of the project (whether it is possible to finish in time, costs, the equipment needed and other practicalities, time needed for supervision). While there are no fixed rules as to what exactly should be included in the structure of a proposal, it is our goal (the authors') that the example in the appendix can be utilized as a template and aid in guiding your own research proposals.

References

Maxfield, M., & Babbie, E. (2014). *Research methods for criminal justice and criminology*. Boston, MA: Cengage Learning.

University Writing Center. (2011). How to write a research proposal: A formal template for preparing a proposal for research methods. Dallas Baptist University. Retrieved from http://www3.dbu.edu/uwc/documents/HowtoWriteaProposal Template.pdf.

Wong, P. T. (2002). How to write a research proposal. Dr. Paul Wong [blog]. Retrieved from http://www.drpaulwong.com/how-to-write-a-research-proposal.

Appendix

Sample Research Paper

Search Strategies of Internet Sex Offenders

Introduction

The Internet has increased access to the population of people sex offenders seek to victimize through solicitations for child pornography and other sex crimes. Previous research on Internet sex offenders has been limited to exploratory studies examining characteristics of Internet sex offenders (Wolak, Finkelhor, Mitchell, and Ybarra 2008; Malesky 2007; Webb, Craissati, and Keen 2007; Young 2005; Burke, Sowerbutts, Blundell, and Sherry 2002; Cooper, Scherer, Boies, and Gordon 1999), their targets (Marcum 2007; Beebe, Asche, Harrison, and Quinlan 2004; Wolak, Finkelhor, and Mitchell 2004), and what characteristics differentiate between Internet sex offenders and traditional sex offenders (Seto, Wood, Babchishin, and Flynn 2011). There is an absence of research explaining the search strategies of Internet sex offenders. This study seeks to add to the body of knowledge regarding Internet sex offenders by examining how they search the Internet for potential targets. The primary research question of this study is: *Can optimal foraging theory explain Internet sex offenders' search behavior?*

Previous studies demonstrated that people have certain patterns they use to search for information online (Nachmias and Gilad 2002; Slone 2003; Thatcher 2004). The time using these searching strategies, time scanning the information found for answers to queries, and the number of steps taken for searchers to reach pertinent information were found to be significant aspects of Internet information retrieval (Nachmias and Gilad 2002; Walraven, Brand-Guwel and Boshuizen 2009). This study examines whether Internet sex offenders also use a specific search strategy when attempting to identify potential targets. We suggest that optimal foraging theory could offer an explanation of Internet sex offenders' behavior. Optimal foraging theory is a search strategy initially used to predict evolutionary fitness of different species of animals, where fitness is enhanced by those foragers who acquired more food, conserved more time and energy, and managed to avoid risk during foraging (Emlen 1966, 615; MacArthur and Pianka 1966, 603). The theory examines four components that are necessary for optimization: An actor, who chooses among patchy alternatives; a currency, by which the actor measures costs and benefits; constraints, beyond the actor's control that limit behavior; and a strategy, specifying the actor's range of available options (Smith et al. 1983; Charnov 1974; MacArthur and Pianka 1966). An actor will adhere to a specific search strategy within a food patch until the point in time when the energy expended in securing the food outweighs the energy obtained from the food, and the patch should be abandoned in what is known as "giving up time" (Charnov 1974; Wellborn 2000).

This study first focuses on one of the principal components of optimal foraging theory, the actor. We will be focused on identifying the actors' patterns of searching and how these actors' (Internet sex offenders) searches vary depending on what they are seeking. We expect the patches (websites) of offenders searching for pictures of child pornography to differ from the websites of offenders searching for a sexual themed chats, and we expect those websites to differ from offenders seeking to make physical contact with a target and so forth. The actor within the foraging model is in search of a specific item to measure costs and benefits by; for this study websites are the currency of choice.

The currency that this study seeks to explore is the different characteristics of a particular website that attract the attention of Internet sex offenders. We will examine different websites, and the different entities or nodes available on those websites that link to different communication outlets, such as chat rooms, instant messaging services, emails, and bulletin boards, to determine what websites (patches) are most attractive to the Internet sex offender (actor). Previous research (Malesky 2007; Young 2005; Wolak, Finkelhor, and Mitchell 2004) revealed Internet sex offenders frequent such websites in an attempt to solicit targets for sexual exploitation. Prey choice and diet breadth are fundamental themes to optimal foraging theory (MacArthur and Pianka 1966; Emlen 1966; Pyke, Pulliam, and Charnov 1977; Smith 1983; Wellborn 2000), and their abundance or lack thereof could have an impact on the where and how offenders search. In determining what websites warrant further allocation of time, Internet sex offenders must have a plan that guides their search. This plan or strategy for searching takes into account all the available options known to the actor (Internet sex offender) so that the efforts of finding and receiving rewards from their currency are optimized, and outweigh the time and energy spent searching for the currency.

The third component required for foraging to be successful is a strategy. Here we are interested in not only what brings the Internet sex offender to a particular website, but what characteristics keep the offender on a particular website for extended periods of time. First, we want to see what content the website displays to determine what offenders use to begin searching. As research has shown, sexually themed websites are popular patches for offenders. We know from foraging literature (Sayers, Norconk, and Conklin-Brittain 2010; Langvatn and Hanley 1993; Lewis 1980) that animals will bypass certain food for others that yield a higher energy return; we expect Internet sex offenders to do the same, meaning offenders would bypass certain websites they considered inadequate for optimization in search of those websites where offenders could gain direct communication with targets, thus optimizing their search. With a set strategy guiding their search, Internet sex offenders need only minimize their risk of being identified.

The final focus of this study will be on constraints facing Internet sex offenders. We examine what factors influence Internet sex offenders to abandon one website in favor of another. We explore if abandonment is due to the risk associated with certain websites and chat rooms, such as being monitored by administrators or guardians, if offenders fear they are being set up by someone claiming to be an underage victim, or if abandonment is due to the depletion of attractive targets. When these risks become greater than the amount of successful targets acquired from a particular website, we expect that website will be abandoned in favor of another one. Previous foraging studies have found support for both high-risk abandonment (Bernasco 2009) and natural depletion of the currency sought (Johnson and Bowers 2004).

In closing, we propose that the concepts and propositions developed in optimal foraging theory will aid in explaining the search behavior of Internet sex offenders. It is expected that Internet sex offenders will search websites that allow more personal interaction with targets, resulting in those websites holding the offenders' attention for greater amounts of time. Finally, we expected that, like animals who can recognize an increase in the risk of predation (Bernasco 2009), Internet sex offenders will abandon a website when the risk of continuing communication with a target or searching for targets within a website increases.

Research Questions

In addressing the primary question of this research, four research questions are examined. These questions provide additional insight into optimal foraging theory's function in the search behavior of Internet sex offenders.

The first research question focuses on one of the main components necessary in optimal foraging theory, the actor. The first research question is: **Do Internet sex offenders' search patterns differ for different exploitations?** For the purposes of this study, the actors choosing among different alternatives will be Internet sex offenders. Just as animals vary their search strategy depending what prey they are in search of, Internet sex offenders may vary their search patterns for different types of targets; for example, how offenders' search for child pornography pictures differ from searches for someone to chat with sexually, and how searches for sex videos differ from an offenders searching for a target for physical contact. While there has been no research on the search strategy for finding these different mediums online, previous research has distinguished between offenders searching for physical contact online, offenders searching for child pornography, and pedophiles (Seto, Wood, Babchishin, and Flynn 2011; Webb, Craissati, and Keen 2007; Young 2005). Salient to this study is not only what offenders are searching for but also where they are searching.

The second research question addresses the next component of foraging, the currency. This research question is: **What characteristics of a particular website attract Internet sex offenders to that website?** For this study, websites and the entities available from them will serve as currency. This research question focuses on what food patches (Internet sites) are more desirable to the actor (Internet sex offender), and provide Internet sex offenders the best chance at acquiring quality food (targets). We are interested in determining what websites or entities available from websites attract Internet sex offenders. We will focus on different websites, and the different entities or nodes available on those websites that link to different communication outlets, such as chat rooms, instant messaging services, emails, and bulletin boards, to determine what forms of media are most attractive in searching for possible targets. Previous research has found that websites and online entities that have increased opportunities for interaction between actor and currency are popular places for Internet sex offender searching (Malesky 2007; Young 2005; Wolak, Finkelhor, and Mitchell 2004). It is expected that websites that allow for more personal interaction, such as the ability to chat or message potential targets, will be favored searching patches for Internet sex offenders.

As foraging animals will pass by some patches of food in favor of others that yield a greater source of energy intake (Sayers, Norconk, and Conklin-Brittain 2010; Langvatn and Hanley 1993; Lewis 1980), we expect Internet sex offenders to bypass certain websites and entities in favor of others. In determining what websites and online entities from those websites warrant further allocation of actors' time, actors must devise a plan to direct their search.

The third research question deals with the searching strategy of an actor. The third research question is: **What characteristics within a website influence time spent at that website?** For this study, the amount of time spent searching within a website and the factors influencing that amount of time will serve as an actor's strategy. The strategy component of foraging entails several factors of focus in this study: the content of the websites and the nodes and links within them, and the availability of targets within websites and entities. In terms of the content of the websites, we examine how sexually explicit a website or entity with a website must be to hold offenders' attention for increased amounts of time. Specifically we examine if social websites and general topic chat rooms are enough to engage the offender in "grooming" targets, or does the website, chat room, instant message, or bulletin board have to be sexual in nature to elicit more search time on the part of the offender. Previous studies (Malesky 2007; Young 2005; Wolak, Finkelhor, and Mitchell 2004) have found that sexually themed websites, chat rooms, messaging forums, and online profiles were frequented by Internet sex offenders searching for targets.

The availability of these targets, albeit to a lesser extent, also influences an offender's search strategy. Just as foraging burglars target more potentially profitable homes that appear in clusters in attractive neighborhoods (Johnson and Bowers 2004; Bernasco 2009), we would expect attractive targets that are clustered within a particular patch (website) to gain more attention and time from offenders. Even with an effective search strategy, Internet sex offenders must still minimize their risk of detection.

The fourth and final research question deals with the risks the actor must contend with within and between patches (the constraints). The final research question is: **What constraints lead to the abandonment of a particular website in favor of another?** For this study, the risks of websites and entities being monitored by administrators, parents, or guardians, and the depletion of attractive targets from the websites and entities will serve as constraints. We are interested in assessing what constraints cause Internet sex offenders to quit searching one website or entity in favor of another.

This research question addresses the marginal value theorem (Charnov 1974) of optimal foraging theory. This theorem states that a forager's (Internet sex offender's) decision about how long to remain in a particular patch (website) harvesting food (targets) before moving to another patch (website) is dependent on the amount of time spent searching for and consuming food (searching for and grooming targets) relative to the amount of energy gained (targets gained) (Bernasco 2009; MacArthur and Pianka 1966; Charnov 1974; Wellborn 2000). At the point in time within the patch (website) when the energy expended (searching for targets) in securing the food (targets) outweighs the energy obtained from the food (successful target acquirement) the patch (website) should be abandoned in what is known as "giving up time" (Charnov 1974; Wellborn 2000).

No studies have examined the marginal value theorem as it relates to Internet sex offender search strategy; so again, inferences will be drawn from other studies. Previous studies examining burglary as it relates to optimal foraging theory (Johnson and Bowers 2004) found that targeting homes near those previously burglarized would indicate a cluster of burglaries spatially but would lead to a depleted population of targets, resources, and a possible increased risk of apprehension over time. To account for this, the foraging burglar would move on to investigate the next cluster of homes that present high returns with limited risks of being apprehended. Bernasco (2009) contended that for criminals, the police, victims, or bystanders can play the role that natural enemies play in optimal foraging theory. This same principle can be found within biological foraging of animals for food. "Birds that seek food on the ground are constantly searching their surroundings for signs of danger ... rabbits will constantly move their ears to detect danger on either side of them. Research indicates that animals can recognize an increase in the risk of predation and suitably adjust their behavior to it by showing increased vigilance" (Bernasco 2009, 12).

It is expected that these same principles can be applied to Internet sex offenders. When an offender has searched a particular website for targets for a significant period of time, that website can become depleted of attractive targets, forcing the offender to begin searching at another website. Similar to birds and rabbits foraging for food, offenders can become aware of increased risk associated with particular websites or targets. This could be because of monitoring of a particular website by administrators, the feeling that the target is not who they claim to be, or increased monitoring on the part of a parent or guardian. The risk of continuing communication with that target or searching within that website would be increased, forcing the offender to search elsewhere for targets.

The four research questions described above assist in answering the primary question of this study, which states, "Can optimal foraging theory explain Internet sex offenders' search behavior?" As discussed in the beginning of the framework, there are four components necessary for optimal foraging theory to function: an actor, a currency, a strategy, and avoiding constraints. Each one of these four components was addressed individually in the preceding research questions. These research questions tied together optimal foraging theory's biological roots with the contemporary search behavior of Internet sex offenders described in this study. Each research question produced a set of concepts that are able to be measured and tested empirically to determine if there is foraging behavior on the part of Internet sex offenders.

Operationalization

The concepts in the primary research question, **Can optimal foraging theory explain Internet sex offenders search behavior?** include optimal foraging theory, Internet sex offenders, and search behavior. These concepts will be operationalized in the research questions that follow. The first concept, optimal foraging theory, is operationalized through analysis of characteristics of websites that attract offenders, characteristics within a website that influence amount of time searching for targets, and the constraints associated with leaving a particular website in favor of another. These concepts will be operationalized in research questions two, three, and four. Internet sex offenders are examined through analysis of what they are seeking and will be operationalized in research question one. The concept of search behavior serves as the dependent variable for this study and is a culmination of all four components of the foraging model. Therefore, search behavior is operationalized throughout all four research questions.

Concepts raised by the first research question, **Do Internet sex offenders' search patterns differ for different exploitations?** include Internet sex offenders and exploitations. For the purposes of this study, Internet sex offenders will be operationalized as any offender who initiated contact with a target on the Internet for sexual purposes, or if the offender was acquiring or distributing child pornography in any fashion. In this study, three categories of Internet sex offenders will be analyzed: offenders searching for or distributing child pornography, coded as (0); offenders searching for targets to engage in sexual communications, coded as (1); and offenders searching for targets to solicit into sexual acts, coded as (2). It is important to note that these categories may not be mutually exclusive. For example, offenders searching for child pornography may also be searching for targets to solicit into sexual acts. The three categories of the variable cannot be ordered. The values 0, 1, and 2 are just labels that assist in the research. It does not matter if 0 is attached to offenders looking for or distributing child pornography, 1 to offenders searching for targets to engage in sexual communications, and 2 to offenders searching for targets to solicit into sexual acts, or if 0 is attached to offenders searching for targets to solicit into sexual acts, 1 to offenders searching for or distributing child pornography, and 2 to offenders searching for targets to engage in sexual communications. This variable is word oriented, where numbers are used to aid with categorical statistical purposes. Because of lack of ordering, this is a nominal level variable.

The concept of exploitations refers to the different sexual media that is searched for by Internet sex offenders. For this study, four categories have been operationalized: searching for child pornography pictures, coded as (0); searching for child pornography videos, coded as (1); searching for targets to chat with sexually, coded as (2);

and searching for targets to solicit into meeting for a sexual encounter, coded as (3). Though similar to the operationalization for Internet sex offenders, these exploitations differ in that they are more specific in their operationalization. For example, within the exploitations we expect the search patterns to differ between offenders searching for child pornography pictures and offenders searching for child pornography videos; therefore, we have distinguished between these two categories for this concept. It is important to note that these categories may not be mutually exclusive. For example, it is possible that offenders searching for child pornography videos may also search for child pornography pictures. The four categories of exploitations cannot be ordered. The values 0, 1, 2, and 3 are simply labels aiding in the research process. It does not matter if 0 is attached to offenders searching for child pornography pictures, 1 to offenders searching for child pornography videos, 2 to offenders searching for targets to chat with sexually, and 3 to offenders searching for targets to solicit, or if 0 is attached to offenders searching for targets to solicit, 1 to offenders searching for child pornography pictures, 2 to offenders searching for child pornography videos, or 3 to offenders searching for targets to chat with sexually. This variable is word oriented, where numbers are used to aid with categorical statistical purposes. Due to the lack of ordering this is a nominal level variable.

Concepts raised by research question two, **What characteristics of a particular website attract Internet sex offenders to that website?** include website and attractive characteristics of websites. The concept website refers to the chat rooms, profiles, and other communication entities found in URLs on the Internet. The concept websites was included in the study because it is the medium on which Internet sex offenders search for targets. For the purposes of this study, websites were operationalized as any specific Universal Resource Locator (URL) addresses that lead to a specific domain, Internet source, email, chat room, or bulletin board.

The concept attractive characteristics of websites refers to what entities of websites enable offenders to maximize their searches for the best chance of acquiring quality targets. Previous studies (Malesky 2007; Young 2005; Wolak, Finkelhor, and Mitchell 2004) revealed that websites offering increased interaction among users were most popular among Internet sex offenders. Based on previous research, attractive characteristics of websites were operationalized into three categories: websites offering chat rooms/instant messaging, coded as (0); websites offering email, coded as (1); and websites offering online profiles/bulletin board postings, coded as (2). The three categories of attractive characteristics have no discernable order. The values 0, 1, and 2 are simply labels aiding in the research process. It does not matter if 0 is attached to websites offering chat rooms/instant messaging, 1 to websites offering email, and 2 to websites offering online profiles/bulletin board postings, or if 0 is attached to websites offering online profiles/bulletin board postings, 1 to websites offering chat rooms/instant messaging, or 2 to websites offering email. This variable is word oriented, where numbers are used to aid with categorical statistical purposes. Due to the lack of ordering, this is a nominal level variable. These concepts were included because they served as the between patches (websites) portion of optimal foraging theory. It was expected that certain websites will be favored by Internet sex offenders over others because of the different characteristics between websites.

The concepts identified in research question three, **What characteristics within a website influence time spent at that website?** include within website characteristics, and time searching. For this study, the concept within website characteristics refers to the nature of the entities (chat rooms, online profiles, bulletin boards) within each website. The concept was operationalized into three categories: sex-themed chat rooms/instant messages, measured as any chat room where discussion between individuals turned toward a sexual nature, including via instant messaging such as AOL chat, MSN chat, and Google chat, coded as (0); email, measured as any communications or exchanging of pictures, literature, or videos of a sexual nature via email, coded as (1); and online profiles/bulletin board postings, measured as gaining contact with an individual (with the intent to communicate in a sexual fashion) through viewing of online profiles and bulletin boards such as Facebook, Myspace, or Hot-or-Not, coded as (2). The three categories of within website characteristics cannot be ordered. The values 0, 1, and 2 are simply labels aiding in the research process. It does not matter if 0 is attached to sex-themed chat rooms/instant messages, 1 to email, and 2 to online profiles/bulletin board postings, or if 0 is attached to online profiles/bulletin board postings, 1 to sex-themed chat rooms/instant messages, or 2 to email. This variable is word oriented, where numbers are used to aid with categorical statistical purposes. Due to the lack of ordering this is a nominal level variable. This concept was included because it served as the within patches (websites) portion of optimal foraging theory. It was expected that certain websites were favored by Internet sex offenders over others because of the characteristics within that website.

The concept time searching was operationalized into the number of seconds an offender spent searching before acquiring a suitable website (between patches) and target (within patches). These categories can be ordered, such that one is greater than the other. Ten seconds searching is more than five seconds searching, and less than 30 seconds searching. The numerical values are not just labels; they are quantifiably representative, and changing order would change the results of the study. There also exists an equal interval of one between the categories. The interval between one and two seconds is the same as the interval between two and three seconds. Lastly, there is no true zero since there is always some amount of time associated with accessing a website. Since the categories can be ordered and there is an equal interval between them, but no true zero, this is an interval level variable.

Concepts identified in the fourth research question, **What constraints lead to the abandonment of a particular website in favor of another?** include constraints and abandonment. For this study, the concept of constraints was operationalized into three categories: monitoring provided by websites/network administrators, coded as (0); monitoring on the part of parents/guardians of young Internet users, coded as (1); and depletion of targets within a website to a point where optimization is no longer achievable, coded as (2). The three categories of constraints cannot be ordered.

The values 0, 1, and 2 are simply labels aiding in the research process. It does not matter if 0 is attached to monitoring provided by websites/network administrators, 1 to monitoring on the part of parents/guardians, and 2 to depletion of targets within a website, or if 0 is attached to depletion of targets within a website, 1 to monitoring provided by websites/network administrators, and 2 to monitoring on the part of parents/guardians. This variable is word oriented, where numbers are used to aid with categorical statistical purposes. Due to the lack of ordering this is a nominal level variable. This concept was included in the study because constraints are directly linked to whether or not an offender will abandon a website in favor of another.

The concept abandonment refers to leaving a particular websites in search of another when the constraints of searching for targets at a particular website outweigh the chances of finding a suitable target. For this study, the concept of abandonment was operationalized as the point in time within the website when the time expended searching for targets outweighs the successful number of suitable targets acquired. That point in time, called "giving up time" (Charnov 1974; Wellborn 2000) was measured by the following formula: $R_{vg} = VG/(T_B + T_W)$, where = rate of targets gained per unit cost; R_{VG} = ratio of targets gained; T_B = total time searching between Internet sites; and T_W = total time "grooming" and seducing targets (Burgason 2011). For example, if an Internet sex offender acquired 2 targets from a particular website, VG = 2. If the amount of time spent searching for that particular website was 30 seconds, T_B = 30 seconds. If the amount of time spent grooming the targets was 2 minutes or 120 seconds, T_W = 120. The final formula would be $R_{vg} = 2/(30 + 120)$, so rate of targets gained is .013. If the offender gained more targets in same time allotted on a different website, for example, then $R_{vg} = 10(30 + 120)$. The rate of targets gained would be .067, increasing the rate of targets gained by .054. The second website would be selected because it maximizes the chances of acquiring targets, meaning one can acquire more targets while expending the same amount of energy. The rate of victims gained with this variable is not simply a label, the differences in the rates are quantifiably representative as R_{vg} = .067 is a higher rate of gain than R_{vg} = .013; and changing order would change the rate of victims gained and thus, the results of the study. There also exists an equal interval of one between the categories. The interval between 1.135 and 1.136 victims gained is the same as the interval between 1.136 and 1.137 victims gained. Finally, there is a true zero because it is possible that offenders acquired no targets from a particular website they were searching. Because the categories can be ordered, there is an equal interval between them, and there is a true zero, this is an interval/ratio level variable. This concept was included because it describes the essence of optimal foraging theory: maximizing one's intake while expending the least amount of time and energy doing so and also avoiding risks.

The research questions operationalized above assist in answering the primary question of this study, which states, "Can optimal foraging theory explain Internet sex offenders' search behavior?" As discussed in the beginning of the study, there are four components necessary for optimal foraging theory to function: an actor, a currency, a strategy, and avoiding constraints. Each one of these four components was addressed individually in the preceding operationalization. This operationalization was organized in a way that the identification of the concepts and discussion on the variables resulting from these concepts was separately addressed within each research question.

Theoretical Path Model

The dependent variable in the preceding model was the search behavior of Internet sex offenders. It is salient to this study to provide the theoretical model that demonstrates how the conceptual elements fit together to explain the primary question of this research. The model illustrates how the four elements required for optimal foraging theory come together and provide explanation for Internet sex offender's search behavior. The model is then linked back to the biological roots of optimal foraging theory to provide a more thorough theoretical understanding of how each of the elements links together to account for actors' search behavior.

The first element of the model is the actor. For the purposes of this model, the actors choosing among different alternatives will be Internet sex offenders. Depending on the form of exploitation offenders search for (child pornography pictures, child pornography videos, chatting sexually online, or searching for targets to solicit into sexual acts) affects what websites offenders (actors) will search for, and thus directly affects the offenders' (actors') search strategy, which in turn has a direct effect on the search behavior of the offender (actor). For example, offenders searching for a website that will allow them the opportunity to solicit a target into sexual acts will generally not stop searching once they find a website with pornographic pictures of children. The exploitation of choice of offenders was a website offering the opportunity to elicit a target for sexual contact; having found a website with pornographic pictures instead, offenders will modify their search strategy to better acquire the sought website, thus affecting their search behavior.

The same modifying strategy can be seen in biological studies of animals. A deer searching for feeding patches (equivalent to websites in our study) with younger swards, which offer higher nutritional value, will encounter patches dominated with older, less nutrient rich swards. Although the deer has encountered a food (website with child pornography) it was not the high yielding food (website with opportunity to solicit) the actor was searching for. Like human beings, deer "are able to recognize and discriminate between feeding patches on the basis of quantity and quality of food" (Langvatn and Hanley 1993, 169). Thus, a deer may graze in the patch for a short period of time, but will ultimately modify its search strategy to obtain a patch (website) containing the young sward (website with opportunity to solicit), which directly affects the search behavior of the deer.

The second element required for optimal foraging theory is a currency for which the actor is seeking. For this model, websites and the entities available from them will serve as currency. The focus is on what patches (websites) are more desirable, and provide the best chance at acquiring quality food (targets). The more lucrative a particular website is in terms of producing opportunities for high returns of successful targets, the more likely Internet sex offenders are to troll that website for targets. Previous research has found that websites and online entities such as chat rooms, instant messaging services, emails, and bulletin boards provide increased opportunities for interaction between actor and currency and are popular places for Internet sex offender searching (Malesky 2007; Young 2005; Wolak, Finkelhor, and Mitchell 2004). The websites (currency) providing these opportunities for interaction are viewed as an attractive currency to Internet sex offenders. For example, websites containing online profiles of individuals such as Hot-or-Not can be considered a form of currency; however, an online website that provides an entity or link to a different URL where communication is available would be considered a higher yielding currency because of the increased rewards (direct sexual chat, real-time video and pictures) now available via direct communication. The search for these websites that offer direct communication (currency) becomes part of the strategy of Internet sex offenders. Knowing this currency exists, offenders may alter their searching strategy with the aim of acquiring websites where direct communication is available, thus modifying their search behavior from searching for any website with online profiles, to searching for websites where direct communication is available. Subsequently, the currency has a direct effect on the strategy of the forager, which has a direct effect on their search behavior.

This modification based on prey choice and diet breadth can be seen in the biological studies of foraging animals. Prey choice and diet breadth refers to an animal's choice of one type of food over another. It has been found in several studies (Sayers, Norconk, and Conklin-Brittain 2010; Langvatn and Hanley 1993) that animals will pass by certain food items (in our study websites) in search of others that will yield greater energy intake. For example, Himalayan langurs eat low-energy in-take foods such as mature evergreen leaves and woody roots "almost exclusively when encounter rates with high-ranking foods were lowest" (Sayers, Norconk, and Conklin-Brittain 2010, 346). Another squirrel gathering nuts (currency) searches for patches that contain the highest energy yielding nut, the red oak acorn; however, these nuts are the least abundant. The majority of the patches available to the squirrel are inundated with white oak acorns and chestnut oat acorns, which yield considerably less energy than the red oak acorn. The squirrel's search strategy is modified to find the high yielding red oak acorn (currency) even though the chestnut oak acorn and white oak acorns are more abundant. The langurs' strategy and the squirrel's strategy is to search for the higher yielding foods (currency) much the same way Internet sex offenders search for websites that provide the best chance of acquiring a target, that is, websites with direct communication (currency).

A third element required for optimal foraging theory is the constraints faced by the forager. For this model, the risks of Internet sites and entities being monitored by administrators, parents, or guardians and the depletion of attractive targets from the websites and entities will serve as constraints. Websites that have increased levels of monitoring will be avoided and abandoned by foragers for websites where risks of being detected are lessened. For example, chat rooms where typing words of a profane or sexual nature result in users automatically being kicked off the website will likely be avoided completely or abandoned by offenders once they have been made aware of this constraint. Offenders would modify their search strategy to avoid such websites. When offenders find a website where they can successfully acquire targets, they may return to this website multiple times as they are aware that it yields high returns (successful target acquirement). This can lead to that particular website (patch) becoming depleted of attractive targets (currency). The depletion of the website of attractive targets is a self-inflicted constraint on the part of the offender, causing the offender to abandon the website in search of another that can yield a higher return (successful target acquirement). The depletion of targets from a website, forcing a moving to another website is termed the marginal value theorem. Specifically, the theory states that a forager's (Internet sex offender) decision about how long to remain in a particular patch (website) harvesting food (targets) before moving to another patch (website) is dependent on the amount of time spent searching for and consuming food (searching for and grooming targets) relative to the amount of energy gained (targets gained). This depletion now becomes an element to be considered in an offender's search strategy, because spending too much time within a patch (website) can deplete it of the sought-after currency (attractive targets) and thus affects the offender search behavior. Consequently, constraints have a direct effect on the strategy of offenders, which directly affects offenders' search behavior.

Constraints faced by the biological forager include terrain, travel time, climate, mobility, and resource density as well as the abilities and skills of the actor, risk of predation, and knowledge of the environment (Sandstrom 1994). For example, deer searching for food must avoid predators searching for food, such as wolves. The wolves in this example would serve as a constraint. The young swards that yield the highest nutritional value to red deer grow atop a steep, rocky mountain located across a fast flowing river. The terrain (rocky, unstable mountain side and fast flowing river) in this instance would serve as a constraint the deer must consider when searching for highly nutritional young swards. Both the severity and abundance of these constraints become part of the foragers' strategy in obtaining food, in that the foragers want to find high yielding food while avoiding most severe and numerous constraints. Subsequently, much the same as the deer modify their search strategy to avoid constraints, thus altering their search behavior, so too do Internet sex offender foragers.

The final component necessary for optimal foraging theory to be a success is a strategy on the part of the forager. For this model, the strategy component of foraging entails all available options to the forager, including the content of the websites and entities within them, the availability of targets within websites and entities, the returns (successful acquisition of targets) the forager receives, and avoiding constraints known to the offender. For example, all previous information obtained regarding the actors (Internet sex offenders) and the exploitations they are seeking, the currency (websites/targets) and whether or not those websites provide opportunities for direct communication, and avoiding the constraints (monitoring of websites/depletion of targets from websites) that can lead to the abandonment of a website for another are coupled with the amount of time spent searching between and within websites, and the successful rate of returns (target acquisition) to form the search strategy of Internet sex offenders. The elements added by the strategy component include time spent searching and rate of return. Without a successful return on the actor's time and energy spent searching for its currency, optimal foraging theory could not exist. The amount of energy taken in by a successful return (in this study's case, an acquired target) must be greater than the amount of time and energy spent searching for said currency.

In biological studies, a forager's decision about how long to remain in a particular patch harvesting food before moving to another patch is dependent on the amount of time spent searching for and consuming food relative to the amount of energy gained (MacArthur and Pianka 1966; Wellborn 2000). At the point in time within the patch when the energy expended in securing the food outweighs the energy obtained from the food, the patch should be abandoned. The strategies for both Internet sex offenders searching for websites and biological foragers searching for food directly influence the search behavior of the actors. Without any strategy to adhere to when searching for food (websites/targets) actors' search behavior would simply be to wander at random and rely on chance alone to provide the currency each seeks.

The above illustration and subsequent explanations represent the final theoretical model for this study. One could argue that effects exist between the actor and currency, or between the actor, the constraints, and search behavior, and also on the placement in the model of the marginal value theorem. One could argue that the marginal value theorem should be placed between the strategy element and the dependent variable. This could be justified within the framework of optimal foraging theory; however, the marginal value theorem directly relates to optimization, or to when the time spent searching for food (targets) outweighs the energy gained from successful acquisition of targets, which is a constraint faced by foragers.

The four elements required for optimal foraging theory and the concepts identified in the four research questions were structured in a theoretical model that aids in answering the primary question of this study, which states, "Can optimal foraging theory explain Internet sex offenders' search behavior?" It is the goal of this study to help the reader understand how each element of optimal foraging theory and the concepts derived from the research questions come together and form a scholarly and coherent interpretation of the theoretical premise of this study. The step-by-step model and subsequent explanations take the reader through the theoretical process necessary for a comprehensive and unbridled understanding of optimal foraging theory's application to Internet sex offender search behavior.

References

Beebe, Timothy, Steven Asche, Patricia Harrison, and Kathryn Quinlan. 2004. "Heightened Vulnerability and Increased Risk-Taking among Adolescent Chat Room Users: Results from a Statewide School Survey." *Journal of Adolescent Health* 35 (2): 116–123.

Bernasco, Wim. 2009. "Foraging Strategies of Homo Criminalis: Lessons from Behavioral Ecology." *Crime Patterns and Analysis* 2 (1): 5–16.

Burgason, Kyle. 2011. From Surfing to Foraging: Optimal Foraging Theory and Internet Search Behavior. [PowerPoint slides]. UALR Graduate Research Symposium and Creative Works Expo.

Burke, Anne, Shawn Sowerbutts, Barry Blundell, and Michael Sherry. 2001. "Child Pornography and the Internet: Policing and Treatment Issues." *Psychiatry, Psychology and Law* 9 (1): 79–84.

Charnov, Eric L. 1974. "Optimal Foraging, the Marginal Value Theorem." *Theoretical Population Biology* 9 (2): 129–136.

Cooper, Alvin, Coralie R. Scherer, Sylvain C. Boies, and Barry L. Gordon. 1999. "Sexuality on the Internet from Sexual Exploration to Pathological Expression." *Professional Psychology: Research and Practice* 30: 33–52.

Emlen, J. Merritt. 1966. "The Role of Time and Energy in Food Preference." *The American Naturalist* 100 (916): 611–617.

Johnson, Shane D., and Kate J. Bowers. 2004. "The Stability of Space-Time Clusters of Burglary." *The British Journal of Criminology* 44 (1): 55–65.

Johnson, Shane D., Lucia Summers, and Ken Pease. 2009. "Offender as Forager? A Direct Test of the Boost Account of Victimization." *Journal of Quantitative Criminology* 25: 181–200.

Langvatn, Rolf and Thomas A. Hanley.1993. "Feeding-patch choice by red deer in relation to foraging Efficiency." *Oecology* 95: 164–170.

Lewis, Allen. 1980. "Patch use by gray squirrels and optimal foraging." *Ecology* 6: 1371–1379.

MacArthur, Robert H., and Eric R. Pianka. 1966. "On Optimal Use of Patchy Environment." *The American Naturalist* 100 (916): 603–609.

Malesky, Alvin L., Jr. 2007. "Predatory Online Behavior: Modus Operandi of Convicted Sex Offenders in Identifying Potential Victims and Contacting Minors over the Internet." *Journal of Child Sexual Abuse* 16 (2): 23–32.

Marcum, Catherine D. 2007. "Interpreting the Intentions of Internet Predators: An Examination of Online Predatory Behavior." *Journal of Child Sexual Abuse* 16 (4): 99–114.

Mitchell, Kimberly J., Janis Wolak, and David Finkelhor. 2005. "Police Posting as Juveniles to Catch Sex Offenders: Is It Working?" *Sexual Abuse: A Journal of Research and Treatment* 17: 241–267.

Nachmias Rafi and Amir Gilad. 2002. "Needle in a hyperstack: Searching for information on the worldwide web." *Journal of Research on Technology in Education* 34: 475–486.

Pyke, Graham. H, H. Ronald Pulliam, and Eric L. Charnov 1977. "Optimal foraging: A selective review of theory and tests." *The Quarterly Review of Biology* 52: 137–154.

Sayers, Ken, Marilyn Norconk, Nancy L. Conklin-Brittain. 2010. "Optimal foraging on the roof of the world: Himalayan langurs and the classical prey model." *American Journal of Physical Anthropology* 141: 337–357.

Sandstrom Pamela E. 1994. "An optimal foraging approach to information seeking and use." *The Library Quarterly,* 64: 414–449.

Seto, Michael C., J. Michael Wood, Kelly M. Babchishin, and Sheri Flynn. 2011. "Online Solicitation Offenders Are Different from Child Pornography Offenders and Lower Risk Contact Sexual Offenders." *Law and Human Behavior* 36 (4): 1–11.

Smith, Eric A. et al. 1983. "Anthropological applications of optimal foraging theory: A critical review." *Current Anthropology* 24: 625–651.

Walraven, Amber, Saskia Brand-Guwel, and Henny Boshuizen. 2009. "How students evaluate information and sources when searching the world wide web for information." *Computers and Education* 52: 234–246.

Webb, L. Jackie Craissati, and S. Keen. 2007. "Characteristics of Internet Child Pornography Offenders: A Comparison with Child Molesters." *Sex Abuse* 19: 449–465.

Wellborn, Gary A. 2000. "Testing Concepts of Animal Foraging Behavior." *The American Biology Teacher* 62 (1): 46–50.

Wolak, Janis, David Finkelhor, and Kimberly J. Mitchell. 2003. "Escaping or Connecting? Characteristics of Youth Who Form Close Online Relationships." *Journal of Adolescence* 26: 105–119.

Wolak, Janis, David Finkelhor, and Kimberly J. Mitchell. 2004. "Internet-Initiated Sex Crimes against Minors: Implications for Prevention Based on Findings from a National Study." *Journal of Adolescent Health* 35 (5): 424.e11–424.e20.

Wolak Janis, David Finkelhor, Kimberly J. Mitchell, and Michele L. Ybarra. 2008. "Online predators and their victims: Myths, realities and implications for prevention and treatment." *American Psychologist* 63: 11–128.

Young, Kimberly. 2005. "Profiling Online Sex Offenders, Cyber-Predators, and Pedophiles." *Journal of Behavioral Profiling* 5 (1): 1–18.

Index